Don't miss these other True Crime Titles
by John Glatt

THE DOCTOR'S WIFE

ONE DEADLY NIGHT

DEPRAVED

CRIES IN THE DESERT

FOR I HAVE SINNED

EVIL TWINS

CRADLE OF DEATH

BLIND PASSION

DEADLY AMERICAN BEAUTY

NEVER LEAVE ME

TWISTED

Available from St. Martin's True Crime Library

FORGIVE ME, FATHER

A True Story of a Priest, a Nun,
and a Brutal Murder

John Glatt

St. Martin's Paperbacks

FORGIVE ME, FATHER

Copyright © 2008 by John Glatt.

Cover photo of man on staircase © Antonio Mo/Corbis. Cover photo of Father Gerald Robinson © Andy Morrison/The Blade/Pool/Reuters/Corbis.

ISBN: 0-312-94646-5
EAN: 978-0-312-94646-3

Printed in the United States of America

St. Martin's Paperbacks edition / February 2008

St. Martin's Paperbacks are published by St. Martin's Press, 175 Fifth Avenue, New York, NY 10010.

10 9 8 7 6 5 4 3 2 1

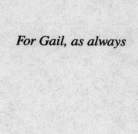

For Gail, as always

ACKNOWLEDGMENTS

When Father Gerald Robinson was ordained as a priest in 1964, he vowed to devote himself to God's work. And to many parishioners in Toledo, where he served the Polish community for more than four decades, he was *the* perfect priest.

So when he was arrested in April 2004 and charged with the brutal stabbing murder of Sister Margaret Ann Pahl a quarter-of-a-century earlier, there was stunned disbelief with many refusing to believe it possible.

By the 21st century the barbaric slaying of the elderly nun on the sacristy floor of Mercy Hospital on the Easter Saturday morning of 1980, was largely forgotten. No one had ever been charged with the murder, which had heavy Satanic overtones, and only a handful of homicide detectives even knew that Father Robinson had once been the prime suspect.

In the 1980s and 1990s Father Robinson had continued preaching God's word around Toledo, as Sister Margaret Ann's murder became a cold case. And the reclusive clergyman probably would have carried on ministering to his flock but for a curious set of circumstances initiated by another nun, who alleged he and several others had once abused her.

Her startling claims of bizarre Satanic rituals led to Sister Margaret Ann Pahl's homicide being reopened by the newly-formed Lucas County Cold Case Squad, using technical advances in DNA and forensics to build its case against Father Robinson.

On May 11, 2006—after a dramatic three-week trial that

made headlines around the world—Father Robinson was convicted of Sister Margaret Ann's murder and sentenced to an indefinite term of fifteen years to life in prison. The verdict came down amidst bitter allegations of a 1980 cover-up, involving top Toledo churchmen and law enforcement officers.

Throughout his trial Father Robinson always maintained his innocence, claiming to have nothing to do with the murder. And in August 2007 his new defense team filed a one-hundred-and-five page appeal to reverse his conviction and set him free.

But whatever the outcome of Ohio's 6th District Court of Appeals, the case of Father Robinson remains one of the most fascinating and unusual murders in American criminal history.

During my exhaustive research for this book I was helped by many of the key protagonists in this case, some wishing to remain anonymous. I am most indebted to Dean Mandross, the Criminal Division Chief for spending hours with me patiently going over every inch of the case and for his continuous support for this project.

I also owe a huge debt of gratitude to Sister Margaret Ann Pahl's surviving family in Edgerton, Ohio. Her sisters Mary Casebere and Catherine Flegal helped me get to know the real Sister Margaret Ann who led such a perfect life as a bride of Christ. Her nephew Lee Pahl and nieces Martha Jane Dietsch and Paula Dockery opened the family photo almanacs and Sister's personal papers to me.

Thanks also goes to the indomitable Claudia Vercelotti of the Toledo Chapter of SNAP, who provided me with valuable background for the book. And if it wasn't for Claudia's valiant work for victims of clerical abuse, Sister Margaret Ann Pahl's murder would have gone unpunished—at least in this world.

I also wish to thank: Lucas County Prosecutor Julia Bates, Judge Mary Chrzanowski, Edith Csizmar, Dave Davison, John Donahue, Sister Phyllis Ann Gerold, William Kina, Father Paul Kwiatowski, Shirley Lucas, Jim Marshall,

Arthur Marx, Jerry Mazuchowski, Stanley Mileski, Det. Tom Ross, Annette Silas, Tom Skeldon, Brad Smith, Jack Sparagowski and Ray Vetter.

Thanks as always goes to my super-editor at St. Martin's Press, Charles Spicer and his assistant Michael Homler and lawyer Henry Kaufman. As always, many thanks to Peter "The Lion" Miller and Adrienne Rosado of PMA Literary and Film Management.

Kudos also to Jerome and Emily Freund, Debbie, Douglas and Taylor Baldwin, GK's BCs, Roger Hitts, Chiquita, Danny and Allie Trachtenberg, Cari Pokrassa, Daniel Lyons—Jolly bartender extraordinaire, Benny and Kim Sporano and Benny Jr., Virginia Randall, Tsarina, Don MacLeod, Gurch, Annette Witheridge and the late Mo Mo Freund.

CONTENTS

FORGIVE
ME,
FATHER

PROLOGUE

SISTER MADELYN MARIE GORDON AWOKE AT 6:00 A.M., savoring the rare luxury of an extra hour's sleep. It was Holy Saturday, the day before Easter, one of only three days in the Catholic calendar when 6:00 a.m. Mass was not held.

By 7:00 a.m., the bespectacled 56-year-old Sister of Mercy nun had washed, dressed and left her room on the seventh-floor convent of Mercy Hospital, situated on the edge of a tough ghetto in downtown Toledo, Ohio. She took the elevator down to the first floor of the main hospital, stopping off at the switchboard in the PBX room to pick up some IBM cards for her morning care.

At about 7:10 a.m., the soft-spoken nun, who had been in the strict order for thirty-four years, left the switchboard area, walking into the main lobby toward the nuns' dining room for her breakfast.

Sister Madelyn knew it would be a relaxed morning. As organist, she just had to prepare music for evening service, to be taken by Father Gerald Robinson, at 42, the youngest of the hospital's two chaplains. She would also assist the sacristan, Sister Margaret Ann Pahl, in removing the decorations in the chapel before cleaning the altar for the somber early evening Mass.

Mercy Hospital—one of several owned and operated by the Sisters of Mercy order—was deserted, as almost all the student nurses had taken the Easter weekend off. But on her way to the clergy dining room, a man in his mid-twenties in work clothes caught her attention. He looked lost, as if trying to find the way out, eventually taking the Madison Avenue exit and waving as he stepped outside.

When Sister Madelyn Marie entered the dining room, several nuns were having breakfast. Some placings were missing from the tables, indicating that others had already eaten and left.

The sister helped herself to toast, coffee, grapefruit and an egg, before sitting down to eat. A couple of minutes later, Father Jerome Swiatecki, the other hospital chaplain, strolled in with a smile on his face.

"Good morning," he said, joining them at the table, his green tray full of breakfast foods.

An enormous bear of a man, the garrulous priest loved to chat, and was well-loved in the hospital as an exceptionally jovial character.

"He was just talking ad-lib with us sisters," she would later remember. "Just the time of day."

At about 7:30 a.m., Sister Madelyn Marie left the dining room with Father Swiatecki and several other sisters, going along the hallway to St. Joseph's Chapel. By the entrance against a wall, she spotted what she thought was a neatly folded white pillowcase. She picked it up and brought it into the chapel, placing it on a pew by the entrance.

Later she would remember an "eerie" feeling coming over her, as she walked into the chapel.

It was now about 7:45 a.m., and Sister Mary Phillip was in a pew, quietly saying her morning office. Without a word, Sister Madelyn Marie walked to the front of the chapel, kneeling down in a pew to say her prayers, to be joined soon afterwards by Sister Clarisena.

The middle-aged nun was in no hurry that morning, as there would be no Mass until evening, so she lingered over her prayers, taking longer than usual. When she had finished, she stood up, walking over to the organ, where she began laying out the music for the evening services. She was not sure about one particular piece of music, so she decided to consult Father Robinson, who would be saying the Mass.

As she got up from her organ to use the sacristy phone, she instinctively looked at her watch, noticing it was 8:20 a.m. Then she walked over to the wooden sacristy door, adjacent to the side altar.

The rest of the year the small sacristy functioned as a storeroom for church items. It was also used by the two hospital priests to don their vestments before conducting Mass in the larger chapel.

But every Easter it was transformed when the Holy Eucharist, also known as the "Blessed Sacrament"—the consecrated wafer that Catholics believe to be the actual body of Jesus Christ—was taken out of the chapel on Good Friday and housed in the sacristy until Easter Saturday evening.

For just a few hours a year, the sacristy became *the* holiest place in the chapel.

When Sister Madelyn Marie tried to open the double doors to the sacristy, they were locked. She thought that strange, as they were always open, so Sister Margaret Ann Pahl, the sacristan, could slip back and forth into the chapel while preparing the altar. Sister Madelyn Marie also distinctly remembered them being open a few minutes earlier, when she had first entered the chapel.

She opened the sacristy door with her own key, walking into the small, dimly lit room, to see what she first assumed to be a CPR dummy lying on the tiled floor. She remembered there had recently been a CPR course at Mercy Hospital, and thought someone had accidentally left it there.

"Why did they bring this mannequin in here?" she asked herself.

She then slowly approached, bending over for a better look, recoiling in horror when she saw that it was Sister Margaret Ann Pahl. The elderly nun's face was horribly swollen, and her spectacles lay nearby on the cold stone floor.

In that split second, she saw that the frail nun's dark blue habit was up above her breasts, and her panties were pulled down to her ankles, leaving her completely exposed. Her arms were unnaturally positioned straight by her side, and her legs were together, as if someone had posed them in some kind of strange ritual. There was also a sliver of blood on her forehead, as if she'd been anointed.

Sister Madelyn Marie then let out a piercing scream, running out of the sacristy and into the chapel. She broke down sobbing in Sisters Mary Phillip and Clarisena's arms, saying that Sister Margaret Ann had been raped and murdered.

SECOND YEAR RESIDENT DR. JACK BARON, WHO HAD JUST finished his Friday night shift, was briefing several colleagues in "Morning Report," when the "Mr. Swift" call—the hospital's emergency code—came through the hospital's P.A. system, ordering all medical personnel to the chapel.

The 32-year-old doctor immediately ran down the stairs to the chapel, mistakenly making a right turn, as he had never been there before. Realizing his mistake, he turned around and passed Father Gerald Robinson, who was walking away from the chapel.

"He looked back at me away from his left shoulder," Dr. Baron later remembered, "and gave me a stare that went right through me."

When Dr. Baron walked into the chapel, Sister Madelyn Marie was still crying uncontrollably, being comforted by Sister Clarisena. He went inside the sacristy to find resident intern Dr. Donald Woodard, 30, who had arrived several minutes earlier, bending over Sister Margaret Ann Pahl's body. Obviously shaken, Dr. Woodard said that the elderly nun was dead and had possibly been raped.

"Life was gone," the intern later told a detective. "I tried to arouse her."

Dr. Woodard was shocked at the terrible way Sister Margaret Ann had been butchered. Her swollen neck was covered in blood and there were numerous stab wounds to her neck, chest and head. It was as if she'd been attacked by a frenzied madman or someone possessed by the devil.

Out of decency, Dr. Baron asked a nurse to cover Sister Margaret Ann's naked body with a blanket.

A few minutes later, an ashen-faced Father Swiatecki entered the sacristy, having heard the terrible news. He was wearing his purple stole and carrying oils, to perform the sacred last rites on Sister Margaret Ann.

As he was performing the sacrament of Extreme Unction, Father Gerald Robinson slipped into the chapel, a blank look in his eyes. He had been summoned from his second-floor quarters by Sister Phyllis Ann Gerold, as he had failed to come down to the chapel like everyone else.

Then, as the unobtrusive priest entered the sacristy, the usually happy-go-lucky Father Swiatecki began trembling with emotion. He slowly stood up, walked over to Father Robinson, and began angrily shaking his finger at him.

"Why did you kill her?" he asked, his voice cracking with emotion. "Why did you kill her?"

But Father Gerald Robinson just stood there rooted to the spot, without saying a word, as the assembly of nuns and medics looked on in astonishment.

PART 1

CHAPTER ONE

Preparing for the Priesthood

GERALD JOHN ROBINSON WAS BORN ON APRIL 14, 1938, THE second son of John and Mary Sieja Robinson. He was delivered by a midwife at the Robinsons' modest home at 1143 Belmont Avenue, in the Kuschwantz section of Toledo, Ohio.

His always-forceful mother had been born Mary Sieja in Poland, before emigrating to America and marrying John Robinson, who was from German descent.

Gerald Robinson's childhood was steeped in the Polish tradition, having little to do with the American way of life.

"He grew up in an entirely Polish community," explained Jack Sparagowski, later to become a close friend. "He spoke Polish fluently."

Toledo's Polish community dates back to 1874, when a Franciscan priest, the Reverend Vincent Lewandowski, was exiled from Poland by the Austrian Emperor Otto von Bismarck. He eventually settled in northwest Ohio, dedicating himself to caring for the spiritual needs of the new wave of Polish immigrants who had settled in Toledo, near the well-established German community.

In the mid–19th century, the arrival of the railway had brought prosperity to the city, creating many new industries, including manufacture of carriages, furniture and glass.

By 1880 Toledo had become one of the largest cities in Ohio, with a population of more than 50,000 and growing. Thousands of Polish immigrants had taken root, drawn by factory jobs and easy accessibility by water or rail.

The first Polish settlers divided themselves into two communities at opposite ends of the city, carving their own distinct identities. In the north, along Lagrange Street, the immigrants from eastern Poland called their community Lagrinka. Western settlers moved a couple of miles southwest to a smaller area, along Junction and Nebraska Avenues. They named it Kuschwantz, which literally means "cow's tail," after the curling of the streetcar tracks at the final stop at Nebraska Avenue.

The vast majority of Poles who moved to Toledo were Roman Catholics, and they immediately began building ornate churches like the ones they had left behind. In 1875, St. Hedwig's church and school, named in honor of St. Hedwig, Duchess of Silesia, opened its doors. Six years later, St. Anthony Catholic Church was established on Nebraska Avenue.

Although Lagrinka and Kuschwantz thrived side by side, there was always a rivalry between them. Both communities were fiercely proud of their heritage, with their own Polish-language newspapers, restaurants and grocery stores.

By the dawn of the 20th century, new parishes were established to cater to the fast-expanding Polish community. In 1907 St. Adalbert Catholic Church was founded on Lagrange Street, followed by St. Stanislaus a year later. Nativity Catholic Church followed in 1922, and St. Hyacinth and Our Lady of Lourdes in 1927.

As young boys, Gerald Robinson and his older brother Thomas were immersed in Polish culture, their mother Mary being a well-respected pillar of the community. Gerald Mazuchowski, a friend of the family and himself well-known in the Polish Catholic neighborhoods, described her as "a very typical Polish woman. They called her Mary. Her real Polish name was Balbina, but you didn't dare call her that."

John Robinson, nicknamed Curly, was a quiet, reserved man, who worked as a custodian for the Toledo Public School system. "He was in charge of the furnaces," said Mazuchowski. "And he was always in the background."

Mary Robinson dominated her family, deciding early on

that her younger son Gerry, a quiet, introverted boy, would enter the priesthood.

He attended the Nativity Elementary School in Kuschwantz, where he learned about his mother's native country, its history and traditions, as well as studying the Bible. When he told his mother he wanted to devote his life to the Catholic Church, she was so delighted, she told all her friends at St. Hyacinth church, where she was in the Altar Society.

"That was her pride and joy," said Mazuchowski. " 'My boy, the priest.' It was like the highest calling you could choose."

In his early teens, Gerald Robinson began a four-year seminary at St. Mary's Preparatory high school in Orchard Lake, Michigan, sixty miles north of Toledo. It was founded by Father Józef Dabrowski in 1885, as a school for Polish-American boys to train for the priesthood, and originally located on the east side of Detroit. In 1909 it moved to a scenic 125-acre campus on the shores of Orchard Lake, taking over the campus from the bankrupt Michigan Military Academy.

In 1969—five years after Gerald Robinson would be ordained as a priest—Cardinal Karol Wojtyla, soon to become Pope John Paul II, visited the campus, declaring, "If the Orchard Lake Schools did not exist, it would be necessary to establish them."

The stated mission of St. Mary's was to "provide deserving young men the moral guidance, discipline, and education necessary to become Christian gentlemen, scholars, and men of service and leadership for the world."

Gerald Robinson easily settled into life at St. Mary's, living on campus and often coming home for weekends. Known by his fellow students as quiet and studious, he tended to blend into the background, mainly keeping to himself.

Classmates still remember him as "very mild" and well behaved, adapting easily to the traditional "monastic" discipline of the seminary.

Gerry Robinson studied English, Mathematics and Science,

also taking a four-year course of Theology, and attending Mass twice a week.

The nervous, rail-thin teenager showed a keen interest in the arts, often taking part in school plays. He was placed in charge of seminary entertainment, responsible for the selection of the students' weekly movies. He was always very careful to ensure that nothing "controversial" was ever shown.

During vacations he and another student would put on theatrical shows for Polish parishes in Toledo, Cleveland and Detroit. These were often Polish-language comedies, and on several occasions, Gerry Robinson even donned female clothes to play women's roles.

Unlike his real life, where he seemed to shrink from all human contact, on the stage he appeared fearless. Years later he would utilize his performance talents to great effect with his firebrand sermons, making him something of a legend in Toledo's Polish community.

AFTER GRADUATING FROM ST. MARY'S IN THE LATE FIFTIES, 19-year-old Gerry Robinson moved across Orchard Lake campus to attend SS. Cyril and Methodius Seminary for the next four years in preparation for the priesthood. He was a handsome young man, bearing a striking resemblance to then-popular crooner—and well-known movie star—Bing Crosby.

Monsignor Stanley Milewski, now emeritus chancellor of the Orchard Lake Schools, was an administrator for the seminary, and he still remembers young Gerry Robinson as a studious young man, pursuing his chosen vocation.

"There was nothing frivolous about Gerry," recalled Milewski. "Very quiet, very pious, very devoted."

The seminary curriculum was highly demanding. Robinson studied Dogmatic Theology, Moral Theology, Spiritual Life, Scripture, the Old and New Testaments, and Polish and English Homiletics.

Each summer, Gerry Robinson returned to Toledo, where his proud mother would take him to St. Hyacinth Parish, telling everyone what a good seminarian he was. Through her contacts, she found her son a summer job. In the early 1960s, at the Toledo Zoo, selling hot dogs, soda and post-cards.

"Gerry's an odd duck," remembered Tom Skeldon, who also worked summers with him on concessions. "He was a loner. He was aloof and I don't recall him being any part of the fun."

Skeldon's father was director of the zoo and a good Catholic, so he was proud to be able to help out a seminarian with a summer job.

In his twenties, Gerald Robinson was older than the other concession workers, rarely socializing with them. He just did his work and went back to his parents' home for dinner.

"He always seemed to be on a mission," said Skeldon. "In a hurry to get someplace. Never having the time to stop and talk to you."

In 1964, Gerald Robinson, now 26, took his final exams. He did well enough for his seminary teachers to recommend him for ordination to his bishop, the Most Reverend George J. Rehring. Monsignor Milewski said that Robinson definitely had "a calling," and was "a worthy candidate" for the priesthood.

On May 30, 1964, Bishop Rehring officially ordained Gerald Robinson at the Rosary Cathedral in Toledo. His proud parents and brother Thomas were all there to celebrate, and he had already been assigned his first posting.

From now on, Father Gerald Robinson would be revered by the tightly knit Polish community, who believed priests were the divine representatives of God on Earth and could do no wrong.

FATHER GERALD ROBINSON WAS ASSIGNED TO ST. ADAL-bert's Catholic Church as assistant pro tem. It was a good start for the young priest, but ironically it was right in the center of the Lagrinka neighborhood parish and not the Kuschwantz one he had grown up in.

The imposing church/school building dated back to October 1909, when Father Józef Wachowski bought property on

Lagrange Street to found a new parish. A convent was added in 1915 and during the 1920s St. Adalbert's grew so fast, the present large church building was built in 1928.

Father Robinson would spend the next three years at Adalbert's, by all accounts remaining a dark horse, opting out of any social events. One fellow priest remembers him as "moody" and "unpredictable," smiling and chatty one minute and refusing to talk to anyone the next.

A few months after being ordained, Father Robinson joined the faculty of the Central Catholic High School on Cherry Street in Toledo, where he taught religion. There he met a pupil named Jerry Mazuchowski, and the two became fast friends.

"Now I never had him as a teacher," explained Mazuchowski, "but some friends of mine did, and I knew him through them. I used to go to confession to him on occasion."

In 1966, the Robinsons bought a small brick corner house at 2401 Nebraska Avenue, and the young priest was a frequent visitor, often staying overnight. Whenever Father Robinson attended birthday parties or other events at his new parishioners' homes, he would always bring his parents with him. Mary Robinson always appeared to overshadow her son, taking center stage on all public occasions.

"They were very, very close," said Mazuchowski, who got to know his friend's mother well. "They would always go on trips together. Once he took her to Hawaii."

The St. Adalbert parishioners liked Father Robinson, being especially impressed by his sermons delivered in fluent Polish. The young priest spent hours preparing them, carefully writing out every word beforehand.

"They were sort of conservative," said Father Paul Kwiatkowski, who first met Father Robinson on a clergy retreat in the late 1960s. "He spoke very loud, very forcefully. That was his stage presence. He had a good sense of humor."

In June 1969, Father Gerald Robinson was transferred to the non-Polish Christ the King church on the west side of the city. His new parish was far more affluent than the blue-collar St. Adalbert's but he got on well with his new parishioners, soon gaining their respect.

Three years later, in June 1972, the Toledo diocese brought Father Robinson back to St. Adalbert's Parish as associate pastor, where he was welcomed back by his original Polish congregation.

"Father was very popular," remembered Mazuchowski. "Very well liked."

But to some, Father Gerald Robinson remained an enigma. Although he was a conscientious, reliable priest, good at his job and never making any waves for his superiors, there was a certain air of mystery about the man.

It would be another thirty years before dark, highly disturbing allegations from six women would implicate him in involvement with Satanic worship and ritual sexual abuse during this period.

CHAPTER TWO

The Sisters of Assumed Mary

IN 1968, 5-YEAR-OLD JEAN MARLOW (NOT HER REAL NAME) became a pupil at St. Adalbert's school. She had been raised a devout Roman Catholic by her parents, celebrating Mass and receiving the Holy Sacraments, She had always been taught that priests were next to God.

Thirty-five years later, Marlow would accuse Father Gerald Robinson, one of her teachers, and his friend Jerry Mazuchowski, a lay preacher, of being part of a bizarre cult of priests who donned nuns' habits to perform bizarre Satanic rituals. Known as "the Sisters of Assumed Mary" (SAM), the drag cult, allegedly founded by then-teenage Mazuchowski, was reputedly active in the 1970s in Toledo, headquartered in St. Adalbert's church basement.

In civil court papers filed in April 2005 with Lucas County Common Pleas Court, Marlow would allege that she had been the victim of systematic "clerical ritual and sexual abuse" from her pre-teens onwards. She claimed that on numerous occasions, Father Robinson and other clergy would dress up in "nun drag," subjecting her to vile atrocities in the name of Satan.

According to Marlow, her mother, a close friend of Robinson and Mazuchowski, was active in the cult, wanting to become "a high priestess of Satan."

Now in her early forties, Marlow alleged that her physical and sexual abuse began back in 1968, but she had "suppressed" all memories of it for many years. Then, after seeing photographs of her two alleged abusers in the newspaper, she slowly began to recall her terrible nightmare.

Under psychiatric care, she began to remember the unspeakable perversions she suffered in St. Adalbert's church basement, including rape, forced participation in animal sacrifices and torture.

In her civil suit, she described bizarre SAM meetings, where the transvestite priests adopted women's names, with Father Robinson becoming "Mary Jerry," and Mazuchowski adopting the name "Carrie Jerry."

"[I] was kidnapped and held either against [my] will or through beguilement in the basement of St. Adalbert's," read her civil action. "While held in the basement, Father Robinson and other clergy colleagues . . . engaged in elaborate, ritualistic ceremonies dressed as nuns."

She described how the "vile" priests would lay her down on a table in the dark basement, chanting Satanic verses, declaring that Jesus was the son of Satan and repeatedly screaming "Son of SAM."

"They cut [me] with a knife as a sacrifice to Satan," she wrote, "and drew an upside down cross on [my] stomach. They forced me to drink the blood of a sacrificed animal."

At some SAM meetings, Marlow alleged, the priests would force her to masturbate them and perform oral sex. There were also orgies involving rape and sodomy.

"[I] would try and escape," she wrote, "but they pulled [me] back into the circle and hit [me]."

At the end of the ceremony, she said, they would "intimidate" her, telling her she was "Satan's child," and forcing her to clean the blood off the basement floor, even threatening to kill her if she told anyone.

Between 1968 and 1975, Marlow claims, her demonic abuse escalated dramatically. By this time she had left St. Adalbert's school, and now, she alleged, Father Robinson, her mother and other SAM members would take her deep into the woods outside Toledo.

"They killed rabbits," she said, "and made [me] drink the

blood. And then [I would be] vaginally raped with a dead snake that had its head cut off."

They would also allegedly tie her down on a table to torture her, burning her feet with lighted matches, before blowing them out and poking them into her eyes.

Her ordeal finally ended when she was 13 years old, and she then buried all memories of it deep into her subconscious. But recurring nightmares eventually led to her undergoing medical treatment, psychological therapy and counseling.

In the years to come, Jean Marlow would not be the only young girl to accuse Father Robinson of Satanic ritual abuse over this period, although nothing has ever been substantiated.

In July 2006, Jerry Mazuchowski maintained that SAM was merely a party joke, claiming Marlow's allegations against him and Father Robinson were bogus. But the openly homosexual lay minister did admit he and some friends had once worn nuns' habits at Halloween, for a fancy dress party.

"The Sisters of the Assumed Mary were a fictitious group of men, who hung around together in the seventies," he explained. "They were given fictitious nuns' names—[they] called me Mother Superior. They don't exist. They never did."

He dismissed any suggestion that Father Robinson was a part of it.

"There were no priests ever involved," he said. "We went to bars, but there were others that did nun drag on a weekly basis."

But Father Paul Kwiatkowski of St. Hedwig's church said the SAM group certainly did exist. He claims to have seen photographs of group members to prove it, even once having a membership list that he has since lost.

"It was an informal fun thing [when it] started out," he explained. "Some of the fellows would dress up as nuns. I don't know whether Father Robinson was part of that group or not."

Father Kwiatkowski said that a young female member gave him a dossier of its activities and members after becoming disillusioned and leaving it. The girl claimed the group was involved in sexual activity at St. Hedwig, prompting him to re-bless it with another priest.

"She couldn't take it anymore," said Father Kwiatkowski.

Soon afterwards, St. Hedwig's church began to be victimized by SAM, leading to Father Kwiatkowski banning its leader, Jerry Mazuchowski, from church property.

"You see, they were pulling all kinds of pranks at St. Hedwig," explained Father Kwiatkowski.

On one occasion, he claimed, Mazuchowski, who also happened to be president of the parish council, drove up to the church late at night, firing BB gun pellets at Kwiatkowski's quarters.

"They went through the storm window of my bedroom," he remembered. "That was quite dangerous."

Another time, he claims, SAM members deliberately poured gasoline on wood directly under St. Hedwig's church.

"It easily could have gone on fire," said the priest. "So we had guard dogs after that."

Finally Father Kwiatkowski summoned Mazuchowski to the church and read him the riot act. He said that he knew all about SAM and its activities. Then he banned Mazuchowski from St. Hedwig's, removing him from the parish council.

Mazuchowski then complained to the bishop, with the matter ultimately going before the Catholic Diocese of Toledo's Court of Equity, which upheld Father Kwiatkowski's ban.

ON JUNE 15, 1973—ONE YEAR TO THE DAY AFTER RETURNING to St. Adalbert's—Father Gerald Robinson was transferred to St. Michael's, a non-Polish church in Findlay, fifty miles south of Toledo. During his year there as associate pastor, he and Jerry Mazuchowski often socialized together.

"I went to visit him there in Findlay," said Mazuchowski. "I remember it was around Easter time, and one of the things he had introduced in Findlay was the Polish Easter custom where the crucifix is unveiled and put in a red stole, representing the high priesthood of Jesus Christ. The people seemed very enamored of this custom."

Whenever Father Robinson visited Toledo, he, Mazuchowski and another Adalbert's Parish priest named Father Bede, would meet at the Northwood Inn, a traditional Polish restaurant on Summit Street.

"It was rather a high-class restaurant run by Polish people," recalled Mazuchowski. "[Father Robinson] would always drink champagne cocktails. It seemed to be his favorite drink. So he introduced me to champagne cocktails."

Mazuchowski said that although Robinson enjoyed alcohol, he never had a problem, unlike some other priests in the diocese. But even on their nights out, Father Robinson never let his guard down.

During this time, Jack Sparagowski, then in his early twenties, also got to know 35-year-old Father Robinson, who was friends with his parents and often came to their home.

"If you didn't know him," said Sparagowski, "you'd probably think of him as being aloof, stuck-up and unfriendly. But that's not the case at all. He was exactly the opposite of that."

But even if Father Robinson's parishioners liked and respected him, the Diocese of Toledo apparently did not. On June 21, 1974, he was transferred back to Toledo to Mercy Hospital, as one of two chaplains.

It was undoubtedly a demotion with little opportunity to progress. Father Robinson would become increasingly bitter at what he considered a dead-end position, subservient to the nuns who ran the hospital.

"He was being pushed sideways," said a Catholic Diocese insider who wished to remain anonymous. "You could tell by his postings that the Church was putting him in places where he wasn't going to have to be mingling with people as much as other priests would be."

"The bishop appointed the chaplains at that time," explained Sister Phyllis Ann Gerold, then in charge of the hospital. "So we really had little say . . . and then we lived with whatever the problems were."

CHAPTER THREE

Mercy Hospital

MERCY HOSPITAL DATED BACK TO LATE 18TH CENTURY Dublin, when Catherine McAuley, an impoverished 18-year-old Catholic orphan girl, was adopted by a wealthy couple named Mr. and Mrs. Callaghan. Over the years she converted her new foster parents to the Roman Catholic religion, and when Mr. Callaghan died in 1822, he left her his vast fortune.

Catherine decided to use the money to help save fallen women from the Dublin slums, providing an education so they could better themselves. On September 24, 1827, on the feast of Our Lady of Mercy, she opened her first House of Mercy on Baggot Street, in Dublin. It consisted of a school, a home for working mothers and later, an orphanage.

Initially McAuley did not intend it to be a religious order, although spiritual exercises were included in the daily routine. But this led to complaints by other Catholic orders, labeling her work "heretical."

Eventually the Archbishop of Dublin intervened, giving her an ultimatum: she must either drop all religious overtones from the House of Mercy, or bring it into the Catholic Church.

McAuley, then 52, capitulated, agreeing to receive her own religious instruction and become a nun. On December 12, 1831, she took her vows to become a Bride of Christ, and the Sisters of Mercy order was born.

"They didn't essentially want single women living together without some kind of religious community involvements in the 1800s," explained Sister Phyllis Ann Gerold, a former executive director of Toledo's Mercy Hospital and a Sister of Mercy since 1945.

Over the next ten years, until her death in 1841, McAuley helped establish ten more Sisters of Mercy Convents in Ireland and England. A year later, one of her pioneer helpers, Sister Frances Ward, sailed to America, founding the first Mercy Hospital in Pittsburgh, followed by one in Chicago.

By the dawn of the 20th century, the Sisters of Mercy operated hospitals all over the world, becoming the largest English-speaking order of nuns in the world.

In 1912, the Sisters of Mercy moved into Ohio, founding a hospital in Tiffin. Two years later, they opened a large seven-story hospital in Toledo. The new hospital was situated a mile away from the city center, dominating the skyline. In 1918 the Sisters of Mercy opened St. Rita's Hospital in Lima, Ohio, to treat victims of the great global influenza epidemic.

At the end of World War II there was a great need to modernize existing hospitals and build new ones. The landmark 1946 Hill-Burton Act provided federal grants for constructing new hospitals, including several new ones for the order.

At one time the Sisters of Mercy order owned and operated nine hospitals in Ohio. They were all run by nuns, who managed multi-million-dollar budgets and were in charge of hiring and firing hundreds of medical and service employees.

By June 1974, when Father Robinson took up his new position, Mercy Hospital, Toledo was flourishing. It had just undergone an ambitious 29-million-dollar expansion, providing a new 250-bed hospital building and a parking garage.

The 36-year-old priest would now be on call around the clock, administering last rites to dying patients and providing pastoral care. He moved into the hospital, and for the next seven years would live in a cramped two-room suite at the end of a dimly lit corridor on the second floor of the school of nursing.

The room he used as an office contained a desk and a couch, with a small bathroom and shower off to one side.

His bedroom next door overlooked a tiny courtyard, and had a bed and a dresser.

"I didn't have much furniture," Father Robinson would later say.

"I went out there visiting with the people and saying Mass," he said. "That was my work."

As part of his daily duties, Father Robinson was expected to conduct morning Mass in the first-floor chapel, run by an elderly nun named Sister Margaret Ann Pahl, now nearing retirement.

She was 66 years old and becoming increasingly deaf, but had once run two Ohio Mercy Hospitals. Now she was scaling down her duties, working in the less-demanding capacity of sacristan. Her job was to ensure that the chapel and sacristy were kept clean, and that there were ready supplies of Communion wine, wafers, holy water and anointing oil available for daily Mass.

But the slender, hard-working nun still demanded a high standard of work from her housekeeping staff, and if they failed to meet her expectations, she would not hesitate to tell them.

From his first day at Mercy Hospital, Father Robinson and Sister Margaret Ann worked closely together in the chapel, preparing for the daily Mass and sacraments. But from the beginning, there was an uneasiness between them, and things would only get worse as Sister Margaret Ann became increasingly suspicious of the priest's strange behavior in and out of Mercy Hospital.

CHAPTER FOUR
"A Sound Mind in a Sound Body"

SISTER MARGARET ANN PAHL WAS PROUD OF HER FAMILY history, carefully writing it down in her personal journal in her perfect penmanship. In January 1978, she and her younger sister Mary jointly compiled a concise Pahl family history, as a labor of love.

They traced their German Catholic roots back to 1790, when their great-grandfather Peter Pahl was born in the small Baden village of Piltshire, in the heart of the Black Forest. In 1817 Peter married 16-year-old Lena Wermerd. They emigrated to America in 1834, staying a year in Buffalo, New York, before settling in Huron County, Ohio. Lena bore seven children, the youngest being Sister Margaret Ann's grandfather Peter, who was born on August 7, 1837.

When Lena died in 1841, Peter Sr. moved to Defiance, Ohio, where he lived with Peter Jr. and his wife Balbina Willman, until his death in 1873, at the age of 83.

Peter and Balbina had twelve children, the sixth being Francis (Frank) Xavier, who was born in 1871, in the Pahl family's two-story log house in Ney, just outside Defiance, Ohio.

"Memories of Frank's early childhood," the Pahl sisters wrote in their family history. "The snow blowing between the logs onto their beds."

Francis' father built houses and barns, some of which are still standing today. As a young boy he had a pet crow that followed him and his brothers when they cut down trees to provide farm acreage.

Frank would often walk ten miles or more to work, or room with the family that employed him. At the end of the week, he'd walk home with a dollar in his pocket.

"At that time my father played violin," remembered Sister Margaret Ann's sister, Mary Casebere. "He never had a lesson in his life."

Most weekends Francis would play the fiddle at local barn dances. At one of them, he met an attractive 26-year-old woman named Catherine Sophia Coressel, and they began courting.

On May 7, 1901, Francis Xavier, then 29, married Catherine at St. Michael's Church in Defiance, in a ceremony conducted by Father John Heiland. The next day, after packing up their wedding gifts and belongings, they tied a cow to the back of their wagon drawn by their horse Charley. Then they drove thirty miles to Edgerton, Ohio, where Francis had recently bought a forty-acre farm, paying $41 an acre.

At that time Edgerton was thriving. Situated three miles from the Indiana State Line, and seventeen from Michigan, it was well situated on the main New York Central Railroad.

The day after they moved into their new house, Francis and Catherine drove their wagon into town, purchasing a range stove and other basic supplies. Then Francis began working as a carpenter, laying down roots for his long and happy marriage.

Fifteen months later, Catherine gave birth to Leo, the first of their seven children. Two years later they had a daughter, Evelyn.

The Pahls were devout churchgoers. Every Sunday they would hitch Charley to a buggy wagon, driving to St. Mary's Catholic Church in Edgerton. The original St. Mary's Church, which the Pahl family attended, dated back to 1855, when Edgerton's growing Catholic congregation decided to build their own, rather than have to make the long trip to Defiance to attend Mass. But it soon became too small for the growing numbers of Catholics settling in Edgerton, and in 1866 a bigger church opened at the corner of Bement and Locust Streets.

In 1905, Francis's carpentry business was booming, and he bought a one-hundred-acre farm with a windmill and a well, nearer Edgerton. It was here in a modest wooden farm-house that he and Catherine would raise the rest of their family.

A year later she gave birth to a second son named Peter and then on April 8, 1908, Margaret Ann was born, and bap-tized three days later. Two years after that came Laura Marie, followed by Clair in 1912, Catherine in 1914, Mary in 1916, and Cletus a year later, completing the Pahl family.

As soon as she could walk, Margaret Ann was expected to help around the farm, milking cows and running errands. She slept in the chicken coop with her sisters, as her brothers had the barn.

The dark-haired little girl grew up without electricity, running water or indoor plumbing. But the tough, Spartan childhood prepared her for the simple religious life she would later lead as a devout nun.

In September 1914, 6-year-old Margaret Ann entered first grade at Edgerton School, where all her brothers and sisters would go. Every morning she would rise at the crack of dawn, helping her sisters milk the cows, while her broth-ers took care of the horses.

Then the Pahl kids would walk one-and-a-half miles across the fields to a red one-room schoolhouse, where they would join the neighboring children, learning the three Rs and memorizing passages from the Bible.

Margaret Ann was one of the best students in her class, excelling at Mathematics and History. Her teachers would come to have high hopes that the ambitious, outgoing stu-dent would enter a profession, rare for a girl in those days. Her outgoing personality and sense of humor endeared her to everyone. And when she wasn't studying, she loved listen-ing to music or riding her bicycle around Edgerton.

On May 9, 1915, 7-year-old Margaret Ann received her First Holy Communion, followed two days later by her Con-firmation.

All the Pahl children had catechism every Saturday,

learning the basics of the Catholic religion. Right from the beginning, little Margaret Ann and her younger sister Laura Marie, who was quieter and more reserved, both decided to one day become nuns.

"We had two cousins in the Mercy order," said their younger sister Mary. "It was through them that Margaret Ann learned about [the Catholic Church]."

Their younger sister Catherine Flegal remembers Margaret Ann first announcing to the family that she had a vocation.

"She always knew that she'd been called to be a nun," said Catherine. "That's what she always wanted to do."

Highly organized and focused, the bespectacled dark-haired girl already kept a detailed journal, adopting many of the mottos she would live her life by.

"She had these little sayings," remembered her sister Mary. "The one that I remember specifically was:

> *'If a task is once begun,*
> *Never leave it until it's done.*
> *But if the task be great or small,*
> *Do it right or not at all.'* "

In May 1926, the pretty 18-year-old graduated Edgerton High School, and was guided toward the Sisters of Mercy by her two cousins, who were already members of the order. Margaret Ann applied to join and was soon accepted to try out as a novice.

So on September 24, 1927, she packed a suitcase and, after neatly labeling all of her possessions, she gave them away to her siblings, saying she would no longer be needing them.

Then her parents drove Margaret Ann and her three sisters Laura Marie, Mary and Catherine, eighty miles east in the family Buick to Our Lady of the Pines Retreat Center in Fremont, Ohio.

There she spent her first six months as a postulant, learning about the religious life to ensure she had a vocation. During this time she was required to wear a three-quarter-length black dress, with a white collar and cuffs and lace headdress.

On March 24, 1928, she became a novice, learning more about the Sisters of Mercy order and its work in America. For the next two years she wore a full-length black dress with a white habit. She attended Toledo Teachers College, taking courses in Psychology, American History, Elementary Spanish, the Modern Novel, Journalism and Public Speaking. She would eventually receive a Bachelor of Arts degree from Toledo's DeSales College.

She also took Saturday classes, where priests instructed her in Ethics, Moral Philosophy and Poverty. Later in her journal she would carefully summarize all her credits, listing 143, including 45 for nursing courses alone.

Margaret Ann made her initial vows, or first profession, on September 2, 1930. A year later she was assigned to St. Rita's Hospital in Lima to begin her nurse's training.

She took her final vows, or perpetual profession, on September 2, 1933, officially becoming a Sister of Mercy. Her parents and sisters Laura Marie, Mary and Catherine all attended the special ceremony at the chapel at the Pines.

From that point on, she would be known as Sister Mary Annunciata, always wearing a wedding ring to symbolize her being a Bride of Christ.

Two years earlier, her younger sister Laura Marie had also joined the Sisters of Mercy order at Fremont, and was now known as Sister Ancila.

For almost fifty years, the two Pahl sisters would enjoy long and distinguished careers, working for Mercy Hospitals all over Ohio, caring for the poor, sick and ignorant.

ON AUGUST 3, 1934, SISTER MARY ANNUNCIATA RECEIVED HER R.N. degree from St. Rita's Hospital, writing a thesis titled "A Sound Mind in a Sound Body." Her first appointment was as second floor supervisor at St. Rita's. Each August, she would receive her orders for the next year from her superiors.

"You had very little say about what you went into," explained Sister Phyllis Ann Gerold, a few years behind her in the order. "You received a little note every August, [telling] you what you were going to do the following year."

But Sister Mary Annunciata was on the fast track to promotion, and on September 15, 1936—nineteen months before Gerald Robinson was born—she was sent to Mercy Hospital, Toledo, as the assistant superintendent of nurses.

OVER THE NEXT TWENTY YEARS, SISTER MARY ANNUNCIATA was assigned increasingly consequential positions within the Sisters of Mercy organization. She moved freely between the order's Ohio Mercy Hospitals in important executive positions, supervising nursing staff and becoming a top executive.

"She had a lot of responsibility," explained her sister Mary Casebere. "She was very efficient and very much loved."

During World War II, Sister Mary Annunciata served as the night supervisor at Mercy Hospital, Tiffin, about forty miles south of Toledo. Late one night, Ruth Alice Steele, a young sophomore from Heidelberg College was in a truck accident in which another girl was killed. Ruth was brought into the hospital with badly cut hands and wrists, and could not even feed herself.

"A beautiful nun all in white, whom I knew as Sister Annunciata, fed me," Ruth would remember sixty-three years later. "To me, she looked like an angel—I shall never forget her kindness and sweetest smile."

In 1948, Sister Mary Annunciata took over the running of Mercy Hospital, Tiffin, essentially serving as CEO. In 1959, she moved to Toledo to run St. Charles Hospital.

Sister Phyllis Ann Gerold was assigned to Mercy Hospital, Tiffin, as a nursing supervisor when she first met Sister Mary Annunciata in 1954.

"She was an administrator at the time," remembered Sister Phyllis Ann. "She was leaving, so she did the orientation for me. She [was] a very lovely lady [who] had done every job in the building besides engineer."

By now her job was so demanding, it consumed every minute of her days. In one letter to her friend Mary Rose

Tiell, Sister Mary Annunciata complained of never having any time to herself:

> I have some splendid reading material now, including your *gift*, a magazine entitled "Review for Religious," also the "Catholic Digest," and a nursing magazine "The American Journal of Nursing."
>
> All I need now is the time to read. The days are so filled with strict duty that we have little time for anything else.

In another letter she wrote in her neat handwriting of the stress of running one of the biggest hospitals in the metropolitan Toledo area:

> We have been quite busy. We're critically in need of nurses . . . the Lord knows how to manage for us. Besides our regular hospital work, we have apples to pick, put up a new fence along the edge of our property, are getting a new guard rail between our driveway and the parking lot, had black-top put in our ambulance entrance, etc. etc.

In those days, the Sisters of Mercy order was very strict, and Sisters Mary Annunciata and Ancila were only allowed to return to Edgerton for family visits twice a year. While there, they were forbidden to spend the night in the family home, having to stay in a convent in Edgerton.

But although Sister Mary Annunciata rarely saw her siblings and their growing army of children, she made a special effort to get to know each of them through correspondence.

"She was always writing letters to me," remembered her niece, Martha-Jane Dietsch, whom Sister Mary Annunciata helped get a scholarship to study Psychology at St. Charles Hospital, Toledo. "She remembered all the details about the family, and that's hard to do in a family as large as ours. But she cared about each of us. . . . She's just warm, just caring."

AT 6:25 P.M. ON SUNDAY, JUNE 10, 1962, FRANCIS XAVIER PAHL died at St. Charles Hospital at the age of 91, with his family at his side. His wife Catherine would die ten years later at the age of 96.

That September, Sister Mary Annunciata was transferred to Mercy Hospital, Toledo, as associate director of nursing services.

"Good-byes are never easy," ran a tribute story to her in a St. Charles Hospital newsletter, "and they are particularly difficult when you bid a farewell to someone like Sister, whose great warmth and kind personal interest has been felt by all."

Soon afterward Martha-Jane joined her aunt there, for a few months before she graduated.

"I remember going down the hall and talking to her," she recalled. "She made time for anybody she met, which is saying something, because she had a lot of responsibility."

In the late sixties, the Sisters of Mercy relaxed their rules in line with the times. Sisters were now allowed to use their birth names and stay overnight with their families.

So in September 1968, Sister Annunciata—now director of patient relations at St. Rita's Hospital—reverted back to using her real name, becoming Sister Margaret Ann Pahl.

Now Sisters Margaret Ann and Laura Marie started coming to Edgerton for regular family reunions.

"Everybody would visit," remembered her niece Paula Dockery. "All the brothers and sisters would come from all over America to attend." Another of her nieces Jo Ann Pahl Saunders, grew up going to the Edgerton family farm.

"In the summertime we would play croquet," she remembered. "Sister [Margaret Ann] had fun playing. But when we ate dinner Sister couldn't eat with us. She would eat in the kitchen."

On one visit home, Sister Margaret Ann asked a nephew, Don Pahl, if she could drive his new Corvette sports car.

"She had a driving license and wanted to go for a ride," remembered her nephew Lee Pahl, who was there at the time. "So she did. Well, unfortunately, she ended up having a fender bender with it. We never forgot about that. Always chuckled about it."

In early 1971, Sister Margaret Ann, now 63 years old,

looked toward her retirement with a less demanding job. She was no longer as strong as she had once been, and was having problems hearing.

But Sister Margaret Ann still felt useful, wanting to end her long distinguished career in pastoral care.

"She wrote a letter asking if we had an opening," recalled her friend Sister Phyllis Ann Gerold: who was now running Mercy Hospital, Toledo. "We were happy to have her."

On April 12, 1971, Sister Margaret Ann Pahl moved into Room 714 on the seventh-floor convent at the east wing of Mercy Hospital, to become sacristan, responsible for the care and maintenance of the hospital's two chapels.

It was a happy time in Sister Margaret Ann's life, and finally she could slow down and catch up with her reading and letter-writing.

But her indomitable work ethic still drove her to set her two alarm clocks, one for 5:00 a.m., and a backup for 5:30, so she could be the first in the chapel to prepare for early morning Mass.

"She was meticulous," remembered Sister Phyllis Ann, "in a sense that, if you do a job, you should complete it."

So nearly fifty years later she was still living the words of her favorite childhood saying: "Do it right or not at all."

CHAPTER FIVE

A Double Life

BY THE TIME FATHER GERALD ROBINSON JOINED MERCY Hospital, Toledo, Sister Margaret Ann Pahl had been sacristan for more than three years. And in her usual efficient manner she insisted the chapels be kept immaculately clean and well stocked with holy sacraments.

"She was very good at cleaning . . . our convent was neat and clean" explained Sister Phyllis Ann Gerold, then in her early forties and Executive director of Mercy and St. Charles Hospitals.

Almost every day Father Robinson would say Mass in the chapel, in the old building directly above the morgue, using the storeroom sacristy to change into his robe. But by all accounts he did not get on with the elderly sister, considering her "dominating."

As she grew older, Sister Margaret Ann had become increasingly deaf, making it difficult for her to communicate. This led to problems with some of her staff, who resented her raising her voice in frustration, to make herself understood.

One of her colleagues, Sister Mary Flora, later told homicide detectives that Sister Margaret Ann was old-fashioned and a "perfectionist."

"She demanded that everything be done exactly as she wanted it done, and on time," said Sister Mary Flora. "If persons she dealt with did not do things as she expected, then she would vocally display her displeasure."

This led to Sister Margaret Ann having several "conflicts" with one particular housekeeper, who did not meet her standards of cleanliness.

When Shirley Lucas joined Mercy Hospital in 1976 as a housekeeper, she had an immediate run-in with Sister Margaret Ann.

On Lucas' first day at work, Sister Margaret Ann gave her instructions before going off to her room. The new housekeeper immediately began cleaning the bathroom and, as the bars of soap were almost finished, she replaced them with fresh ones. She then changed the toilet paper rolls, some of which only had a couple of sheets remaining.

The next day, Sister Margaret Ann admonished Lucas for being wasteful.

"She proceeded to tell me that when nuns take an oath, they waste nothing," remembered Lucas. "When a bar of soap was real little, she told me to wet it and stick it on a new one."

"She was from the old school," explained Lucas. "Everything just had to be done right. She was very quiet and stern, and very strict."

One afternoon, Lucas was cleaning the convent bathroom when she heard the strains of a Verdi opera coming from Sister Margaret Ann's room. A few minutes later, the elderly nun came in, asking if Shirley liked opera, and who her favorite singer was. The housekeeper said her favorite song was Elvis Presley's version of "How Great Thou Art," and immediately sensed the sister's strong disapproval.

"Catholics should not listen to that," snapped Sister Margaret Ann, before walking out in disgust.

"I just basically did my job and minded my own business," Lucas reflected.

DURING HIS TIME AT MERCY HOSPITAL, FATHER GERALD Robinson kept to himself, saying very little to anybody and not making any friends.

"He did not exude happiness, that's for sure," averred Sister Phyllis Ann. "He's an introverted person, and very timid, I thought."

The former Mercy Hospital CEO remembers the shy priest as being theologically ultra-conservative, something that occasionally created minor problems for her.

Nevertheless the young chaplain did his work well, distancing himself from the emotional toll of performing last rites up to ten times a week. He soon gained a reputation as a loner, with people steering clear of him.

But he seemed strangely active at night, after the rest of the hospital had gone to bed. And this led to much gossip.

On one occasion well after midnight, Mercy Hospital security guard Robert Wodarski was making a routine key check of the parking garage, when he caught Father Robinson on the top floor.

"I think we scared each other," remembered Wodarski. "It was the first time that I'd seen Father Robinson. I asked him what he was doing up there. He said he was meditating."

At least half a dozen times over the next few years, Wodarski would catch the furtive priest lurking suspiciously in the parking garage or the courtyard in front of the hospital, between midnight and six in the morning.

TWO DECADES LATER, A 41-YEAR-OLD NUN WOULD ACCUSE Father Robinson of being linked to the Circle of Darkness, a sinister cult of priests allegedly engaging in murder, rape and torture. Sister Annie Louise (not her real name) would then complain to the Catholic Diocese of Toledo that she was repeatedly abused over a fifteen-year period until she was 18. And in her complaint she would name Father Robinson and disgraced priest Father Chet Warren, who was later thrown out of the Oblates of St. Francis de Sales order in 1993 after five women accused him of sexual misconduct.

Born in 1963, the youngest of three girls, Sister Annie Louise moved to Toledo with her parents when she was 2 years old. She grew up in an affluent neighborhood, attending church and going to Catholic school.

To all appearances she had the perfect childhood, with Barbie dolls and pet dogs, but from the age of 3 she claims to have been used as a sexual plaything, repeatedly tortured and abused by the Circle of Darkness. Her horrific descriptions of Father Gerald Robinson and the cult are remarkably similar to allegations from Jean Marlow and at least four other women.

All the alleged victims describe cult meetings in church basements and rectories, where members engaged in demonic rituals, donning black robes and praising Satan. And like Marlow, Sister Annie Louise blacked out all the horrific memories until 1992, when she sensed having been sexually abused as a child. Then she started having flashbacks and, over the next few years, with the help of counseling, started filling in the horrific blanks.

In 2003 she wrote a four-page letter to the Toledo diocese, describing secret depraved "cult-like ceremonies," naming Father Gerald Robinson as one of her sexual abusers.

"I've had nightmares about this since I was a child," she told the *Toledo Blade*. "I didn't think anyone would believe me."

She said Father Warren, who led the cult, was a trusted family friend, who was helping her mother overcome depression. She also alleged that her parents and grandfather were all cult members, actively participating in the ceremonies.

The Toledo diocese took her allegations so seriously that it assigned two diocesan detectives to interview her and investigate her startling claims.

The nun described, in harrowing detail, being taken across the state line to a campground in Michigan when she was 5 or 6. She was brought into a cabin with a stone fireplace, and stripped naked. Then she was forced to lie on the floor by a blazing fire, as three men in black robes stood around her.

As the ceremony began, according to the nun's allegations, the men started making "clicking" sounds with their mouths, and slowly twisting and twirling ceremonial knives. They began stroking her bare skin with the blades and poking her, but were careful not to cut her.

One of the robed men started slowly beating a drum, as the other members danced around her. Then one of them approached, lifted up his black robe and started to have sex with her.

Sister Annie Louise described in gruesome detail how she was forced to participate in similar ceremonies as she was growing up in Toledo. But her most horrific memories were of what she called "the House of Blood," a run-down wooden farmhouse at the end of a long dirt driveway on Raab Road, just outside Toledo.

On one occasion in 1972 when she was 9, she claims to have been taken out of her elementary school class at midday by one of the cult. She was then driven to the farmhouse in her grandfather's car, and taken down into the basement, where a man with a crew cut was waiting for her with the rest of the cult.

"You will get to know what happens to little girls that talk about the Circle of Darkness," he warned, leading her into a small room off the basement with shelves and a tiny window.

There, to her horror, she says she saw the bodies of six young girls between the ages of 6 and 11, dangling from meat hooks.

"Their eyes were open," recalled Sister Annie Louise, "and there were no marks on their bodies."

Then the man told her to pick one of the girls. At first she refused, but eventually selected a little girl of about 6 with short blonde hair.

The man removed the dead girl's body from the hook and carried it back into the basement, laying it on a table. He then handed Annie Louise a handsaw, ordering her to start cutting up the body. When the terrified little girl refused, two men held her arms, forcing her to start sawing.

She remembers regurgitating in disgust and one of her torturers made her lick up the vomit as punishment.

"Damn you!" he screamed at her. "Can't you do anything right?"

On another occasion, when she was 11 years old, she says

she was driven to the House of Blood at 1:00 a.m. and brought into the basement, where seven men and three women clad in black robes were waiting.

"A bowl containing an eyeball was brought in," she wrote. "It looked like a human eye. One of the leaders said, 'Take it, eat it, chew it, and swallow it.' He said the eyeball would always be with me and that I would always be a part of them. The group would always be watching me."

She was then stripped naked and a dark curly-haired little girl of about 3 years old, whom Annie did not know, was brought in. Sister Annie Louise later told Toledo diocesan investigators that she believed the child had been drugged, as she seemed very tired and moved so slowly.

"They tied the girl to a wooden chair," she said. "And they put a machete in my hands. They told me to kill her, but I couldn't do it."

Then one of the robed men held her arm tightly, she later told investigators, forcing her to swing the machete into the girl's neck, causing a deep cut. The child collapsed on the chair, as blood began pouring from the wound. Then he repeatedly forced her to strike the girl again and again, until she was dead.

When he finally let go of Annie Louise's arm, another man pushed her to the cement floor and raped her.

Afterward they all left, locking the basement and leaving her alone with the little girl's mangled body. Annie Louise told the investigators she was so traumatized that she was physically sick, dropping down to the bloody floor, where she found a cardboard box.

"The cardboard was a little island," she explained. "I told myself if I stayed on the cardboard, I wouldn't go crazy. I wish I had died."

At dawn the cult members returned to the basement, and began cleaning the blood off the floor with bleach. They put the girl's body in black plastic bags and drove Annie Louise home.

Although Sister Annie Louise told diocesan investigators she could not be certain if Father Robinson had been one of her torturers at the House of Blood, she claimed he had used her as his sex slave and violently beaten her on another occasion.

She tearfully told the investigators how, in the late 1970s, Father Chet Warren had operated a "little prostitution ring" at St. Vincent Hospital, where he worked as a chaplain. Every couple of months she would be taken to Father Warren's bedroom, where various men would have sex with her.

"I also remember Robinson being there when Warren took pornographic photos of me when I was about 15," she said.

She described one afternoon in September 1978 or 1979, when her father had driven her to St. Vincent Hospital. In the car park they had been met by Father Warren, who then brought her to his quarters, taking her into the bedroom and leaving.

A few minutes later, she claimed, Father Gerald Robinson walked in, wearing a dark jacket and black pants. She saw him hand Warren a white envelope with money in it for an hour of sex.

"She's all yours," Warren told Father Robinson. "Have fun."

The nun told the investigators how Father Robinson had first ordered her to strip naked, before getting a black leather jacket and a pair of spiked black leather cuffs out of a closet, and putting them on. He then proceeded to tie her to the bed with ropes, leaving her spread-eagled and helpless.

Then he started licking and biting her breasts, arms and thighs, calling her "whore" and "pussy."

"The foreplay was painful," Sister Annie Louise told the diocesan investigators. "He was pinching me and saying disgusting things."

At one point he took out a black whip from the closet and began thrashing her, becoming increasingly angry. Suddenly he stopped, holding out the handle toward her.

"You deserve this, you whore," he declared, as he penetrated her vagina with the handle.

"He's a maniac," Sister Annie Louise tearfully told the investigators. "He wanted to humiliate me."

She said Father Robinson had ejaculated twice on her before walking out of the bedroom.

A few minutes later, she continued, Father Chet Warren returned and untied her, according to Sister Annie Louise's allegations, asking if she had enjoyed herself. He then told her to dress, and took her to the hospital's main entrance, where he handed her father an envelope with cash in it.

"That was the only time I saw Father Robinson in the chaplain's quarters," said Sister Annie Louise. "There were a lot of different men. I didn't know them all."

CHAPTER SIX

"Why Do They Cheat God?"

IN 1977, FATHER JEROME SWIATECKI WAS ASSIGNED TO MERCY Hospital as the new junior chaplain. And although both he and Father Robinson were of Polish descent, they could not have been more different.

The son of a Toledo police officer, Father Swiatecki was well over 6 feet tall, weighing about 300 pounds. The always outspoken chaplain, then in his mid-fifties, towered above the introverted and skinny Father Robinson.

"Father Swiatecki was Friar Tuck," recalled former Mercy Hospital security officer Robert Wodarski. "He was a big man."

The larger-than-life priest with thick glasses and receding slicked-back hair had spent eight years at St. Augustine Catholic Church in Napoleon, Ohio, but a serious drinking problem had sidelined him into rehab. Now he was in a twelve-step program, and had been transferred to Mercy Hospital as a last resort.

"Father Jerry's commanding voice," read a tactfully worded tribute when he left St. Augustine, "combined with a sensitive manner, allowed him to serve many in need."

The good-natured priest was rarely seen without a cigar in his mouth, and was an avid sculptor and woodcarver, considering himself something of an artist.

"He was big, overpowering and bombastic," remembered Sister Phyllis Ann Gerold. "The biggest thing was that he was a former alcoholic and he spoke about it at great length.

That he'd gone through the program and that he'd been off drink for many years."

Father Swiatecki now drank only coffee, and each morning after Mass, he'd go to the Mercy Hospital security office to talk sports over a few cups.

"The man loved coffee," said Wodarski. "We always had coffee in our office, and we'd go outside and have a cigarette and talk."

Former Toledo Police Officer Dave Davison, whose regular beat included the hospital, got to know Father Swiatecki well in the staff canteen over breakfast.

"He was what you would call a police groupie," remembered Davison. "He liked police. He would come down and smoke cigars and shoot the breeze down in the emergency room with us. I mean, everybody liked him at the hospital."

But the only person he did not get along with was Father Gerald Robinson, who took an immediate dislike to his new junior chaplain. Although the two priests divided their duties and ate meals together, they rarely talked, and kept out of each other's way whenever possible.

"They detested each other," said Father Robinson's friend Jerry Mazuchowski. "There was an animosity between them because they came from the two different Polish communities. Father Robinson was from Kuschwantz and Father Swiatecki was from Lagrinka, and there was always that silly, silly tension."

Sister Phyllis Ann also noted how differently they were regarded by Toledo's Polish congregation.

"Father Robinson was loved by the Polish people," she remembered, "while Father Swiatecki did not make any efforts to court the Polish population in Toledo. I would presume it was just the opposite."

ON MARCH 20, 1977, SISTER MARGARET ANN PAHL CELEBRATED her golden anniversary as a Bride of Christ at a special ceremony at the Pines in Fremont, where she had first entered the Sisters of Mercy order half a century earlier. Six months later, she celebrated again with her family in Edgerton.

Later, in her journal, she would proudly list the items she had purchased with gift money. She was especially proud of a new $59.95 silver Bulova watch she had bought from Heumann's Jewelers, proudly noting her 20 percent discount. She also bought a radio/tape recorder and a digital alarm clock at Edgerton Hardware.

On her return to Mercy Hospital, Sister Margaret Ann knew she was nearing the end of her long career. Yet in addition to her duties as sacristan of the facility's two chapels, she had recently taken on the additional responsibility of being moderator for the Mercy Guild, a volunteer support group for the hospital. Although she had recently been hospitalized for a short period, she never complained or eased up on her daily workload, still, for example, making daily afternoon orange juice runs, carrying a heavy full pitcher from the kitchen to the nuns who worked in the hospital.

"She had some medical problems that were minor, and hearing difficulty," remembered Sister Phyllis Ann, "but her mind was good."

ALTHOUGH FATHER GERALD ROBINSON WAS NOT PARTICU-larly popular at Mercy Hospital, he was well-loved in the Polish neighborhoods. Mary Chrzanowski, now a judge, grew up in Detroit, but regularly visited her Aunt Sophie Domanski, a prominent member of the Toledo Polish community. She got to know Father Robinson, who often brought his parents to her aunt's house on religious occasions.

"He was the epitome of a priest," remembered Judge Chrzanowski. "He was a very holy man. Very spiritual."

She fondly remembers Father Robinson presiding over baptisms, weddings and Holy Communions, and attending birthdays and holiday celebrations.

"He was very loyal to his mother and father," she recalled. "I never heard him raise his voice. Ever. Even as kids, if we did something to maybe upset him, like throw a baseball in his direction, he was never somebody to become quickly angered."

"He was really considered *the* priest," said Jack

Sparagowski, later President of St. Anthony's church council. "As laid-back as he was, if you simply heard him presenting a homily . . . his voice bellowed. He projected very well. In fact, he did a eulogy for one of our parishioners that was almost spellbinding. He was just that much of an orator."

Father Robinson was also chaplain to a local Catholic scout group. On one occasion in the mid-1970s, the scouts took a trip to Washington, D.C., bringing him back a souvenir dagger-shaped letter opener from the National Historical Wax Museum, complete with a nickel-sized medallion of the Capitol building on the handle.

After thanking them, Father Robinson put it in the desk in his room for safekeeping.

IN MID-JANUARY 1980, THREE MONTHS BEFORE HER 72nd birthday, Sister Margaret Ann Pahl attended a Pahl family reunion in Edgerton. It was the first time she had seen many of her new grandnieces and grandnephews, including Lee Pahl's baby son Randall.

"She was at the point she was going to go back to the Pines to retire," remembered her younger sister Mary Casebere. "She was all excited. She says, 'I got my stocking cap and I'm getting ready to go to the Pines . . . It's such a beautiful spot.' "

One night over dinner, Sister Margaret Ann had a long conversation with her younger sister Laura Marie, now with the Sisters of Mercy in Jamestown, Virginia, and told her she would be retiring. She spoke of a "power struggle" among two senior nuns for the top job at Mercy Hospital, and also confided that she had recently been warned not to go into the chapel alone, as a suspicious character had been lurking around. She said the Mercy Hospital chapel was open to the public, and the other sisters did not want her to risk any type of confrontation.

The next morning Sister Margaret Ann returned to Toledo to make final preparations for her retirement. It would be the last time she would ever see Edgerton and her family.

AT NOON ON GOOD FRIDAY, APRIL 4, 1980, FATHER ROBINSON said Mass in St. Joseph's Chapel, with Sister Margaret Ann Pahl among the small congregation. A few hours earlier, the Holy Eucharist—the body and blood of Jesus Christ—had been placed in sacristy. In *the* most solemn service of the year, Catholic tradition dictates a series of meditations and readings, as well as the highly dramatic Passion account from the Gospel of St. John, involving the priest and the congregation.

But today Father Robinson inexplicably shortened the service, without consulting anyone else. Sister Margaret Ann Pahl became so indignant, she challenged him on it.

As the elderly nun berated him, Father Gerald Robinson remained silent, merely staring at her through thick black-rimmed glasses, before walking out of the chapel, leaving her distraught by St. Joseph's altar.

"I think this was the final straw," Lucas County Lead Prosecutor Dean Mandross later claimed. "A lot of things had been building with him over time. And he just snapped."

After composing herself, the distraught nun took the elevator seven floors up to the convent, leaving a note for Shirley Lucas on the main door to meet her in the chapel. Then she began her preparations for Holy Saturday services.

When Shirley Lucas walked into the ground floor chapel, Sister Margaret Ann motioned for her to remain outside until she came out. A few minutes later the elderly nun appeared, telling the housekeeper to go back and clean the convent and come down again when she had finished. The sister said she was waiting to talk to Father Robinson, who was on his way back.

She then took the convent key, pinning it to the inside of Shirley Lucas' uniform, before dismissing her.

"She made me feel like a little kid in kindergarten," Lucas later remembered.

After cleaning the convent, she returned to the chapel, waiting outside in the hall for Sister Margaret Ann, who eventually came out looking visibly distressed.

"When I handed her the key, she grabbed my hand," remembered Lucas. "Then she wished me and my two daughters a peaceful and blessed Easter."

Suddenly Sister Margaret Ann became emotional, something the housekeeper had never seen before.

"She squeezed my hands," she recalled. "She had tears in her eyes. You could tell she was upset. Then she says, 'Why do they cheat God out of what belongs to him?'

"I said, 'Sister, I don't know.' Then she gave my hand a squeeze and walked away."

The housekeeper was surprised by Sister Margaret Ann's uncharacteristic emotional display. In all the years she had known her, Shirley had always considered her boss on "the cold side," never even wishing her a merry Christmas or asking after her children, as the other nuns did.

When Sister Margaret Ann went back into the chapel, the housekeeper was also overcome by emotion.

"I lost it," she later recalled. "I cried after she turned around. I had to go to the bathroom. I don't know if it was because it was the first time that she ever touched me and held my hand. She just looked so pitiful and emotional.

"Maybe she had a feeling that something was going to happen to her."

CHAPTER SEVEN

Holy Saturday

AT 5:00 A.M. ON SATURDAY, APRIL 5, SISTER MARGARET ANN
Pahl's digital alarm clock went off. It was Easter Saturday—
one of only three days in the Catholic calendar with no 6:00
a.m. Mass—and she could have stayed in bed for several
more hours. But Sister Margaret Ann was a creature of habit,
and, although tomorrow would be her 72nd birthday, the
thought never crossed her mind. Even if she had accidentally fallen back to sleep, there was always a second clock
set for 5:30 a.m., as a backup.

As there would not be services until the Easter Vigil Mass
that evening, her only task would be taking down the religious decorations from the chapel altars, a sign of mourning
for the death of Jesus Christ.

After showering, she put on her uniform—a blue smock
with a cross pinned on the left side over a white long-sleeve
blouse—and laced up her blue oxford shoes. Then she carefully arranged her veil over her snow-white hair. Now she
was ready to start the day that Catholics consider the qui-
etest and calmest of the religious year.

Sister Margaret Ann left her room at about 6:00 a.m.,
locking the door behind her. She walked out of the convent,
taking the elevator down to the first floor. The hospital was
unusually quiet—most of the student nurses had gone home
for the Easter holidays, and it was running on a skeleton staff.

She first stopped off at the telephone switchboard to pick
up some papers before walking to the sisters' dining room
for breakfast.

It was 6:15 a.m. and cafeteria worker Audrey Garroway, 31, wished her good morning. The elderly sister apologized for being late unlocking the canteen door, as she usually did. But Audrey told her not to worry, as she had gotten in with a spare key.

"She was going to the chapel," the cheerful Jamaican-born canteen worker would later remember. "She asked to borrow a green tray."

After leaving the cafeteria, Sister Margaret Ann walked down the hall to St. Joseph's Chapel, unlocking the door to let herself in. Then she went into the adjoining sacristy, turning on the ceiling light. She loaded the tray with incense, linens, a paschal candle cover, a brown paper bag and some Reynolds Wrap, carrying it back into the chapel and leaving it on the front wooden pew.

Then she returned to the dining room for breakfast, ordering coffee, grapefruit and raisin bran.

"She said she didn't have time to eat," remembered Audrey Garroway, "but she'd have coffee."

At about 6:45 a.m., Sister Margaret Ann walked back to the chapel, passing ambulance drivers Jerry Tressler and Robert Powers, who were coming off the night shift. She bade them good morning and then hurried toward an exit door. Tressler would later tell detectives he had looked at his watch after seeing her. It had been 6:50 a.m.

Back in the chapel, Sister Margaret Ann began removing the decorations from the tall statue of St. Joseph, which towered above her. In order to reach the drapes behind it, she had to stand on a wooden chair. So after putting her keys and purse in a small cabinet by the window, she carefully positioned the chair sideways, placing a small footstool in front of it with a newspaper on top to protect it from her shoes.

Then she slowly climbed up on the chair, taking down the gold crucifix and chalice. She came down again, bringing the items into the sacristy, and placing them in a cabinet drawer for safekeeping.

Returning to the chapel, she got back on the chair to remove the pins and masking tape, freeing the drapes behind the altar. Then she went back into the sacristy to put away the candles and finish preparations for the evening services.

But the hard-of-hearing nun never heard someone enter the chapel, lock the door and then come into the sacristy.

PROSECUTORS WOULD LATER THEORIZE FATHER GERALD Robinson hardly slept that night. Since Sister Margaret Ann Pahl had admonished him the previous afternoon, he had seethed with anger. How dare she order him around like that, telling him how to organize his services? Now all the years of slow growing resentment for her and her damned hospital were boiling over.

The priest, frustrated by his stalled career, had come to a decision. He was not going to take it anymore. He'd had enough of Sister Margaret Ann's dominating attitude, and had decided to teach her a lesson once and for all.

All that night he had lain awake, preparing himself for what he had to do. He was well acquainted with the sister's routine, knowing she would be in the chapel early, removing Easter decorations. Well, it would be there that he would finally get his revenge.

Just after 6:00 a.m. he got out of bed, washed and dressed in his black cassock and a pair of rubber-soled shoes. He walked over to his desk, taking out the dagger-shaped letter opener that his scout group had brought him from Washington, D.C., placing it in a duffle bag.

A little before 7:00 a.m. he left his second-floor quarters, walking slowly down the corridor. There was no one around as he took the stairs down to the first floor to an enclosed bridge linking the professional building to the hospital.

The door to the chapel had been open, as it always was, and he had slipped in. He crept up to the sacristy door and peered in, seeing Sister Margaret Ann Pahl already hard at work. He stood there for a few seconds, steeling himself for what he had to do.

Then, using his key, he locked the chapel door behind him. He saw a long white linen altar cloth lying by the altar and picked it up, walking softly into the sanctuary. He felt relieved that Sister Margaret Ann was too deaf to hear him.

Now inside, he saw Sister Margaret Ann standing on a chair, removing drapes. He put down his duffle bag and watched her for a while, gripping the altar cloth tightly in both hands.

When she came down from the chair, he came up behind her. Suddenly, he threw the cloth over her neck, pulling it as hard as he could, sending her spectacles smashing to the stone floor. The elderly nun had no time to scream or defend herself against the powerful younger priest, as he viciously choked her with all of his strength. For two long minutes he suffocated her. The sheer force of his attack snapped two bones in the side of her neck and burst the tiny blood vessels in her eyes.

Finally she went limp. Father Gerald Robinson laid her body out on the floor in front of the Holy Eucharist. Now he was ready to perform a Satanic, bastardized version of the last rites, as he had so many times before. Only this time, the last anointing would be to the devil.

He first covered her with the long white linen altar cloth, placing an upside-down crucifix over her heart. He relished the knowledge that the inverted cross was a blasphemous insult to God, the ultimate degradation and humiliation.

Reaching into his duffle bag, he drew out the dagger-shaped letter opener, gripping it tightly in his hand. Then, positioning it over the inverted cross, he thrust down hard, repeatedly, around the upside-down crucifix. Because Sister Margaret Ann's heart had stopped beating, there was no blood.

Again and again he brought the blade down hard, nine times through the white altar cloth, piercing deep into her flesh. Furious at the lack of blood, he ripped off the altar cloth, ferociously stabbing her face, neck and chest. Later, no fewer than thirty-one deep stab wounds would be discovered all over her body.

When he'd finally finished his work, the blade of his letter opener had found enough blood to anoint her with.

He carefully pressed the handle of the letter opener, with its embossed medallion of the Capitol building, against the sister's bloody blue smock until it was covered in blood. Then he lifted it up, pressing it down hard on her forehead, leaving an imprint.

Father Robinson then proceeded to deliver his bastardized version of the last rites, anointing the Bride of Christ with her own blood to the glory of Satan.

But Father Robinson had still not finished. He had one unspeakable final act of humiliation to complete.

Returning the bloody weapon to his duffle bag, he knelt down on the cold tiled floor and began to undress her. He neatly rolled up her habit over her brassiere, almost up to her throat. Then, using all his strength, he pulled her pantyhose and girdle down to her ankles, and, after a struggle, removed her left shoe.

He then spread her legs apart and, taking the crucifix he had used to stab her, penetrated the virginal nun in defilement of her vows of chastity.

After he had finished, he straightened up her arms and legs, carefully posing her body to leave a clear message for everyone to see. Then he slowly stood up, surveying his bloody work. His small beady eyes scanned over her defiled body, lying naked and exposed, as if in a coffin on the cold sacristy floor.

She lay inches away from the Holy Eucharist—the very flesh and blood of Jesus Christ on the anniversary of his crucifixion. Tightly wound around her neck was her silver chain and cross with the words "I AM A CATHOLIC. PLEASE CALL A PRIEST."

Then, composing himself, Father Robinson picked up the bloody altar cloth he'd stabbed the sister through and left the sacristy.

A LITTLE AFTER 7:00 A.M., FATHER GERALD ROBINSON CAME out of the chapel. To his horror, he saw a young laboratory assistant named Grace Jones waiting for the elevators. He froze, uncertain of what to do, accidentally dropping the altar cloth on the floor outside the chapel.

Then he instinctively walked toward Jones, nodding as he passed, leaving the hospital through the Madison Avenue exit. A few minutes later, Father Robinson came back into the hospital, running back to the safety of his quarters and closing the door behind him.

CHAPTER EIGHT
"Mr. Swift" Call

LESS THAN AN HOUR LATER, SISTER MADELYN MARIE GORdon's anguished screams brought Mercy Hospital to a standstill.

"I heard this terrible screaming," remembered Sister Phyllis Ann Gerold, who was eating breakfast with Sister Mary Flora. "I left the dining room and ran to the chapel."

Inside she found Sisters Mary Phillip and Clarisena, trying to comfort their hysterical colleague. It was several minutes before she was composed enough to tell them that Sister Margaret Ann had been raped in the sacristy.

Then Sister Phyllis Ann went into the sacristy, where she found Sister Margaret Ann's exposed, mutilated body, lying on the polished terra-cotta floor.

"It was terribly strange," she would later recall, "and sad and horrifying."

The head of Mercy Hospital immediately noted the strange, ritualistic way Sister Margaret Ann's body had been left.

"She was posed," Sister Phyllis Ann later testified. "The weirdness of it. The horror. Why the ritualistic layout of a dead body? She was laid out on the floor very neatly with her clothes pulled up."

Her nurse's training instinctively told her that the sister's swollen face meant she still had air in her chest, and needed immediate attention.

"I don't think at the time I realized she was dead," she would explain. "I went into nurse mode. I was going to save her, but I couldn't find that phone in that room. I did not touch Sister. I did not see any blood. I still don't understand that."

Finally, unable to find the phone, Sister Phyllis Ann ran out through the chapel and back to the dining room, telling Sister Mary Flora to initiate an emergency "Mr. Swift" call to summon medical help.

BACK IN HIS QUARTERS, FATHER GERALD ROBINSON WAS BUSY cleaning Sister Margaret Ann's blood off his letter opener and trying to calm himself. Fifteen minutes after returning to his room, he'd suddenly realized he had dropped the bloodstained altar cloth somewhere by the chapel. He would have to go back and retrieve it, as it was so incriminating.

So at about 7:50 a.m. he came out of his quarters and down the stairs to the first floor, retracing his steps along the tunnel to the chapel. He was searching for the altar cloth in the hallway, when the "Mr. Swift" call came through the hospital's public address system.

Suddenly he saw Dr. Jack Baron coming toward him in response to the emergency code call. Confused and not knowing what to do, Father Robinson walked past the doctor, and then looked back at him over his left shoulder.

Later Dr. Baron would testify that he would "never forget" that chilling stare, which went "right through" him.

Father Robinson then ran back to his room without encountering anyone else. Once inside, he locked the door behind him, waiting to be summoned to administer the last rites to Sister Margaret Ann Pahl.

A FEW MINUTES EARLIER, DR. DONALD WOODARD, A 30-YEAR-old resident intern, had been walking toward the chapel, when he heard Sister Madelyn Marie's piercing screams.

"I saw two of the sisters," he told detectives several hours later, "run out of the dining room toward the chapel."

Dr. Woodard followed them into the chapel, where he saw Sister Madelyn Marie in the first pew, crying uncontrollably.

"She was in hysterics," he remembered. "I thought something was wrong with her."

One of the sisters said Sister Margaret Ann was "hurt" in the sacristy, and Dr. Woodard went straight in.

"I saw Sister Margaret Ann lying faceup on her back. Her neck was swelled and bloody," he later remembered. "I can't recall if her glasses were on at the time. Her underwear was down around her ankles, her dress was up over her breast. From the waist down her naked body was exposed."

Dr. Woodard then desperately tried to resuscitate her. "I put my ear to her mouth, checked for breath, heartbeat and pulse, but there was none. Her eyes were fixed and dilated. Life was gone."

He then pulled down the sister's collar from her neck and was horrified by what had been done to her.

"That is when I noticed," he told detectives, "and told one of the sisters to call security."

Then Dr. Baron and the rest of the "Mr. Swift" team arrived. Dr. Woodard told them that the sister was dead and had possibly been raped.

Dr. Baron noted how the nun's hands were both by her side. He reached down and clasped her wrists, noting they were "slightly cold, with no pulse." He felt her chest, but there was no heartbeat. Out of respect, he asked a nurse to cover the sister's body with a white blanket from the medical supply cart.

Then Father Swiatecki entered and started administering the last rites, as emergency medical staff began clearing people out of the sacristy.

Meanwhile, from her office across from the chapel, Sister Phyllis Ann Gerold informed the Catholic Diocese of Toledo. As she was speaking, a nurse rushed in to tell her that Sister Margaret Ann Pahl had died. Sister Phyllis Ann then returned to the chapel, where all the nuns and other key personnel were—with the exception of Father Gerald Robinson.

"News in hospitals travels fast," Sister Phyllis Ann later explained, noting how she'd thought it strange he was missing. "So I called him."

Later, Father Robinson would tell detectives he was buttoning up his cassock when he'd received Sister Phyllis

Ann's call. He'd immediately run to the chapel, where Father Swiatecki was in the sacristy, administering the last rites.

A terrible change came over Father Swiatecki as soon as he saw Father Robinson come in. He stopped anointing Sister Margaret Ann and slowly rose to his feet, shaking his finger at Robinson.

"Why did you kill her?" he asked, his voice breaking with emotion. "Why did you kill her?"

But Father Robinson just stood silently, to the astonishment of the other nuns and doctors.

"I just looked at him," Father Robinson would later explain, "because it's the first I'm seeing Sister—and to say something like that . . . I had no idea what he was talking about."

AT 8:15 A.M., TOLEDO UNIFORMED POLICE OFFICERS DAVE Davison and Dan Deeter were eating a breakfast of eggs and bacon at Mercy Hospital, after working the night shift. They were on a punishment detail for "attitude problems," assigned to the area around the hospital, surrounded by four dangerous housing projects.

"It was Toledo's ghetto," explained Officer Davison. "The hospital was the only place you could go into to use the restrooms or clean up. And it was the only place to eat breakfast."

Suddenly the canteen telephone rang and Davison answered. On the other end was an excited nun, telling him to come straight to the chapel.

"We have a dead nun up there," she said, before hanging up.

At that moment a nurse burst into the canteen, shouting that there was a dead nun in the chapel. As neither officer knew where the chapel was, a nurse took them there.

When they walked into the chapel, they found a crowd of curious nurses, doctors and nuns standing around, who pointed them toward the sacristy.

Later Davison would explain how he had initially thought the elderly nun had suffered a stroke or heart attack.

"She's covered in white sheets," he remembered. "All we

could see was just from a little above the knees down to her feet. Her panties were down around her ankles.

"Then somebody blurted out, 'She's been stabbed!' Then we knew it was a murder."

As the more experienced of the two, Davison took charge, telling Deeter to protect the crime scene at all costs, although it was obviously already contaminated. They ordered everyone out of the sacristy and chapel, and began separating them.

"Then we called the police dispatcher," said Officer Davison. "I said, 'We need assistance up here immediately, as a nun's been murdered.'"

While waiting for detectives to arrive, the two officers shepherded the twenty possible witnesses into the hall outside the chapel, sitting them on chairs ten feet apart.

"I tried to get initial statements," he explained. "What I wanted was people's names, because they were already trying to get out. They didn't want to get involved."

For the next few minutes, Davison and Deeter took down as many names as possible, and brief statements.

"I kept saying, 'Who's capable of this?'" Davison later remembered. "They all said, 'Father Robinson.'"

CHAPTER NINE

The Investigation

AT ABOUT 8:30 A.M. THE CODE 18 CALL CAME IN TO THE Toledo police headquarters in the Safety Building at 525 N. Erie Street. Within five minutes Detectives Arthur Marx, Tom Staff, Dan Foster and Sergeant Larry Przeslawski were on their way to Mercy Hospital to investigate.

"The victim was a Catholic nun," said Detective Marx, who was immediately assigned the role of lead detective. "She had been stabbed to death and possibly sexually assaulted."

At 8:40 a.m., the detectives met Sister Phyllis Ann Gerold at the Twenty-third Street entrance of Mercy Hospital. The Mercy Hospital CEO then escorted them to the chapel, to be briefed by Officers Davison and Deeter, who gave them a list of hospital personnel and a summary of the interviews they had already conducted.

"Then they sent us away," remembered Officer Davison. "Told us to go to the bus station in downtown Toledo, to look for people covered in blood [who] were trying to get out of town."

Soon after arriving at the hospital, Lead Detective Marx cordoned off the chapel area, where he was joined by Toledo police evidence technician Ed Marok. Then at 8:40 a.m., Marx and Marok went into the chapel, spending the next hour processing the murder scene, while the other detectives began interviewing possible witnesses.

"The body was found lying on her back on the floor, in the approximate center of the Sacristy," Detective Marx later wrote in his report. "The body was covered with a white sheet-type blanket."

He then partially removed the sheet, checking for any signs of life.

[Her body] was "cold to the touch," he wrote.

Detective Marx also tested Sister Margaret Ann for signs of rigor mortis by slightly raising her right arm, but found none.

The lead detective then drew a detailed crime-scene sketch, as Detective Marok began taking numerous black-and-white photographs of the murder scene, using a state-of-the-art German-made Horseman camera, specifically designed for recording crime scenes on large format 120 film.

At 8:50 a.m. Tim Fish, an investigator for the Lucas County Coroner's office, arrived at the chapel. He viewed Sister Margaret Ann Pahl's body before arranging for its transportation to the Lucas County morgue.

"A detailed examination of the body revealed the following information," Marx later reported.

> The body was positioned as follows: head to the west, feet to the east. Her veil, which is black in color and worn as part of the Sister's uniform, was lying under the back of her head, with the end of the veil extending out and to the right.
>
> There were visible traces of what appeared to be dried blood on the bridge and tip of the nose. There were also numerous puncture type wounds on the right side of the face and neck. The blood that apparently seeped from these wounds appeared to still be wet and was dark in color.

Marx also noted that a white altar cloth from St. Joseph's Chapel had been wrapped around the sister's right forearm one time, the remaining material lying along the right side of her body, extending to just below her right knee.

> "There were several red stains visible on the lower section of the cloth that appeared to be blood," he wrote. A closer examination of the cloth revealed several punctures . . . in the

area near the right forearm. It appeared that the victim's right arm had been resting across the front of her chest when she was stabbed.

This could be determined by comparing the punctures on the altar cloth with the visible punctures in the dress in the area of the chest.

From the way the victim's two hands were positioned palm-up, her fingers forming a loose fist, he deduced that she had not been able to defend herself. He also reported that both her legs were straight, but spread apart at the ankles approximately twelve inches, with no visible injuries.

Her gray plastic-framed glasses lay on the tiled floor, about eight inches from her right hand. There appeared to be smudges of blood on the right lens.

Detective Marx observed that Sister Margaret Ann was wearing a "blue jumper-type knit dress," with a cross pinned above her left breast.

"The dress had visible stains on the front that appeared to be blood," he wrote.

The stains were concentrated above the left side of the upper chest. The dress was saturated with the stains which were still moist. Numerous punctures were also visible in the dress in the area of the upper left chest.

The victim was also wearing a white long-sleeved blouse, gray panty hose, a white rubber elastic panty girdle that had been pulled down and was now resting around the right ankle. The girdle would have been slid over the left ankle and foot to be found in this position. The victim was also wearing blue Oxford type shoes (laces both tied).

Later, at the morgue, it was determined that she was wearing a white bra and blue slip.

After photographing Sister Margaret Ann's body and the 11′ × 17′ sacristy from all angles, evidence technician Marok searched for latent fingerprints at the murder scene and around the hospital, paying special attention to exit doors.

He also began collecting evidence, placing it in sealed envelopes, which he later stored in the property room of the Safety Building.

"There was a large white altar cloth," he remembered. "The one that was draped over the nun with the blood and holes in it. And her personal glasses. I secured those. Those were the only items that I took in addition to the latent prints at the hospital."

Detective Marx's subsequent report noted that a window shade on one of the two sacristy windows had been pulled all the way down, making him think the murderer was well acquainted with the sacristy.

"[It's] usually kept halfway down," he wrote.

It appears that the suspect responsible for the homicide may have pulled the shade down to avoid being observed. It is this investigator's opinion that a stranger to the surroundings in the chapel/Sacristy would not normally have the incentive or initiative to lower the window shade to avoid being detected.

At about 10:00 a.m., Marx left the sacristy and walked through the chapel, where he noticed a white altar cloth lying on the first pew. It was the one that Sister Madelyn Marie Gordon had found outside Sister Phyllis Ann's office, placing it there just before she found the body.

"The cloth was neatly folded," wrote Marx. "It was given to Sister Kathleen who later unfolded [it] and found what appeared to be blood stains."

The lead detective then marked and tagged the blood-stained altar cloth, before putting it in the evidence safe, where it would remain untouched for almost a quarter of a century.

WHILE ART MARX AND ED MAROK WORKED THE MURDER scene, Detectives Tom Staff and Dan Foster commandeered the St. Joseph Conference Room to interview possible witnesses. The interviews began at 9.30 a.m. with Sister Mary

Phillip, who was in the chapel when Sister Madelyn Marie had made her terrible discovery.

Still in shock, Sister Mary Phillip said she had arrived at the chapel between 7:45 and 7:50 a.m., finding the doors unlocked and one standing open.

When she'd entered the chapel, Sister Mary Phillip told Detective Staff, there was no one else there and no sign of Sister Margaret Ann. She had then walked to a front pew, kneeling down to say her morning prayers. About ten minutes later, Sister Madelyn Marie had come in, walking over to the organ to arrange some music scores for the evening Mass. She had then walked toward the sacristy door, Sister Phillip recounted, unlocked it with her key and let herself in.

"She heard Sister Madelyn Marie scream," wrote Detective Staff, "and then say Sister Margaret Ann had been raped."

Sister Phillip had then comforted the distraught nun, asking Sister Clarisena to summon help immediately.

Detective Staff then finished the interview, deciding that Sister Mary Phillip had little more to add.

AT 10:10 A.M., DETECTIVE ART MARX AND CORONER'S Investigator Tim Fish walked across the hall to Sister Phyllis Ann's office, asking the hospital CEO to formally identify the body. After doing so, she checked Sister Margaret Ann's personnel records for the detectives, finding that she had relatives in Edgerton, whom Sister Phyllis Ann agreed to notify immediately.

Sister Phyllis Ann told Detective Marx how Sister Mary Phillip had already checked the victim's alarm clock, discovering that she had gotten up at about 5:00 a.m. The hospital CEO then asked hospital coordinator Sister Kathleen Mary Maross to take over in assisting the investigators.

Detective Marx then interviewed canteen assistant Audrey Garroway, one of the last people to see Sister Margaret Ann alive. The Jamaican-born dietician said she had arrived at the sisters' dining room at approximately 6:00 a.m., finding the door locked. Normally Sister Margaret Ann would have unlocked the door for her, but as she was late, Garroway had obtained another key from the dietary department.

She remembered Sister Margaret Ann coming into the dining room at 6:15 a.m., apologizing for being late, and borrowing a green tray before leaving for the chapel. About five minutes later she had returned, and eaten a grapefruit and some raisin bran and drunk a cup of coffee. Then she had left at about 6:45 a.m., telling Garroway she had to go and fix up the chapel.

Sister Kathleen Mary then took Detective Marx and Investigator Fish up to the seventh-floor convent, to inspect Sister Margaret Ann's living quarters in Room 714. It was exactly as she had left it four hours earlier, and nothing appeared to have been disturbed. Marx noted the electric alarm clock was set for 5:00 a.m. and a manual one for 5:30. Both alarms had been turned off.

Sister Kathleen then retraced Sister Margaret Ann's path to the first-floor dining room for detectives. On the way she explained that the entrance door to the seventh-floor convent was always locked for security. Sister Margaret Ann, she told them, would have stopped off at the first-floor switchboard before proceeding to the dining room. The first floor would have been empty at that time, as the security guards opened the hospital entrance doors between 6:00 and 7:00 a.m.

Detective Marx carefully timed the journey between her room and the sisters' dining room, determining it would have taken her between three to five minutes to walk.

Sister Kathleen Mary then returned to her duties, leaving Detective Marx at the main security office, to interview security guards Robert Wodarski and Robert Iler, who had been on duty. Wodarski gave him copies of the hospital watch records for that morning, saying nothing unusual had happened.

The investigators' next stop was the sixth-floor records office, to review personnel records, as well as interview several nurses who had been on duty earlier that morning.

At 10:30 a.m. a team from the Lucas County Coroner's office arrived, to collect Sister Margaret Ann Pahl's body and transport it to the county morgue on Detroit Avenue. As Investigator Fish supervised the removal of the body from the sacristy floor, Detective Marx closely observed.

"As the body was removed," he later wrote in his report, "a pool of blood (dried) was observed on the marble floor under the right side of the victim's head and shoulder."

After it was cleared, Detective Marx asked Father Jerome Swiatecki to search the sacristy to see if anything was missing, as theft was still a possible motive. The assistant chaplain duly did so, later reporting that none of the valuable golden chalices or Communion plates were missing, and nothing had been taken. Detective Art Marx then ruled out robbery as a motive.

Soon after Sister Margaret Ann's body was carried out, investigators finished investigating the sacristy. A young housekeeper named Valerie Berning was then told to clean up the floor with detergent. Later she would recall there was a lot of blood, which had "pooled" in the middle of the floor, with more blood in the sink.

By midday, all physical evidence from the sacristy had been obliterated. There was no sign that Sister Margaret Ann Pahl had been murdered there.

FOUR HOURS AFTER TOLEDO HOMICIDE DETECTIVES BEGAN investigating what would prove to be the most sensational murder in city history, Deputy Police Chief Ray Vetter had still not been informed. The tall crew-cut Toledo police veteran, who had worked his way through the ranks from beat patrolman, had spent the morning at Bowman Park, watching one of his five boys play baseball in a Catholic Youth League.

When Detective Marx finally reached him at about midday with the news that a nun had been butchered in the sacristy of Mercy Hospital, Vetter was furious he had not been told earlier.

The deputy chief, who was in charge of every Toledo Police Department investigation, immediately took control. He assigned four detectives to the case full-time, vowing to find Sister Margaret Ann's killer however long it took. From then on, Deputy Chief Vetter maintained a personal interest in the case.

Born and raised a devout Catholic, Vetter, then 57, had been taught by nuns until he was 12. He was a regular churchgoer with close ties to Mercy Hospital, where all his six children had been born. He believed priests and nuns were next to God, so the idea of a holy sister being butchered and sexually assaulted was beyond belief.

It was not long before Art Marx realized that the deputy chief planned to take more than a supervisory interest in the case. He says he became uneasy when his boss ordered him to type all further police reports on the homicide in triplicate, sending them all straight to his office. Under normal procedure, the investigating officer kept a pink copy, his department received a yellow one, and a white one went to Vetter.

Though Marx would later testify he had no alternative but to comply with the unprecedented order, already he wondered why Vetter would request this.

EARLY SATURDAY AFTERNOON, FATHER GERALD ROBINSON asked a doctor friend of his at Mercy Hospital to prescribe him Valium, to calm him down. The priest explained he had "a bad head" in the aftermath of the terrible events that morning.

"He gave it to me after Sister was murdered," he would later tell homicide investigators. "I had headaches from the stress of that day."

CHAPTER TEN

Few Leads

AFTER LEAVING MERCY HOSPITAL, DETECTIVE ART MARX drove to the Lucas County Coroner's office to meet Assistant Coroner Dr. Renate Fazekas. She brought him into the morgue, where Sister Margaret Ann's body was already laid out on a surgical procedure table. Also present were Detective Ed Marok, to collect evidence and bodily samples, and Dr. Fazekas' husband Steve, the Lucas County Coroner, to observe.

The assistant coroner began by cursorily examining the nun's butchered body, individually counting all the stab wounds. She initially found twenty-seven, but that figure would later be amended to thirty-one. She also observed visible petechiae, or broken blood vessels, on the face, leading Fazekas to conclude that the sister had first been strangled, before the frenzied stabbing attack.

"The doctor also stated," Detective Marx later wrote in his report, "that it appeared that the victim was strangled from behind by an individual with large hands. This was the doctor's opinion, due to the fact that a rather large bruise was noticed on the back neck."

Dr. Fazekas then informed Marx that she would be unable to determine the cause of death, or if the victim had been sexually assaulted, until after the following morning's autopsy.

Marx then returned to the Safety Building, leaving Detective Ed Marok to begin collecting evidence under the assistant coroner's supervision.

"The nun was on the processing table," Marok would later testify. "[I was there] for more additional processing, searching for evidence. Again, we wanted to take more photographs, to be more specific."

He first collected nail clippings, placing one from each finger in carefully labeled yellow evidence envelopes, for later testing in the crime lab. Then he gathered hair samples from her skull and pubic regions, also taking swabs from her mouth, vagina and rectum, and blood samples.

Then Sister Margaret Ann's clothes were removed, each item being carefully listed before it was logged into evidence: blue shoes, white girdle, pantyhose, white bra, blue slip, white blouse, blue sleeveless dress, black habit and necklace.

The detective then secured all the evidence in appropriate containers before taking them to the property room at the Toledo Police Department, where they were assigned Property Number 14330.

His final task that day was to fill out a Toledo Police Regional Crime Laboratory form, requesting tests for the presence of any foreign blood or sperm on her clothes.

SHORTLY AFTER MIDDAY, THE TOLEDO *BLADE*'S CITY DESK received an anonymous telephone tip that a nun at Mercy Hospital had been brutally murdered. But when a reporter checked the crime log sheet at the detectives' bureau, there was no record of it. So the city editor asked reporters to call their police sources, to see what they could come up with.

At 3:00 p.m., after *The Blade* had verified that it was true, the Toledo Police Department released a terse one-paragraph statement, confirming the murder of Sister Margaret Ann Pahl. It just gave the time and place of the killing, identified the victim and said that four detectives had been assigned to the case, but no arrest had yet been made.

EIGHTY-FIVE MILES AWAY IN EDGERTON, MARY CASEBERE was at home when she received a phone call from Sister Phyllis Ann Gerold.

"The telephone rang," she would remember. "And they quietly said Sister Margaret was murdered. It was very soft. I just barely got it."

By the time Sister Phyllis Ann had offered her heartfelt condolences and put down the phone, Sister Margaret Ann's younger sister was in deep shock, unable to comprehend the horrific news.

"I was in hysterics," she later remembered. "I called my husband Paul at his Chrysler dealership and told him."

After telling his staff there was a family emergency, Paul Casebere came straight home to comfort his wife, and they discussed how to break the news to the rest of the family.

"The first thing we did was to go down and tell Catherine," said Mary, "and then she went with us out to tell the family."

Over the next few hours the Caseberes visited various members of the Pahl family, who were scattered around the Edgerton area. They started off with their oldest brother Leo, finishing up with the youngest brother Cletus, who lived miles away on a rural farm.

"Everyone was just shocked," said Catherine. "I just couldn't grasp it. How could something like that happen to her?"

LATE HOLY SATURDAY, DR. RENATE FAZEKAS PERFORMED AN autopsy on Sister Margaret Ann Pahl, at the Detroit Avenue morgue. Also present were her husband, Dr. Steve Fazekas, and Detective Marok from the Toledo Police Department's Scientific Investigations Unit.

Dr. Renate Fazekas' subsequent autopsy report described Sister Margaret Ann as being 5'2" tall, weighing 134 pounds. First she sketched out diagrams of the sister's face and neck area, marking the numerous stab wounds and other injuries. Then she began taking photographs, holding down the lower eyelids to reveal petechial hemorrhages on the insides of the eyes, clear signs that the sister had been strangled.

Dr. Fazekas described the sister's chain and cross, bearing the inscription "I AM A CATHOLIC. PLEASE CALL A PRIEST," which caused such heavy bruising to her neck.

"This is consistent with strangulation," explained Dr. Diane Scala-Barnett, who reviewed the autopsy report and later succeeded Dr. Renate Fazekas as Lucas County Assistant Coroner. "We have three linear bruises on the back that tells me that the skin is pinched. That could be consistent with a soft ligature strangulation, because it's not leaving any other marks."

Dr. Fazekas also described bruising above and below the clavicle, as well as two fractures of the hyoid bone, a little U-shaped bone at the base of the tongue.

"That is commonly seen in strangulations," said Dr. Scala-Barnett, "from side-to-side pressure applied. These little bones break. It's easier to break them in an older person, because they have more calcification."

The autopsy report also described hemorrhaging in the right vocal cords and trachea, further signs of strangulation.

Then Dr. Fazekas had turned her attention to the nun's horrific stab wounds. There was a cluster of six to the left side of her face, which she described as being "oriented obliquely." These wounds varied in size from a quarter of an inch to a half-inch, reaching a depth of one-and-a-half inches. She also noted that all the wound edges were sharp, ruling out scissors and other weapons that have one sharp edge and one blunt one.

She then focused on the left side of the neck, counting fifteen further stab wounds, ranging in size from three-sixteenths of an inch to one-half inch. The assistant coroner also noted that the wounds' trajectory went from front to back, leading her to deduce that the murderer was stabbing downward.

Dr. Fazekas counted nine more stab wounds on the chest, plus another to the shoulder. These wounds were between an eighth of an inch to one-half inch in length.

"She describes some of these wounds as having an irregular outline," said Dr. Scala-Barnett. "She doesn't on the others but she does make that extra note about the chest."

There were also numerous internal injuries caused by the furious stabbings. Sister Margaret Ann's carotid artery in the left side of her neck had been damaged, as well as her larynx and trachea, which had three stab wounds apiece.

"So that's six internal [injuries] right there," explained Dr. Scala-Barnett. "When you breach a trachea, you are going to have an air leak."

The escaping air went into the soft tissues under the skin, causing a buildup that, similar to crisped rice, will crackle if pressed.

"It's called subcutaneous crepitance," explained Dr. Scala-Barnett. "It can make you look bloated and swollen."

In her autopsy report, Dr. Fazekas described other internal injuries to the esophagus and several vertebrae, and the left lung had two stab wounds. One of the deepest stab wounds had ripped through the breastbone, right into Sister Margaret Ann's heart through the right ventricle.

"There was only one into the heart," said Dr. Scala-Barnett, adding that the sister could not have survived more than five to ten minutes with such terrible injuries.

There were no defensive wounds on the victim's body, showing that she had been unconscious during the attack.

Dr. Fazekas also concluded from the nature of the puncture wounds that the murder weapon had a blade at least three inches long and half an inch wide. It was also highly distinctive, having four sides with a cross-section resembling the shape of a kite or a diamond.

Finally, Dr. Fazekas found a small scratch inside Sister Margaret Ann's vagina, although she had not been penetrated and her hymen was intact. It was impossible to know exactly what had caused the scratch, leading to speculation that it could have been caused by a finger or an instrument like a crucifix.

At the end of her report, Dr. Fazekas stated the cause of death:

This 71-year-old white female, Sister Margaret Ann Pahl, died of multiple—31—stab wounds to the left side of the face, neck and chest. There was also evidence of strangulation.

CHAPTER ELEVEN

"Father, Forgive Them for They Know Not What They Do"

ON EASTER SUNDAY, ON WHAT WOULD HAVE BEEN SISTER Margaret Ann Pahl's 72nd birthday, Toledo residents woke up to the horrific news of her murder.

"Nun At Mercy Hospital Is Murdered In Chapel," was the headline on the front page of the *Toledo Blade*. "Robbery Discounted As Motive After Valuables Are Left."

The sensational story, alongside a recent smiling picture of Sister Margaret Ann, described in gory detail how the sacristan had been brutally stabbed to death.

"From all appearances," Dr. Harry Mignerey told *The Blade*, "she was sexually assaulted," adding that she had been strangled prior to the stabbing.

Mercy Hospital public relations director Sarah Fisher said no extra security measures had been introduced since the murder, although guards were now conducting "special" patrols. Fisher maintained that hospital security was "adequate," saying it was "normally a safe place."

"She was a most sweet and gentle person," she told the Associated Press, who ran a report on its national wire, "with a really quiet sort of strength and a very peaceful demeanor. She was very loving. It's a great loss."

Early Sunday morning, Detective Art Marx and his team returned to Mercy Hospital to continue interviewing all hospital staff. Over the next three weeks they would conduct more than six hundred interviews, a few yielding valuable clues, but most leading to dead ends.

As there were no official suspects, detectives concentrated

on finding a motive for this apparently senseless murder. The only clue so far was the murder weapon, which Dr. Fazekas had informed them was at least three inches long and no wider than half an inch. It was also unusual in having four edges, resembling a diamond on a deck of cards.

"A rather lengthy investigation has begun," Detective Art Marx told a reporter at a press briefing that afternoon. "We are interviewing and are going to interview all employees who worked on the afternoon and night shift."

He added that police were also questioning all the nuns who lived in the convent, and were looking for any "disgruntled" hospital employees. But the lead detective discounted any doubts about hospital security.

"If you can't be safe in a chapel," said the devout Catholic detective, "then I don't know . . ."

In the aftermath of the murder, the nuns and medical personnel at Mercy Hospital were in shock and disbelief. Emotions were running high, and for several days there was lots of hugging, and discussion about the murder and who might have committed it.

Auxiliary Bishop James Hoffman agreed to come and reconsecrate St. Joseph's Chapel and the sacristy. But ultimately the bishop performed a toned-down "reconciliation ceremony" the following day, after the sacristy was deemed not to be part of the chapel.

Toledo Diocesan Director for Health and Hospitals Father Donald Hunter described the ceremony as a public demonstration of "faith versus evil," as well as a memorial for Sister Margaret Ann Pahl.

"Essentially it was an exorcism," explained Sister Phyllis Ann Gerold, who was present. "It was scary. You see, the chapel was desecrated because of the murder, and so it was re-consecrated."

Father Gerald Robinson attended the ceremony, along with several other priests. But during the rededication service he suddenly became upset, physically grabbing a fellow priest named Father Doplar, begging him to hear his confession as they left the chapel together.

"That was the story that ran around the hospital," said Sister Phyllis Ann.

Many years later she would tell homicide detectives the story, but by then, Father Doplar was long dead.

ON THE HOSPITAL GRAPEVINE, FATHER GERALD ROBINSON'S name was frequently whispered as the probable killer although some suspected Father Swiatecki.

"Mercy put a gag order around these people," claimed former Toledo Police Officer Dave Davison, who frequented the hospital cafeteria. "So if they talked to the police or the press, they'd be fired. But people did talk to us, because we were friends. They all kept saying Robinson did it. It was like a mantra."

Many years later, Mercy Hospital CEO Sister Phyllis Ann Gerold agreed there were "rumors" pointing the finger at Father Robinson, but denied placing any gag order on her staff.

"Of course everyone was horrified, and there was a lot of talk," she explained. "I believe everyone cooperated with the police. Things were reported as they were discovered. Essentially there was a list of potential people who may have done it, but the continuous grapevine at the hospital said it was [him]."

On Sunday night, Deputy Police Chief Ray Vetter held a press conference, admitting no "startling" evidence had yet turned up. So far, he told reporters, the only definite lead police had to follow was that they were looking for a man.

Vetter said his investigators would pursue two possible theories: that the killer was connected to the hospital with knowledge of Sister Margaret Ann's routine, using it to plot his attack; or he was "some screwball" off the street, and Sister Margaret Ann was "in the wrong place at the right time."

A FEW HOURS EARLIER, SISTER MARJORIE BOSSE OF THE Cincinnati-based Sisters of Mercy Provincialate, wrote a moving letter to her fellow Sisters of Mercy, informing them of the murder and trying to make some spiritual sense of it.

Dear Sisters,

I write this letter on a beautiful, peaceful Easter morning. It is a time to experience the mystery of the joyful hope of the resurrection while we experience hurting hearts. The sudden violent death of Sister Margaret Ann Pahl on Holy Saturday morning almost seems to call forth for a cry of vengeance yet our Lord's words from the cross have such deep meaning to grasp, "Father, forgive them for they know not what they do."

We pray that in God's mercy Sister was unconscious before she died from strangulation or before any multiple wounds were inflicted. Sister was a prayerful, loving, deeply committed Sister of Mercy.

As the women on Calvary were persons of deep faith and strength, so [too] are our Sisters at Mercy Hospital, Toledo, and Sister Laura Marie Pahl. May we, as a believing community, unite with them in the Eucharistic Liturgy. It is Our Lord's invitation to be in communion with Him and one another.

May the promise of Easter help us to share God's boundless love together, believing that Sister Margaret Ann is with Him, her family, and us in a special way. The resurrection alleluia brings new life to all who believe. We pray that Sister enjoys this new life fully.

> In the Risen Lord,
> Sister Marjorie Bosse, R.S.M.

CHAPTER TWELVE

Closing In

LIEUTENANT BILL KINA OF THE TOLEDO POLICE DEPART-
ment's homicide bureau, was at a Saturday afternoon baby
shower when he first heard about Sister Margaret Ann's
murder.

"Why aren't you on this homicide?" asked another guest.
Assuming that, as he hadn't been summoned, someone else
must have been assigned the case, Kina didn't bother to contact the department.

But when he arrived at the Safety Building Monday
morning, Deputy Chief Vetter immediately summoned him
into his office, closed the door and put him in charge of the
high-profile murder hunt.

A twenty-seven-year veteran of the Toledo Police Department, Lieutenant Kina had begun his career as a patrol
officer, riding scout cars and patrol wagons. He had worked
his way up through the ranks to sergeant in charge of uniform patrol units, and his dogged determination paid off
when he was promoted to the detectives' bureau in the late
1970s. He was soon put in charge of twenty-seven officers,
overseeing homicides, robbery and sexual assault units. By
April 1980, Lieutenant Kina had worked for sixteen years
under Deputy Chief Vetter, whom he considered a close
friend.

"He told me to oversee the case and direct the investigation," remembered Lieutenant Kina. "He gave me a short
briefing that a nun had been murdered—just a [smattering] of
information."

Lieutenant Kina immediately drove over to Mercy Hospital to be briefed by Marx and the other three detectives, who had been working the case since Saturday. He then began setting up a command center in a hospital boardroom.

"We set aside a room for them," remembered Sister Phyllis Ann Gerold. "We sent out a note to the employees, asking them to cooperate." Typewriters were brought in for police reports, and a section of the room was cordoned off for interviews.

Lieutenant Kina decided to leave Marx in place as lead detective. He was a strict Catholic, and knew all about the workings of the Catholic Church, which would later prove invaluable.

"So I just left him [there]," explained Kina. "And I just kind of laid back and watched."

Lieutenant Kina knew he had a daunting task ahead. Mercy Hospital had 1,400 employees, but initially only the ones working on the midnight and day shifts at the time of the murder were contacted. Over the next several weeks, Lieutenant Kina and his team would conduct more than one hundred interviews.

As the first interviews started in the boardroom, Lieutenant Kina and Detective Dave Weinbrecht drove to the Lucas County Coroner's office for a briefing by Dr. Renate Fazekas.

"She felt that the body was in a staged position," Lieutenant Kina remembered. "They were trying to make it look like it was a sexual molestation to throw us off. She said there was no rape or trauma in the vaginal area [to] indicate any type of molestation."

Dr. Fazekas told the detectives that the killer had sneaked up on Sister Margaret Ann from behind, strangling her with his bare hands. Later, it was believed that the attacker had used a ligature, throttling her so hard that both bones in the side of her neck had snapped under the pressure. Then, after she fell to the floor unconscious, her frenzied killer had begun stabbing her over and over again.

After stabbing her thirty-one times, he'd pulled her panties and underwear down to her ankles, and her smock up over her breasts. But Dr. Fazekas told them that she had found absolutely no evidence of rape, or any other type of sexual assault.

"This was done," said Kina, "as far as I'm concerned, only to defile her."

The assistant coroner also pointed out the tiny scratch inside the nun's vagina, which could have been caused by her murderer's finger, or a small object like a crucifix.

By the time he left the coroner's office, Lieutenant Kina was certain Sister Margaret Ann had not been murdered by a stranger.

"The victim knew her assailant," he explained. "A stranger would not have killed the victim in such a vicious manner. It would take somebody with a very strong vendetta to go in and kill a person in that ferocious manner. I mean, if a stranger comes in and his intention is to rob or rape the victim, he's going to stab them once or twice, or maybe cut their throat. But he's not going to stand there and stab them thirty-one times."

BACK AT MERCY HOSPITAL, DETECTIVE ART MARX AND HIS team were busy interviewing potential witnesses. One of the first was a 20-year-old resident nursing student named Karen Raszka, who had worked a double shift, finishing at about 7:30 a.m. on Holy Saturday. After punching her time card in the basement, she'd taken an elevator to the first floor to say her morning prayers in the chapel.

"It was my habit to stop at the chapel," she later told Toledo *Blade* religion editor David Yonke. "But that day, for the first time ever, the chapel doors were closed."

Then, as she was walking along the hallway by the chapel, she saw a man she had never seen before come out of an office. When she turned around, she saw him staring at her.

She described him to detectives as a slim white male between 24 and 30 years old, about 5 feet, 8 inches tall, with collar-length blonde hair. She also remembered him wearing a beige, camel hair sports coat.

"I didn't know him," she said, "from either the school or the hospital."

A police artist then made an Identi-Kit drawing of the man, from her description. A bodyguard was also assigned to escort her to and from the hospital, in case she was in danger.

At 2:30 that afternoon, Detective Dave Weinbrecht conducted a twenty-minute interview with Sister Kathleen Mary Maross, the convent's coordinator of sisters. Later during their inquiries, detectives would learn from other nuns that Sister Kathleen was somewhat unconventional. The high-ranking nun was said to often dress like a "truck driver," wearing blue jeans and plaid shirts outside the hospital on her days off.

Sister Kathleen Mary said she was showering at about 8:20 a.m. Holy Saturday morning, when someone knocked on her door, yelling about a sister being murdered in the chapel. She had hurriedly dressed and rushed down to the chapel, one of the last nuns to arrive.

Sister Kathleen Mary explained that there had been no pressing need for Sister Margaret Ann to prepare the altar so early, as there were no services Holy Saturday morning. She thought it "a bit unusual," as the fifteen-minute job could have been done at any time during the day.

Then Detective Weinbrecht asked Sister Kathleen Mary about the victim's personality.

"She stated that she was a very docile person," Weinbrecht later wrote in his police report, "and that she would not try to struggle or fight back."

She thought the victim would avoid confrontation and would probably faint in a dangerous situation. But as the interview progressed, Sister Kathleen Mary became more and more emotional, fixating on whether or not Sister Margaret Ann had been sexually assaulted.

When Weinbrecht asked why she believed the victim had been raped, the nun said she was just repeating what others were saying.

"Sister Kathleen seemed to become upset with the idea

that it may have not been a man and that there may not have been a rape," Detective Weinbrecht wrote in his police report four days later. "She spontaneously stated it could have been me, I have big hands, and I could have done it. She then stated, 'but I was in my room after it happened'."

Then, she began rambling, telling the detective that Sister Margaret Ann was more popular than she was.

"A lot of people dislike me," she said "because I can't hold back with words and I am a lot tougher on people. You would think they would pick on me instead of her."

At one point Sister Kathleen Mary became so excited, she speculated on whether the murderer could have been a nun.

"You know what they say about nuns?" she told Detective Weinbrecht. "What they do together when they are alone? They will say this is what caused the death."

Sister Kathleen Mary also said a pair of old scissors that Sister Margaret Ann had kept in the sacristy to trim candles was missing. She gave the detective a similar pair of scissors from which he made a tracing, attaching it to his subsequent report.

At 3:21 p.m. Detective Weinbrecht interviewed Sister Mary Phillip in the boardroom. The elderly sister recounted going into the chapel just before 8:00 a.m. Holy Saturday to say her morning office. Soon afterward Sister Clarisena had come in, taking a pew behind her.

Then Sister Madelyn Marie had come in, going over to the organ to look through some musical arrangements.

"Sister [Madelyn] Marie was only at the organ for a few moments," read Weinbrecht's subsequent report. "[She] then walked toward the sacristy . . . using her key to unlock the door. She then heard Sister Madeline [sic] Marie scream and she said something about Sister Margaret Ann being raped."

That afternoon, Deputy Chief Ray Vetter announced at a press briefing that he had set up a special hotline. He appealed to anyone who had been in the vicinity of Mercy Hospital chapel early Saturday morning to come forward. He was "encouraging" possible witnesses to contact police, as they may have seen something without realizing it at the time. Any new information, pieced together with what they already knew, could prove vital in catching the murderer.

The investigation, he told reporters, was at a pivotal stage, and detectives were not ruling out any possibilities. As yet, he admitted, no murder weapon had been found, but he was refusing to disclose if any useful fingerprints had been discovered.

A FEW DAYS LATER, SISTER MARGARET ANN PAHL'S FAMILY composed a card of thanks, which was printed in a local Toledo newspaper with a typo.

> *The Family of Sister Margaret Ann Pal [sic] would like to express ou[r] appreciation for the consoling words and deeds extended to us at this time when our Lord took Sister to her reward in heaven. Our thoughts turn to Christ's last moments on the cross on Good Friday, the day before Sister died. And this brings us to say, "Into your hands we commend her spirit." By the grace of God we feel no need for revenge and are able to say, as He said, "Forgive them for they know not what they do."*

CHAPTER THIRTEEN

"A Violent, Tragic, Traumatic Death"

AT 11:00 A.M. ON TUESDAY, APRIL 8, MORE THAN TWO HUN-dred people attended Sister Margaret Ann Pahl's funeral. The sister's closed coffin, draped in a white cloth embroidered with a cross, lay on a metal trolley in the aisle at the front of the St. Bernardine chapel, on the grounds of Our Lady of the Pines in Fremont, Ohio. Ironically, it was the same retirement home that the sister had been so looking forward to spending her final days in.

It was an unseasonably warm, overcast day, and the Pahl family drove in from Edgerton to pay their final farewells.

There had been no hint of bad weather when the mourners first entered the chapel, but as soon as the doors closed, a tumultuous lightning storm descended on Toledo, knocking out the electricity to more than 20,000 homes.

And when Father Gerald Robinson, who was conducting the funeral Mass, entered to the organ strains of J. S. Bach's "Jesu, Joy of Man's Desiring," the sky turned black, and dark clouds lowered overhead. Then there was a loud crack of thunder, a flash of lightning, and the church doors flew open, blowing dozens of dead leaves inside, onto the red floral-print carpet.

"I thought the roof was going to fall in," remembered Catherine Flegal. "It just kept rattling."

As the storm raged outside, Father Robinson, standing under a statue of Jesus Christ on the cross, looked visibly anxious. He was wearing holy white vestments with the words "Peace" and "Love" stitched into them, and would be presiding over Sister Margaret Ann's Mass of the Resurrection.

Directly to his right was Father Jerome Swiatecki, who would deliver a homily, and the two were flanked by eight other priests.

"Father Robinson was decidedly nervous," recalled Sister Margaret Ann's niece Martha-Jane Dietsch. "I got a bad feeling about him."

"Praised be God, the father of our Lord Jesus Christ," began Father Robinson in a shaky voice, trying to maintain his composure as flashes of lightning illuminated the chapel. "He comforts us in our afflictions and thus enables us to comfort those who are in trouble, with the same consolation we have received from him."

Then as Father Robinson blessed Sister Margaret Ann's body with holy water, the storm outside grew even more menacing, the church doors banging loudly.

"We thought it was a tornado," said Lee Pahl. "It was that severe. The church rumbled and shook. I mean, it just came out of nowhere and was a surprise to everyone."

Sister Margaret Ann's younger sister Mary Casebere was frightened by the violence of the storm.

"It was eerie," she remembered. "The storm came up right at the time of the Mass, and the wind came in, rattling the cross on the roof."

After finishing the blessing, Father Robinson placed the pall on the casket, and began reciting in a shaky voice that could barely be heard above the storm, "On the day of her baptism, Sister Margaret Ann put on Christ. In the day of Christ's coming, may she be clothed with glory."

Father Jerome Swiatecki, a look of deep sorrow in his eyes, then moved to the microphone to deliver his homily.

The visibly emotional priest invited the mourners to seek a meaningful message in what he called a "violent, tragic, traumatic death. A death not only blasphemous, but patently absurd. It stirs up within us a deep repugnance at death." He explained that a day after the murder, while searching for a message himself, he had reached over to pick up his prayer book. Suddenly the answer had "leapt up" at him, in verses 19 to 21 of the 118th Psalm.

"'Open the gates of virtue to me,'" he intoned. "'I will come in and give thanks to Yahweh [the Old Testament name for God]. This is Yahweh's gateway, through which the virtuous may enter.'"

Father Swiatecki interpreted the passage, telling the mourners that the sister's "violent, blasphemous death" had opened the gateway to heaven for her, and no one had the right to question God's method.

"On Good Friday, Sister Margaret Ann did everything she possibly could," he continued, "to help me with the Celebration of the Lord's Passion. The orderly person she was, she prepared everything well and became intimately involved with this Celebration. She was deeply concerned that everything should go well for me, the celebrant. Everything did, because she was so much a part of it."

Father Swiatecki told the congregation that after he had read the Passion, he had made a few remarks.

"I wanted to underscore the fact that in reality, this Good Friday and this reading of the Passion was our own preparation toward eternal life in our suffering and dying and death.

"There before me sat Sister Margaret Ann, listening thoughtfully. I'm sure it was her own preparation she was thinking about, unknowingly preparing to accept a violent and tragic death, such as that of her divine bridegroom to whom she was wedded for more than fifty years. For he and she had celebrated a golden jubilee in a marriage only he could make in heaven.

"Then on this last Holy Saturday, the Lord, her divine bridegroom, demanded of her one last great act of love, the one he so poignantly describes in these, his words, 'The greatest love a man can have for his friends is to give his life for them.' Sister Margaret Ann's last greatest act of love was tragically violent because it was for her greatest friend, the Lord Jesus Christ himself, her own groom.

"She became willing to discover that love in the tragic

violence of giving, then she entered into the silent tomb of his divine love on Holy Saturday that she might rise with him to a new birth date on his glorious day of Resurrection. Her happiest birthday.

"No longer would she have to worry about clean altar linens, and candles, and altar bread, and flowers, and my clean albs."

From now on, Father Swiatecki told the mourners, he would always see Saturdays as a special memorial to her.

"Sister Margaret Ann came into my life these past few years as a priest-chaplain at Mercy. Each Saturday, at least most of them, in the past three years, Sister Margaret Ann and I were the only two at the early morning celebration of the Eucharist, the sacrifice of the Mass.

"As she knelt there before me, I was mindful that here was a woman who offered herself generously. Kindly and graciously offered her time and her ministry to the patients that morning, so her Sister Religious could rest a little longer, and later participate at Mass in the convent that Saturday morning."

Finishing off his homily, Father Swiatecki said the risen Lord had cried out to Sister Margaret Ann, "Cling to me!" and she no longer had to follow him as she was with him in heaven.

"The only report we have from Sister Margaret Ann today," he said, "is the one last experience of her life in which she cries out to us from the blasphemous violence—'I HAVE SEEN THE LORD.' "

AFTER THE SERVICE, LEE PAHL AND THE OTHER FIVE FAMILY pallbearers solemnly carried Sister Margaret Ann's coffin down the aisle of the chapel and out through the back doors. As the storm was still raging, everyone except the pallbearers and several of the nuns were instructed to remain inside the church.

Sister Margaret Ann's simple wood coffin was then carried the short distance to the St. Bernardine cemetery, where she was laid to rest, alongside so many other nuns of the Toledo Sisters of Mercy order.

And as her coffin was gently lowered into the ground, the storm subsided, just as abruptly as it had begun, and the sun came out.

"It was so quiet," remembered Mary Casebere. "To me, it was God telling us not to worry. That she's made it to heaven."

AFTER BURIAL, THE PAHL FAMILY HOSTED A MEMORIAL lunch in the glass solarium that ran across the entire length of St. Bernardine's dining room.

During the meal, Catherine Flegal sat near Father Robinson and had an uncomfortable feeling about him. Others there still remember him sitting by himself, his face as white as a sheet, staring into space and not eating anything.

"Father Robinson was very upset," said Flegal. "He wasn't able to eat."

Lee Pahl also noticed the priest's strange behavior, and later, with hindsight, it made more sense.

"I think after going through that storm," he said, "knowing what he had done, he was shook up . . . I know I would be too."

CHAPTER FOURTEEN

Reward

ON WEDNESDAY MORNING, A $10,000 REWARD WAS POSTED BY the Lucas County Commissioners for information leading to the arrest and conviction of Sister Margaret Ann Pahl's killer. The reward was initiated by Prosecutor Anthony Pizza, who called a special meeting, telling commissioners that the Toledo Police Department was frustrated by the lack of any leads in the case.

The previous afternoon, Detective Dave Weinbrecht had conducted "an extensive search" outside by the Madison Avenue and Twenty-third Street sides of Mercy Hospital, looking for clues. He had scoured bushes, grass, sidewalks, garbage cans and alleys, but had come up empty-handed.

"I spent approximately forty-five minutes searching the outside area of the hospital," he wrote in his report, "with negative results."

Later that morning, Toledo Police Chief Walter Scoble admitted that his homicide task force was praying for a "lucky break" in the case, as there was no "substantial evidence."

He told reporters his "only hope" was that Lieutenant Kina and his team would discover valuable leads from the "scores of interviews" now being conducted, which would tie in with other information.

Detectives close to the investigation told the Toledo *Blade* there were no fingerprints, footprints, clothing fabric or even a weapon to focus the investigation on. Any evidence that might have existed, they admitted, had probably been destroyed during the "Mr. Swift" team's frantic attempts to save her life.

Deputy Chief Ray Vetter also revealed that his team was no longer limiting its search to men, while conceding the newly set-up murder hotline had so far received few calls from the public.

BUT A FEW HOURS LATER, THE BIG BREAK IN THE CASE CAME, when Mercy Hospital housekeeper Shirley Lucas walked into the clergy dining room for her scheduled 12:40 p.m. interview with Detective Art Marx. The 44-year-old divorcee said she'd worked at the hospital for a year, cleaning the convent and mainly working for Sister Margaret Ann.

She described Sister Margaret Ann as "a very fussy individual" and a "very strict and devoted Catholic."

She told the detective that the sister had "always treated her very coldly," and was "not as open" as the other nuns she discussed her personal problems with.

Lucas said she spent mornings cleaning the VIP office on the first floor, before attending to the other administrative ones on the ground floor. After lunch she would go to the seventh-floor convent, where Sister Margaret Ann would hand out her assignments for that day.

She told Marx that the sister's only hobbies were opera music and her duties in the chapel, recalling one particular conversation when the nun had been "somewhat disturbed" about her failure to take enough personal care of convent property.

At the end of the interview, Detective Marx asked about any other "serious conversations" she had ever had with the victim. Lucas said there actually had been one on the afternoon of Good Friday, just a few hours before her murder.

"Sister Margaret was very serious about her religion," Marx wrote in his report, "and she was very upset because the Good Friday services had been shortened. She mentioned that one of the priests had changed the Good Friday services and that this upset Sister Margaret to no end."

Then the elderly sister had become uncharacteristically

emotional, clasping the cleaner's hand before breaking down in tears.

"Why do they cheat God out of what belongs to him?" she sobbed.

After the interview, Detective Marx immediately informed Lieutenant Kina in the boardroom about the breakthrough. Both men presumed that Father Gerald Robinson had said the Good Friday service—something that has never been disproved.

"I found that to be very significant," Kina would later say. "[Sister Margaret Ann] was very upset with Father Robinson because of the fact that he was trying to cut the Good Friday services short. And he was going to cut the Holy Saturday and Holy Sunday ones short too. She was crying on Shirley Lucas' shoulder."

This was a turning point in the investigation. Over the next few days Lieutenant Kina and his team interviewed the remaining nuns, student nurses and other hospital employees, eliminating them one by one. They searched rooftops, car parks, trash cans and every conceivable place for clues. And they ran down numerous tip-offs, many of which proved fruitless.

One strong lead that detectives had initially pursued came from Sister Madelyn Marie Gordon. She said that on her way to breakfast, before finding the body, she had seen a strange man leaving the hospital through the Madison Avenue exit. He had been a "neat, light-skinned man" with "small lips," in his middle twenties, and had even waved to her on his way out.

But like scores of other leads dutifully followed up by Lieutenant Kina and his team, this went nowhere.

Several weeks into the investigation, frustrated detectives interviewed Maumee psychic Beverly Holmes, who claimed to have seen the killer in her dreams, describing him as a Caucasian flower delivery boy from Delaware.

"This person knows music," Weinbrecht duly noted in an interview report, "and plays a string instrument. He has a mental history, caused by the way he was treated by his parents. He is a negative person."

At the end of his report Weinbrecht wryly noted that Holmes "appears to have no knowledge of the case whatsoever . . . The investigation continues."

The detectives also received a slew of anonymous letters offering advice and help, all of which would be tested for fingerprints and then logged into evidence.

"Here's a tip on the Mercy Hospital Nun Murder," began one received by homicide detectives on April 18, 1980.

> He has a perverse hate for the Catholic Church and especially nuns (a bitter [and] imbalanced ex-Catholic himself)
>
> He's very sick and needs help—a psychopath with a great potential for violence
>
> He's a woman hater—also sexually deviant
>
> He's into devil worship
>
> Many times, he has "jokingly" threatened exactly this kind of crime
>
> I hope you can help him and stop this before it happens again—It's in your hands!
>
> Christ help us.

AS THE INVESTIGATION INTO SISTER MARGARET ANN PAHL'S murder continued into the second week, the Toledo homicide team fell into a routine. Every morning at 8:30 a.m. the detectives met in the hospital command post for coffee and donuts, bringing each other up to date on developments.

"We critiqued," explained Lieutenant Kina. "We [discussed] the day before, so everybody was aware what the other detectives were doing."

At the meetings, Lieutenant Kina handed his detectives their assignments for the day. And then in the evening, if they were not too busy, the homicide team met again for a further update.

Toledo Police Chief Walter Scoble was under increasing pressure to solve the murder, which by now had become a national story. Every day the increasingly frustrated chief and Deputy Vetter met with the press, with no significant developments to report.

"After scores of interviews," Chief Scoble told reporters more than a week after the murder, "we are still lacking the kind of evidence we need to solve this crime."

Deputy Vetter reminded the press how the "Mr. Swift" team had moved the body, perhaps obliterating key evidence. But he refused to criticize them.

"The first priority is to try and save a person's life," he explained. "Preserving evidence is secondary. And we don't even know if there was any evidence to be destroyed."

CHAPTER FIFTEEN

Frantic Footsteps

ON SATURDAY, APRIL 12, A WEEK AFTER THE MURDER, DETECtive Dave Weinbrecht interviewed Mercy Hospital receptionist Margaret Warren, who had startling information. She said she had arrived at work on Holy Saturday at 7:30 a.m., and on her way to her reception desk in the professional building, encountered janitor Wardell Langston, who was staring up at an exposed balcony.

When she asked what he was looking at, he explained that he had just heard "fast and very frantic" footsteps running along it. She suggested he go and investigate further, but the 32-year-old worker refused, saying he was no hero.

A few minutes later, Warren also heard loud running footsteps overhead.

"She described the footprints [sic] as being very rapid and frantic," Weinbrecht wrote in his report.

> They started westbound from the hallway that comes down from the bridge and turned left . . . to the point at the end of the L-shaped hallway in front of Father Robinson's quarters. These footsteps excited and scared [her]. She thought they were frantic."

After checking with Lieutenant Kina, it was decided Weinbrecht would conduct an experiment, to try to determine what kind of shoes could have made the sound of the footsteps. So he had Margaret Warren stand by her reception desk, while two police officers ran along the same overhead route she had described.

"One was wearing leather-soled shoes," explained Detective Weinbrecht, "and one wore rubber. And I had them each run at approximately the same speed and the same direction."

After listening to both sets of shoes, Warren said the footsteps best resembled the rubber shoes.

Then Weinbrecht turned his attention to the emergency exit door at the end of the corridor by the priest's quarters, which Warren had not heard open or close.

"We found that door to be much heavier than any other doors in the hallway," Weinbrecht later testified. "It was a very loud door . . . like a fire exit push bar. We opened and closed the door, just to see if anybody heard what door the footsteps may have gone out of."

After repeatedly opening and closing the door, the detective satisfied himself that it was loud enough to have been heard if someone had exited the hospital. So the only alternative was that whoever had run through the hospital after the sister's murder had ended up in Father Robinson's living quarters.

On Sunday morning, Detective Weinbrecht interviewed Wardell Langston at the command center. The janitor said he had been with a colleague, Jimmy Harris, cleaning carpets under a balcony by the main entrance, when he'd heard the frantic footsteps.

He described them as running along the second-floor balcony, down a hallway toward Father Robinson's quarters. He too had not heard the clang of the panic bar hit the fire door.

"[It sounded like] something was terribly wrong," he told the detective.

Langston was also able to fix the time of the footsteps as 7:35 a.m., straight after seeing Margaret Warren arrive for work.

"That was significant," explained Lieutenant Kina. "They fell within the timeframe of the homicide. The balcony and the entrance to the nurses' quarters is actually where the priest lived. And he [Langston] heard frantically running footsteps up on the balcony and running down that hallway to Robinson's room."

AT 1:00 P.M. ON SUNDAY, DETECTIVE DALE VAUGHAN INTER-viewed Sister Laura Marie Pahl in the convent community room at Mercy Hospital. It was her seventieth birthday and Sister Margaret Ann's younger sister was still in deep shock.

Detective Vaughan began by asking if her late sister had had any enemies, or if anyone had a vendetta against her. Sister Laura Marie, who was presently living at St. Bernardine's retirement home, said she and her elder sister had been extremely close. She described her as "a very quiet person" who seemed "very content" with her job in the chapel.

Although she could not think of anyone with a vendetta against Sister Margaret Ann, she did tell Detective Vaughan about their last-ever conversation three months earlier at a family reunion in Edgerton. Sister Margaret Ann had mentioned a warning to nuns not to go to the chapel alone, after an incident where a "black male had been seen hanging around the chapel area."

At the end of the interview, Detective Vaughan handed Sister Laura Marie her sister's personal property. But a small silver Bulova watch, purchased out of her golden anniversary gift money, was still missing.

Later Dave Weinbrecht unsuccessfully checked Toledo pawn shops, to see if anyone had brought in a Bulova watch recently.

At 1:52 p.m., Detective Vaughan interviewed cardiac care technician Leslie Kerr, who had been on duty Holy Saturday morning. Kerr said she had arrived at the Heart Center, located at the other end of the hallway leading to the chapel, at 6:59 a.m. She had not seen anything unusual, except she had noticed the chapel doors open.

Then, after typing up the morning list, she and her girlfriend Candy had gone to the coronary unit, where they had worked for about twenty minutes. At about 7:40 a.m., they had walked back to the Heart Center and were checking cardiograms when they heard Sister Madelyn Marie Gordon's harrowing screams.

Kerr had immediately "spun around" and started running toward the chapel, noticing the clock on a nearby wall read 8:10 a.m. Then she and Candy went in, discovering Sister Madelyn Marie being consoled by a nun. Kerr had then gone into the sacristy and seen Sister Margaret Ann lying on the floor, as if asleep.

Nearly a quarter of a century later, Kerr would remember seeing Father Gerald Robinson standing by the chapel doors at about 7:00 a.m. when she had first arrived. When asked why she hadn't told detectives at the time, Kerr said she had not considered seeing the priest by the chapel unusual, as she had probably seen him there more than a hundred times.

AT MONDAY MORNING'S STATUS MEETING, LIEUTENANT Kina assigned Detective Art Marx to re-interview Wardell Langston and Margaret Warren, and Detective Dale Vaughan to interview all the student nurses who had remained at the School of Nursing over the Easter holiday weekend.

"There were only four or five nurses there," Kina said. "So he interviewed them. And then he searched all the rooftops and the bushes and grass areas right by the hospital."

The next day, Lieutenant Kina personally inspected the hallway leading to Father Robinson's apartment, where the frantic running footsteps had been heard. He paid particular attention to the exit door just past the priest's quarters.

"There was a panic handle on it," he later testified, "and it would only open from the inside. You couldn't get in from the outside. You had to push the handle down and then the door would open. And then, when it closed, it had a terrific clanging noise."

Repeating the test Detective Dave Weinbrecht had conducted, Kina opened and closed the noisy exit door again and again, until he was satisfied that whoever Warren and Langston had heard running down the hallways could not have exited the door without the loud clanging sound being heard. He became certain that the murderer had to be Father Gerald Robinson.

But as the priest came increasingly under suspicion, some in the Toledo Police Department were decidedly uneasy about accusing him of such an unspeakable crime against a nun.

On Wednesday at 12:40 p.m., Detective Dan Foster interviewed Dr. Jack Baron, one of the first members of the "Mr. Swift" team to rush to the chapel. The 32-year-old second-year resident had just finished his Friday night shift, and was briefing two other doctors in Morning Report, when the "Mr. Swift" call had come over the public address system.

He had rushed down the stairs, making a right instead of a left, as he'd never been to the chapel before. Realizing his mistake, he turned around to pass a priest in a black cassock going the other way. Dr. Baron told Detective Foster how the priest had glanced back, giving him an icy stare. He described the clergyman to the detective as being between 35 to 45 years old and of medium height, with brown hair.

At this point in the interview, Dr. Baron realized that Detective Foster was not taking any notes, and asked why.

"That always bothered me," Dr. Baron would relate years later, adding that the detective seemed more concerned about the position of the window shades than his strange encounter with Father Robinson in the wake of the murder.

But even without this eyewitness account of Father Robinson leaving the chapel, Lieutenant Bill Kina had already decided to bring the priest in for questioning and a polygraph test.

"By that time we had solidified our original thoughts that Robinson was our suspect," explained Lieutenant Kina, "because he was the only one we could not account for."

Later that day, Detective Art Marx telephoned Father Robinson, asking him to come to the Safety Building for an interview as soon as possible. The priest said he was busy Thursday, but would be available Friday evening, promising to be at the detectives' bureau at the corner of Erie and Jackson at the appointed time.

CHAPTER SIXTEEN

The Interrogation

AT 8:00 P.M. ON FRIDAY, APRIL 18, FATHER GERALD ROBINSON walked into the detectives' bureau wearing his black clerical jacket. He had driven himself there from Mercy Hospital.

He was immediately brought into a small interview room on the second floor, where Lieutenant Bill Kina and Detective Art Marx were waiting. The only furniture was a table and three chairs. In accordance with Toledo police policy, the interview was not audiotaped, although Detective Marx took notes, which have long since disappeared.

Prior to Father Robinson's arrival, the two detectives had agreed on a game plan. Kina decided to go for a confession, assigning Art Marx, the former Catholic altar boy, to the role of lead interrogator. The previous day, Detective Marx had interviewed Father Swiatecki, who'd then passed a polygraph test. The junior chaplain, having also been seen in the clergy dining room eating breakfast at the time of the murder, had been cleared, leaving Father Robinson the prime suspect.

"I left it entirely in Marx's hands," explained Kina, "because he had so much knowledge of the Church and the priesthood."

After twenty-seven years with the Toledo Police Department, Lieutenant Kina was well aware of his superiors' sensitivity to anything that might embarrass the Catholic Diocese.

"There was an unwritten rule," he explained. "When you caught a priest in a homosexual or a pedophile situation, you didn't book them like you did any other individual. You took them down to the vice squad, who then called in the Monsignor. He'd then come down and put a collar on them and take them away and do whatever was appropriate with the Church at that time."

The wayward priests would then quietly be transferred to an out-of-state parish.

But Lieutenant Kina believed that in the case of a priest murdering a nun, different rules might apply.

The two homicide detectives began by trying to put Father Robinson at ease, standard practice at the start of an interrogation.

"We might talk for an hour about baseball," explained Kina, "just to get the guy to relax a little. But I don't remember what we spoke to Robinson about."

Slowly, Detective Marx steered the conversation around to the murder, asking about the victim and where he had been on Holy Saturday morning. And as soon as Father Robinson answered one question, Marx followed up with another, looking for any inconsistencies.

"I mean, Art was really nailing him," remembered Lieutenant Kina. "It was a serious interrogation and everything the priest would say, he would counter it."

Over the next few hours, Father Robinson became more and more unnerved by the "forceful" questioning. Marx repeatedly asked about his movements at the time of the murder, slowly wearing down the priest, who became increasingly evasive.

"He was getting pretty uptight," said Kina. "You could just see the tension. But he wasn't angry. He didn't show any emotions."

Suddenly, out of the blue, Father Robinson claimed that Sister Margaret Ann Pahl's murderer had confessed to him two days earlier.

This statement stunned both detectives, who knew that if true, he had broken one of the Catholic Church's cardinal rules, never to reveal anything about a confession—punishable by automatic excommunication.

"He says, 'I'll tell you what happened,'" remembered Lieutenant Kina. "One of his parishioners had come in and confessed to killing the nun, and he took his confession. Then Marx jumped all over him, telling him there was "no way that you, as a priest, could come out and divulge details of a confession.'"

Detective Marx then demanded to know who had confessed and under what circumstances, but he refused to elaborate further. Finally the priest threw up his hands, admitting he had made it up just to get them off his back.

"Here's a Catholic priest [who] would lie to police during an interview," explained Marx years later. "He said, 'Oh, I just made that up.' That's critical."

When Marx asked why he would lie about someone making a confession, Father Robinson shrugged his shoulders, saying he was exhausted and just wanted to go home.

"I was trying to protect myself," he told the detectives meekly.

Just after midnight the interrogation came to an end. A polygraph test, scheduled to be administered by Lieutenant Jim Weigand, was postponed until the following afternoon, as the priest was too upset to provide a meaningful baseline reading.

But before he left the interrogation room, he signed a waiver of search warrant, allowing detectives to immediately search his living quarters without a court order:

I, Father Gerald Robinson, do hereby authorize and agree to allow members of the Toledo Police Department, to wit Detective Arthur Marx, to search my living quarters at Mercy Hospital, for a weapon, clothing or cloth materials that might contain blood, and/or any other evidence that might prove to be connected with the death of Sister Margaret Ann Pahl.

I understand that I have a constitutional right to refuse to have my quarters searched, and have been under no threat or promises made to me, and that I'm giving permission free[ly] and voluntarily.

By that point Father Robinson was in no state to drive back to Mercy Hospital, so a detective brought him back, careful not to get him there before the search had finished.

STRAIGHT AFTER THE INTERROGATION, LIEUTENANT KINA and Detective Marx drove to Mercy Hospital to search Father Robinson's two cramped rooms. The priest had agreed not to be present during the search.

They started in his bedroom, opening up his closet, before moving on to his front room/office. Then as Lieutenant Kina looked on, Detective Art Marx opened the center drawer to his wooden desk, peering inside. "Oh, what have we got here?" he declared triumphantly.

"We found this dagger-type letter opener in there," remembered Kina. "It had a diamond-shaped blade on it, and then on the handle was a knuckle-guard thing like a sword would have."

Immediately both detectives realized that the eight-inch letter opener, bearing a circular bronze medallion on the handle with an embossed picture of the U.S. Capitol building, fitted Dr. Renate Fazekas' description of the murder weapon.

Marx then put the souvenir from the National Historical Wax Museum in Washington, D.C., given to Father Robinson years earlier by a local scout troop, into a white evidence envelope. He neatly marked the date on it, before sealing it up and placing it in his briefcase.

When the detectives left Father Robinson's room to return to the Safety Building, they were certain they had found the murder weapon.

"I put it in the safe in the detectives' bureau," said Kina. "Then we went home, as we had been working all day."

The following day Father Robinson's letter opener was sent out to the police laboratory for forensic analysis, but it would be another week before it would be examined for traces of Sister Margaret Ann Pahl's blood.

FATHER GERALD ROBINSON HAD LITTLE SLEEP THAT NIGHT. All the tough questions must have shaken him to the very core, and he knew there would be more in a few hours, when the lie-detector test had been rescheduled. So he took one of the Valium tablets that he had been prescribed on the day of the sister's murder, to calm down enough for a few hours' sleep.

By Saturday lunchtime—the two-week anniversary of the murder—Father Gerald Robinson was a nervous wreck. In desperation, he asked Sister Phyllis Ann Gerold for help.

The Mercy Hospital CEO was eating lunch in the clerical dining room with several other nuns when Father Robinson suddenly burst in.

"He was very upset," Sister Phyllis Ann would remember in January 2007. "And I can still see him leaning against that wall, saying what happened to him. That the police had taken him down to the station and he had been interrogated. He also said Father Swiatecki was accusing him. He spoke about the lie-detector test, and that Swiatecki was screaming at him."

Sister Phyllis Ann felt that Father Robinson desperately needed legal help and advice.

"He was naïve," she said. "He just did not have any street knowledge, and he didn't seem to understand that he needed somebody. I thought, 'This is not going right, and . . . you had better have an attorney.'"

So she told the anxious priest to cooperate with the detectives, and called the diocese after lunch, asking if their attorney would be representing him.

"And they said no," said Sister Phyllis Ann. "That priests are on their own. After that, I made the decision to get him an attorney. I called the hospital attorneys, who are corporate and not criminal."

That afternoon Toledo attorney Henry Herschel was officially appointed to represent Father Gerald Robinson, going straight to work on behalf of his client.

CHAPTER SEVENTEEN

Intervention

AT 12:40 P.M., FATHER JEROME SWIATECKI BROUGHT HIS SENIOR chaplain to the Safety Building, waiting with him in a second-floor detectives' bureau interrogation room, until he could take his lie-detector test. Father Robinson would later admit taking Valium earlier that morning, to feel more relaxed.

A few minutes after their arrival, they were joined by Lieutenant Dave Roberts, who would be conducting the brief pre-test interview.

"When I came in to collect Father Robinson," remembered Roberts, "Father Swiatecki suddenly pointed his finger at him and said, 'You tell the truth!' His voice was very stern and it was like he was giving him an order. Father Robinson showed absolutely no reaction. He was very stoic."

After Lieutenant Roberts had finished the pre-interview, Father Robinson was brought into another room, where Lieutenant Jim Weigand was waiting to administer the polygraph. He first asked the priest to remove his cassock, so various wires and tubes could be attached to his chest, to measure breathing and blood pressure. Father Robinson was then read his Miranda rights, which he signed.

Lieutenant Weigand began by asking simple biographical questions about the father's family and life, to ensure that the machine was working properly and would provide a baseline score. When he was satisfied that everything was OK, he asked Father Robinson about his movements the morning of Sister Margaret Ann Pahl's murder.

Father Robinson was evasive, hesitating before answering any questions. Even the simplest ones were met by long pauses, leading the detective to suspect he was lying.

Finally, Lieutenant Weigand asked if Robinson had any idea who had murdered Sister Margaret Ann. The priest said he had "none at all" and then Weigand asked why someone would have wanted to kill her.

"Well," replied Father Robinson, "she had a dominant personality."

Surprised by this statement, Lieutenant Weigand asked him to elaborate.

"She was a dominant woman," he repeated.

Weigand finished the test at about 4:45 p.m., going next door, where Detective Art Marx and Lieutenant Bill Kina were waiting to resume the interrogation from the night before.

"He told us that there were some real shaky, questionable responses," said Kina, "which indicated there was some lying."

Art Marx, who would start his own polygraph business after retiring from the police department, was later shown the priest's test charts.

"I had the opportunity to look at them," he said. "And to me, being trained, they were very deceptive."

In his official report, Lieutenant Weigand noted how Father Robinson had contradicted himself several times during the questioning. When first asked what he was doing when he had been summoned to the chapel by Sister Phyllis Ann, he said he was finishing his shower and drying himself with a towel. But a few minutes later he claimed to have been buttoning up his cassock.

"Truthfulness could not be verified," Lieutenant Weigand concluded in his report. "Deception was indicated on relevant questions, concerning the murder of Sister Margaret Ann Pahl."

ARMED WITH THE RESULTS OF THE POLYGRAPH TEST, LIEUtenant Kina and Detective Marx now believed it was only a matter of time before Father Robinson would break. Aware that polygraph test results were not admissible in Ohio courts, they felt certain the priest was now ready to confess to the murder.

"So we took him back into the interrogation room," said Kina. "I felt that after that polygraph and the fact he showed deception, as well as the letter opener and all the other stuff we had, like the running and the shoes, we were close to a confession. We needed a confession bad, but there is no way you are going to get a confession other than just talk to him."

As the interrogation resumed, Art Marx went straight to the point, accusing Father Robinson of murdering Sister Margaret Ann and telling him that the polygraph test proved him a liar.

An hour into the interrogation, Father Robinson had still not admitted a thing, and Detective Marx left to get more notepaper. Left alone with the priest, Kina made small talk to try to relax him.

"Then there was a knock at the door," remembered Kina. "So I got up and answered it."

There stood Deputy Chief Ray Vetter, flanked by Monsignor Jerome Schmit of the Toledo diocese and Mercy Hospital attorney Henry Herschel.

Vetter asked Kina to step out of the interrogation room, and the three men went inside, closing the door behind them.

When they were in there with Father Robinson, Kina walked across the hall, where Father Swiatecki sat waiting. About ten minutes later, the interrogation room door opened and out walked Deputy Chief Vetter, Monsignor Schmit, chomping a cigar, Father Robinson and his newly appointed attorney Herschel.

"I was livid," said Kina. "Then they walked out of the Safety Building with Robinson."

Shocked by what he had just witnessed, he turned to Father Swiatecki, who had observed everything.

"I said, 'Where are they taking him?'" recounted Lieutenant Kina. "'What are they going to do with him?' And he said, 'They'll put him on a funny farm someplace and you'll never see him again.' So I just threw up my hands in the air."

When Detective Marx learned what had happened, he was furious, but knew once Father Robinson had lawyered up, there would be no confession.

"That stopped everything," he said. "For all practical purpose[s] our investigation was done. We did not come back and re-contact him, for there was no way an attorney was going to allow us to meet with him."

"There was a lot of steam taken out of the investigation when they pulled him out of there," Kina recalled in July 2006. "We later found out Deputy Chief Vetter had gone down to the diocese to pick up Monsignor Schmit and bring him down to the Safety Building. He brought the attorney along to take care of police." Lieutenant Kina was bitterly disappointed by Vetter's intervention, feeling it breached all police procedure.

Vetter and Kina's friendship suffered a bitter blow, and they stopped socializing, and drifted apart. Although, more than twenty-five years later, he still considers the long-retired deputy chief one of the most "honest" and "upstanding" men he has ever known, Kina still questions his course of action.

"I don't believe anybody," Kina said, "no matter what their rank is, has the right to interrupt a completely lawful interrogation of a prisoner. But he chose to do it."

Kina believes that his boss was swayed by his deep religious conviction, placing it above his responsibilities as an officer of the law.

"I don't think he was trying to protect the priest or justify the killing of a nun," explained Kina. "He was trying to protect the sanctity of the Church. Even today I don't think you could get him to admit he did anything wrong, because he was such a devout Catholic, he thought he was doing right."

Years later, Deputy Chief Vetter would vehemently deny doing anything to protect Father Robinson.

"Absolutely not, absolutely not," he maintained in June 2006. "I did absolutely nothing to try and reduce the charges against the father."

Vetter claims he only brought his close personal friend Monsignor Schmit to the Safety Building to aid the investigation.

"I told him," Vetter would later testify, " 'All I want you to do is to talk with Father Robinson, make him feel sort of at home. Whatever you can find out. And if you find out anything, let's talk.' "

Vetter claims he no longer remembers taking Father Robinson out of the interrogation room.

"I wouldn't do that," he said, bristling at the accusation. "They're coming up with the idea that I fixed the case, and that's bullshit. I would never do that. I wouldn't put my job at risk, my pension.

"And it's illegal. It's immoral. In fact, if we had capital punishment, and if we had more evidence, and if they had put him in the electric chair, I would probably have pulled the switch."

CHAPTER EIGHTEEN
Going Through the Motions

WHEN THE HOMICIDE TEAM MET ON MONDAY FOR ITS DAILY status meeting, morale was at an all-time low. Father Robinson was now back at Mercy Hospital, and his attorney Henry Herschel had agreed to allow detectives to conduct a second search of his client's living quarters. Additionally, the attorney had arranged for Father Robinson to take a second independent polygraph test that afternoon in Dearborn, Michigan.

On Monday morning, Detectives Art Marx, Dale Vaughan and Dave Weinbrecht returned to Father Robinson's quarters.

"The first thing I found," Detective Weinbrecht would later testify, "was a bottle of Valium that was issued on the day of the murder out of the hospital pharmacy."

The detectives then searched Robinson's desk again, discovering a metal pry bar, along with some other items they seized as possible evidence. In his closet was a black cassock with a stain, and a new pair of brogues with rubber soles, matching the type of footwear Margaret Warren had described hearing about the time of the murder.

When the detectives told the priest they were confiscating the shoes and his cassock, he protested.

"I remember him telling us that was the only one he had and he needed it back," said Weinbrecht. "He said he only had one robe."

A few hours later, Father Robinson was driven 55 miles north to Dearborn for the polygraph test arranged by his attorney. This time he passed, although the results were deemed to be "inconclusive." A subsequent report found Father Robinson highly emotional during the test, providing "inconsistent" responses to many questions.

Years later Father Robinson would claim the second lie-detector test had totally vindicated him.

"It showed I was definitely not in the vicinity of that murder," he would tell detectives. "There was nothing to indicate that I was part of that murder whatsoever. Absolutely nothing."

THE NEXT DAY FATHER ROBINSON'S LETTER OPENER WAS examined by senior criminologist Josh Franks at the Toledo police crime lab. He was testing for the presence of blood, and first put it under the microscope.

"It was sumptuously clean," remembered Franks. "It didn't have any fingerprints, no stains, no smear marks. It appeared as if it had been polished, and that was interesting."

He then turned his attention to the circular nickel-sized medallion of the Capitol building, embedded between the handle and the blade. It was glued on to the opener and Franks pried it off, noticing a small spot, possibly blood, under one of the notches below the medallion.

He carried out a standard presumptive test, coating the area with a chemical called phenolphthalein. It immediately turned pink, indicating the presence of blood.

In his subsequent report the criminologist concluded:

> The wax museum medallion affixed to Exhibit 1 (letter opener) gave a weak positive result to a presumptive screening test for blood, indicating the possible presence of blood.

But unfortunately there was not enough of the substance remaining for a second test to confirm blood, and the preliminary test alone would be inadmissible in court.

Detectives had still not ruled out the possibility that a pair of surgical scissors, missing from the sacristy, could also be the murder weapon. So that afternoon, Josh Franks examined a pair of sample scissors, provided by Sister Kathleen Mary the previous day, similar to the ones used by the victim. The criminologist first compared the scissors to the holes found in Sister Margaret Ann's dress, determining that they had been made by an instrument similar to the scissors.

Then Detective Weinbrecht, who had witnessed the test, brought the scissors to the county morgue, to be examined by Dr. Renate Fazekas.

"She had sample pieces of flesh preserved from the victim," Weinbrecht noted in his police report," "as well as photographs and slides."

The assistant coroner first compared the scissors with the flesh samples, making test cuts into the flesh and using photographs for comparison.

"The opinion of the doctor is that the scissors very well could have been the weapon," reported Weinbrecht. "But she [would] not say with 100 percent certainty."

Dr. Fazekas also observed that some of the wounds to the victim appeared to have been made with the scissors closed, and others with them open, especially the ones to the neck.

But she thought the terrible wounds to Sister Margaret Ann's face had been made with a weapon far sharper than the scissors.

Detective Weinbrecht then asked the deputy coroner to examine Father Robinson's letter opener, comparing its depth and width to the puncture wounds on the sister's body.

"Her conclusion was that the instrument was compatible with each of the wounds found in the body, and could have been the weapon used," Weinbrecht would later testify.

A FEW HOURS LATER, DEPUTY CHIEF VETTER SUMMONED Lieutenant Bill Kina into his office, asking if there was anything left for the homicide investigators to do at Mercy Hospital.

"I told him no," recalled, Kina. "We don't have to be at Mercy Hospital. He said, 'Have the guys come back and reassign them to their regular duties, and you and Marx carry on for the rest of [the investigation].' "

Then Vetter called a press conference, announcing that the investigation would be scaled down within the next few days. But he emphasized Sister Margaret Ann Pahl's homicide would remain under active investigation, with more detectives being reassigned back to the case if and when new leads demanded it.

"[The investigation] is getting to the point," he told the Toledo *Blade*, "where we're getting down to the bottom of the pile of things to do."

He explained that although his five-man task force had spent "hundreds of hours" conducting "dozens of interviews," they had not been able to develop any concrete leads.

Once again Deputy Chief Vetter appealed to anyone with any information about the murder to contact the homicide unit.

The next day, as the Mercy Hospital trustees put up a further $5,000 reward for information leading to the killer, Vetter ordered Lieutenant Kina to take the complete case file to Lucas County Prosecutor Curt Posner, to see if they had enough evidence to indict Father Robinson.

"I knew there wasn't enough to indict before I even took it over there," said Kina. "Posner told me, 'You better go back and see what else you can develop'. That's all he said."

WITH THEIR CASE AGAINST FATHER ROBINSON AT A DEAD end, Lieutenant Kina and Detective Marx merely went through the motions for the rest of the investigation.

"That was the handwriting on the wall," explained Kina. "I knew the investigation was over with, and it wasn't going anywhere. It was extremely stressful."

In early May, the two detectives received a promising lead from Ohio prison inmate Archester Neal, claiming that another prisoner had confessed committing the murder to him. According to Neal, the killer and a friend were transvestite hustlers, working the streets by Mercy Hospital the morning of the murder. They had sneaked into Mercy in full drag, going into the chapel, where they were confronted by

Sister Margaret Ann Pahl. Then one of them began stabbing her repeatedly with a knife.

Neal claimed that the murderer had then buried his bloody clothes and the murder weapon in the backyard of a house in downtown Toledo, and even provided an address.

After Neal was brought to Toledo and passed a polygraph test, Lieutenant Kina and Detective Marx obtained a search warrant for the backyard.

"So we went home," said Kina, "changed our clothes and came back with shovels, and dug up the backyard. But we found nothing."

OVER THE NEXT FEW MONTHS, THE INVESTIGATION SLOWED down, as the two detectives turned their attention to other homicides. The case was still considered open, though not under active investigation. Still, whenever a fresh lead came in, Kina and Marx would investigate.

Back in Edgerton, Sister Margaret Ann Pahl's family was becoming increasingly frustrated at the lack of progress being made.

"They always say that after a certain time you come to closure on your grief," said her sister Catherine Flegal. "But there was none here."

On May 23, the medical staff at Mercy Hospital offered an additional $9,000 to the reward fund, now totalling $24,000.

By now Father Gerald Robinson had resumed his duties at Mercy Hospital as if nothing had happened, working side by side with Father Swiatecki.

"[Father Robinson] was just his quiet self," recalled Sister Phyllis Ann Gerold. "There were no problems that I knew of between him and Father Swiatecki."

Sister Phyllis Ann said that at the time, she never believed Father Robinson was the murderer.

"I knew the police suspected him," she said. "And he was their main prime suspect. In fact, we all believed that if it was a priest, it had to have been [Father Swiatecki]."

In the months following the killing, recalled Sister Phyllis

Ann, paranoia was rife at Mercy Hospital, with no resolution to the murder.

"It was totally unreal," she explained. "You begin to think of all the other people [who] could have done it internally. Well, because of the time of day, the front door was probably open, and someone from the outside could have gotten in.

"There was a consistent rumor at the hospital that it was a Satanic killing, and part of a Satanic rite."

ON JULY 2, 1981, THE NEWLY APPOINTED BISHOP OF Toledo, James Hoffman, moved Father Gerald Robinson out of Mercy Hospital, reassigning him as pastor of three Polish churches in Kuschwantz: St. Anthony, St. Stanislaus and Nativity.

"The Bishop took me out of there a year after this all happened," Father Robinson later explained. "He said, 'I just want to move you out because things would be better.'"

From then on, Father Robinson faded back into the Polish community, where he was still much admired and respected.

Jack Sparagowski, who had first met him years earlier, now got to know Father Robinson well at St. Anthony's.

"I don't think anyone from our parish," said Sparagowski, "was aware that he was ever a suspect in Sister's murder."

By this time the Toledo Police Department had put its investigation on the back burner. With an average sixty murders a year in Toledo, Lieutenant Kina and his four-man homicide squad were woefully undermanned, and he was fast burning out.

"I was trying to lead a group of detectives in a situation where it was impossible to do a good job," he explained. "We just did not have the manpower to look into these cases the way we should have. You get bad results."

On Thursday, October 22, 1981, Detective Art Marx visited Ypsilanti State Hospital near Ann Arbor, Michigan, to meet Dr. Harley Stock, a renowned FBI-trained forensic psychologist. He had read about the case and contacted the Toledo homicide task force, offering his help pro bono, to prepare a criminal profile of the killer.

"During [our] meeting," Detective Marx later reported, "the homicide of Sister Pahl was discussed in detail."

After explaining that criminal profiling was not "an exact science," Dr. Stock reviewed the entire case file.

He told Marx he should be looking for an "extremely strong" Hispanic male in his mid-twenties, with a tenth- to eleventh-grade education. The suspect had a history of family violence, and was possibly abused as a child. He is heterosexual, but has "very poor social relations" with women.

"The suspect is very repulsive," wrote Marx in his meeting report. "He can be violent and is easily provoked. According to Dr. Stock, the original motive was robbery and not sexual assault or rape."

The profiler believed the killer did not take responsibility for his behavior. He was mentally ill but not insane, and "sophisticated" enough to blame others for his acts.

Then Dr. Stock advised Marx on the best approach to interview the suspect and get a confession. The detective noted:

> The doctor felt the interviewer should be well rested, thus giving him a definite advantage. There should first be some general conversation, followed by questions about what kind of person would do something like this. Questions should then be directed toward the suspect's last response. This should keep the subject talking freely. The doctor felt that there is a good possibility that the subject needs to talk to somebody about the incident and with the proper application of subtle pressure, he would confess his guilt.

Two weeks later, Bill Kina, still angry at how his superiors had shielded his prime suspect so close to a confession, took retirement from the Toledo Police Department, after twenty-nine years of service.

"I felt that the job was getting me down," he later admitted. "And morale was very low. I mean, you don't give anybody, including priests, a carte blanche ticket to do anything they want. Now running a red light, I can see looking the other way, so you don't get a priest involved. But as far as homicide, you don't give anybody a green light to just go ahead and carry on with their life after that."

OVER THE NEXT FEW YEARS, THE INVESTIGATION VIRTU-ally ground to a halt. About once a year, Sister Phyllis Ann Gerold would receive a call from homicide detectives requesting information. And every few months the Toledo *Blade* would run a recap of the murder, appealing for any new information. But police had given up hope of ever bringing anyone to justice.

In late 1981, a 22-year-old man was arrested in Chicago, accused of stabbing and raping a New York nun. Toledo detectives investigated any ties to Sister Margaret Ann Pahl's murder, but could find none.

Detective Art Marx never stopped following up sporadic leads, regularly meeting with Father Jerome Swiatecki, who, Marx was convinced, knew the truth about what had really happened in the sacristy that 1980 Holy Saturday morning.

"I would meet with him on a monthly basis for coffee after the investigation was curtailed," explained Marx in June 2006. "We'd talk, and there were some things that he shared with me that made me feel that Father Robinson had probably confessed to him. Although he could never tell me that . . . he was telling me indirectly that's probably what happened."

On June 2, 1982, Father Swiatecki received an anonymous birthday card. Inside was a note, claiming to be from Sister Margaret Ann Pahl, imploring him to confess the sin of murder to the bishop. Father Swiatecki handed it to the police, who duly checked the envelope and card for fingerprints, but found none.

Later that year, Father Robinson himself called the police, after being mugged by two men on the way to the bank to deposit St. Anthony's church funds.

OVER THE NEXT TWO DECADES FATHER GERALD ROBINSON faded into the background, keeping a low profile. As he grew older and his hair turned white, he carved out a reputation as a hard-line priest, always delivering ultra-conservative sermons in fluent Polish. His knowledge of the old traditions and folk songs made him much loved in the Polish community.

But few outside the Toledo Police Department and the diocese knew that the outwardly shy, mild-mannered clergyman had once been suspected of murdering a nun.

IN JULY 1989, SISTER PHYLLIS ANN GEROLD RECEIVED A call from a representative of the Toledo diocese, wishing to reassign Father Robinson to Mercy Hospital. The CEO of Mercy, now two years from retirement, was amazed that the diocese would ever contemplate bringing back Father Robinson after all that had happened.

"And I said," she remembered, " 'I don't think it's such a great idea, because he was the prime suspect.' And he said, 'Oh really?' He didn't know that story, and that was very strange. And after I told him, he assigned somebody else."

ON SEPTEMBER 5, 1989, FATHER ROBINSON WAS APPOINTED Associate Pastor of St. Joseph, Sylvania. Six months later he transferred to a part-time ministry at Flower Hospital and Lake Park Nursing Home, with residence at St. Hedwig Parish.

"He lived at my rectory for four years," said Father Paul Kwiatkowski, then the parish priest of St. Hedwig. "He's a very shy and quiet person—like a Caspar Milquetoast in a way. A bit of a pushover, and wishy-washy."

Semi-retired by this time, Father Robinson performed pastoral care at nursing homes and hospitals around Toledo. He also conducted Sunday Mass at St. Hedwig, while Father Kwiatkowski strummed hymns on his guitar with his folk group.

"He was a good preacher," said Kwiatkowski. "His sermons were OK. They were sort of conservative, and he always had everything written out. He spoke very loud and very forcefully. That was his stage presence, I guess."

One day he was talking to Father Robinson, when the subject of Sister Margaret Ann Pahl's murder came up.

"I was sitting at one corner of the table," he remembered, "and Father Robinson was at the other. And he just looked at me and said, 'You know they *even* questioned me on that.'

"I mean, there was no sense of guilt or anything like that. No guile at all. Just that they questioned him."

On weekends, Father Robinson preached at various churches around Toledo. One Sunday in the early 1990s, Detective Art Marx walked into his church, to find his one-time murder suspect conducting Mass.

"And I'm not walking up to the Communion rail," he remembered. "I'm leaving church early."

ON JUNE 20, 1985, LUCAS COUNTY SHERIFF JAMES TELB AND A team of investigators spent two days digging up a wooded area in Lucas County. Acting on reliable information, they were searching for the bodies of more than fifty babies, reportedly sacrificed over the years in Satanic rituals involving priests.

"We hear these things for months," Sheriff Telb told reporters at a hastily called 7:00 a.m. press conference to announce the search. "We had to act on it."

The sheriff explained that he had finally moved in, after information that there was to be another human sacrifice on the following day, the summer solstice.

He told reporters that his reliable informants had claimed the existence of a group of several hundred Satan worshippers, who had been sacrificing babies and young children in bizarre black magic ceremonies. The bodies were then buried in a dense wooded area in Spencer township, just west of Toledo—where Jean Marlow would later accuse Father Gerald Robinson and the Sisters of Assumed Mary of taking her to as a child.

Before going into the wood to search for bodies, investigators raided the home of a 59-year-old man who had reportedly disappeared with his daughter two years earlier. But instead of finding the shotguns and drugs they were expecting, they only came up with a Bible, two Ozzy Osbourne albums, an animal bone and a poster for the movie *Raiders of the Lost Ark*.

After two days scouring the woods with a backhoe and bulldozer, no evidence of any human or even animal sacrifices was found. They did uncover a headless doll with a pentagram attached to its wrist and an eight-inch black-handled ceremonial knife. Two weeks later Sheriff Telb conducted a second search of the area, producing no further evidence of Satanic activity.

IN SUMMER 1992—TWELVE YEARS AFTER THE MURDER OF Sister Margaret Ann Pahl—Bill Kina ran into Deputy Chief Ray Vetter at a Toledo Police Department social event. It was the first time that they had seen each other in more than ten years. As soon as Vetter spotted him across the room, he came over.

"Hey, Bill," he exclaimed. "What was the name of that nun?"

"Sister Margaret Ann Pahl," Kina replied.

"I can never remember what her name was," Vetter said, shaking his head. "That's the biggest mistake I ever made."

Then without another word, retired Deputy Chief Vetter walked away.

It was the last time the two former friends would ever see each other. Years later, when a reporter challenged him about his remark to Kina, Vetter said he had no memory of that statement.

Dave Davison, the first Toledo police officer at the murder scene, never forgot the case. Throughout the 1990s, he waged a one-man campaign to bring Father Robinson to justice.

In November 1994, he wrote to the popular television show *Unsolved Mysteries*, sending newspaper clippings about the case and asking them to feature Sister Margaret Ann Pahl's unsolved homicide.

"Although the case was never solved," wrote the long-retired law enforcement officer in a pitch letter, "I and a good many others are firm in the belief that the killer was a priest, who was in chapel with her getting ready for Easter services."

After the murder, he wrote, Father Robinson had been moved out of Mercy Hospital "in very short order.

"Every priest prior to him was given a going-away party," wrote Davison. "Not him!"

A few weeks later, he wrote to Pope John Paul II, informing him about a murderous Roman Catholic priest with the blood of a nun on his hands. He offered to make all his files available to any investigator the Pope wished to assign:

> I seek only the truth and justice for the murder victim. I stood over the body of Sister Margaret Ann Pahl. I saw the marks on her throat where the killer had strangled her, until she stopped fighting for her life. I saw the thirty plus stab wounds and the puddles of blood, and I saw that her clothing was taken from her lower body, leaving her naked to add to the shame of the deed.
>
> With or without your help, I will not let this murder rest. I will bring the killer to light.

On March 24, 1995, he received an official reply on Vatican letterhead, signed by Pope John Paul II's Assessor Monsignor L. Sandri, on behalf of the Holy Father.

"Dear Mr. Davison," it began.

> I am directed to acknowledge the letter which you sent to His Holiness Pope John Paul II and I would assure you that the contents have been carefully noted.

PART 2

CHAPTER NINETEEN
The Cold Case Squad

IN DECEMBER 1997, JULIA BATES, THE NEWLY APPOINTED LU-cas County Prosecutor, attended a law enforcement confer-ence in Cleveland. At a cocktail party one night, she was speaking to the Cleveland prosecutor, Stephanie Tubbs Jones, when the conversation turned to the latest twist in the notorious Dr. Sam Sheppard murder case.

In 1954, Dr. Sheppard's pregnant wife Marilyn had been found bludgeoned to death in the couple's Cleveland home. Subsequently, Dr. Sheppard had been convicted of her mur-der, spending ten years in jail before the U.S. Supreme Court overturned his conviction. He was later acquitted at a retrial.

The legendary case had inspired the hit television series and movie *The Fugitive*. Now, twenty-seven years after Dr. Sheppard had died penniless, his son Sam Reese Sheppard was suing the State of Ohio for $2 million for his father's wrongful imprisonment.

Jones, who was representing the city of Cleveland in the civil action, told Bates about the new genetic DNA tests, which Sam Reese Sheppard claimed provided "conclusive evidence" that the blood found on Dr. Sheppard was not his own, and would prove him innocent.

"This was on my mind when I went to bed," Bates remem-bered. "And at about three o'clock in the morning I woke stark awake, sat up and thought, 'Oh my gosh. If they can do DNA on Sam Sheppard to exonerate him, we should be doing it too.' It was like an epiphany. With modern technology and DNA testing, we can look at old unsolved homicides."

There and then, Bates decided to apply DNA testing to the most perplexing case of her career—the notorious Lovers' Lane serial killings, which had terrorized Toledo in the 1970s and 1980s.

For more than twenty years the brutal murders of nine young people, mostly young lovers parked in deserted areas, had gone unsolved. The innocent victims had been brutally tortured, raped and stabbed, before being shot execution-style, their bodies stuffed in car trunks or dumped in nearby drains. But one young female victim, Sandra Podgorski, who witnessed her boyfriend Tom Gordon's savage 1980 murder, had survived. And Julia Bates, who had worked the case as a young prosecutor, now realized that Podgorski might hold the key to catching the serial killers.

"The rest of these people were all dead and buried," said Bates. "They're bones. But she had survived. We can get her DNA if we still have the evidence— Oh my God. Because she was raped by both men. And if we saved that evidence, we can test it, and even though we can't prosecute the rape case, we could prosecute the murder."

When she returned to Toledo, Bates called a friend on the homicide squad, who discovered that the old case evidence still existed.

"We reopened the case," Bates said, "and found the evidence still contained samples of the semen found in the panties of the victim. And we tracked down the victim, who's now got two teenage kids and [is] a grown woman."

Then Bates had Podgorski's DNA compared to Anthony Cook's and his brother, Nathaniel's, the original suspects, who were never prosecuted due to lack of evidence.

"We got a DNA match," said Bates. "So we indicted the two brothers for aggravated murder."

Just before their trial, the Cook brothers took a plea bargain, with Anthony confessing to nine murders, and Nathaniel three.

"We cleared up all these cases," Bates related. "Finally the victims' families had some closure."

Delighted with her success in finally bringing the Lovers' Lane serial killers to justice in 1999, the Lucas County Prosecutor now joined forces with the Toledo Police Department to establish a permanent Lucas County cold case squad, its stated mission to reinvestigate old cases using DNA and other modern technologies.

"It's a new concept to America, and most of us have seen it on television," said Detective Tom Ross, a founding member of the cold case squad, who helped investigate the Cook brothers' case. "We try to apply new technology to old cases to try and bring them to a successful conclusion."

Initially the cold case squad consisted of Detective Ross, an investigator with the Lucas County Prosecutor's office with thirty-seven years' experience in law enforcement, and Sergeant Steve Forrester of the Toledo Police Department. They were soon joined by Lucas County Assistant Coroner Dr. Diane Scala-Barnett, the husband–wife forensic anthropologist team Drs. Frank and Julie Saul, as well as members of the DNA Team from the Bureau of Criminal Investigation and Identification (BCI) in Bowling Green, Ohio.

"It started kind of loosey-goosey," explained Julia Bates. "It's not like a really structured team. But now we have this nice little core group of people. You've got the medical component. You've got the detectives. The DNA experts. You've got all that—so pray start."

The cold case squad began meeting monthly to discuss new cases, reporting progress on the ones already underway.

"We've looked into close to fifty cases," said Detective Tom Ross in 2006. "And we've probably resolved thirty cases out of that."

But there was one particular cold case in Toledo that had always intrigued veteran law enforcement officers—the unsolved murder of Sister Margaret Ann Pahl. Detective Ross, who had played a minor role in the investigation, was well aware that homicide detectives had always believed Father Gerald Robinson was the killer.

In November 1999, Lieutenant Rick Reed of the Toledo

Police Department decided to have Father Gerald Robinson's dagger-shaped letter opener, long thought to be the murder weapon, reexamined by the BCI crime lab.

"He called me into his office," remembered Sergeant Steve Forrester of the cold case squad, "and told me that he had decided to send the letter opener to the attorney general's office for some scientific testing."

Lieutenant Reed attempted to interview Father Robinson about Sister Margaret Ann Pahl's murder, but was declined.

A month later, Cassandra Agnosti, a forensic scientist working in BCI's serology DNA unit, and a member of the cold case squad, performed a presumptive blood test on the letter opener, similar to the one conducted almost twenty years earlier by Josh Franks. She too received a presumptive positive result for blood in the area surrounding the Capitol building medallion.

But there was no way of tracing who the blood belonged to, or even if it was human. It would be three years before there would be another review of Sister Margaret Ann Pahl's murder.

IN 1992 SISTER ANNIE LOUISE, NOW 29 AND A NUN, BEGAN TO suspect that she had been sexually abused as a child. At first she had only snippets of memories, but then she began having flashbacks of horrific incidents involving clergymen in robes, and strange ritual ceremonies.

Sister Annie Louise, who taught children with special educational needs in Catholic schools around Toledo, began seeing a counselor, subsidized by her holy order. Gradually she began to remember specific incidents of abuse.

In early 1993, she wrote to Bishop James Hoffman of the Toledo diocese, naming Father Chet Warren as her main abuser. Unknown to Sister Annie Louise, five other women had already accused Father Warren of inappropriate sexual behavior, leading to his expulsion from the Oblates of St. Francis de Sales.

On June 23, 1993, Bishop Hoffman replied with a handwritten letter, expressing sadness that she had been "abused by a priest as a child." He promised "to meet this reality of clergy sexual abuse with compassion, sensitivity and honesty."

Five months later, after receiving no further word from Bishop Hoffman, Sister Annie Louise wrote a second letter to Father Warren's superior, Father James Cryan, head of the local oblates. She told him how Father Warren would visit her home to counsel her mother when Annie was a pre-schooler.

"She would be in a different part of the house," she wrote, "and he would abuse me."

She said the abuse had continued in a church rectory and sacristy soon after she started grade school.

On December 1, 1993, Father Cryan replied, writing that the terror he felt reading her letter could not compare with what she had gone through, rendering him speechless. A few weeks later she wrote a second letter to Bishop Hoffman, also forwarding copies to several members of a recently appointed diocesan commission investigating how to handle the recent allegations of clerical abuse of children.

"I am particularly devastated spiritually," she wrote, after explicitly outlining her sexual abuse. "I find it difficult to attend Mass. Some days it's excruciating. I walk up to Communion and think about oral sex . . . it's not fair."

Sister Annie Louise never received a reply from Bishop Hoffman or his commission.

Over the next few years she bravely struggled with her demons in therapy. Slowly she began to fill in the nightmarish blanks of her childhood, remembering more and more details, including the name of a second abuser—Father Gerald Robinson.

CHAPTER TWENTY
SNAP

BY EARLY 2002, AFTER TEN YEARS OF THERAPY, SISTER Annie Louise was finally making steady progress dealing with her torturous childhood memories. Almost daily she would read newspaper reports about Catholic Church scandals involving pedophile priests, making her realize that many other young children had also been victims of clerical abuse.

But on March 21, 2002, after reading an article in the Toledo *Blade* where Bishop James Hoffman declared that there were no abuse problems in *his* Toledo, she was outraged. The article, by *The Blade*'s religion editor David Yonke, headlined "Toledo Diocese Tries to Stem Abuse Fears—Bishop Hoffman Says Plan in Place to Protect Children," included a letter from Hoffman to his Toledo parishioners, addressing the growing national scandal of sexual abuse by priests:

> As your bishop, I am saddened and embarrassed by these acts of abuse affecting our children. Past vigilance has been found wanting. Catholics feel betrayed by those who have committed these actions. I sense the deep anger of many of our people as they read of these revelations.

Bishop Hoffman appealed to anybody who had been molested by someone in the Church to contact the diocese.

The article also quoted Frank DiLallo, a diocesan-employed licensed counselor, working full-time with alleged clerical sexual abuse victims, saying there were no problems in Toledo.

"In the six years that I have been doing this," he told *The Blade*, "there have been absolutely no allegations of priests abusing children."

He claimed that all four cases he was presently handling were allegations of child sexual abuse going back more than twenty years, with one dating back half a century.

"Two priests, in the history of our diocese," he said, "were diagnosed as pedophiles."

After reading the article, Sister Annie Louise was furious. She felt Bishop Hoffman had dismissed everything she had told him nine years earlier, so she decided it was only just that the diocese pay for her decade of counseling.

At a meeting with DiLallo, the diocesan case manager, she demanded $50,000 compensation for therapy that she and her order had paid for. When DiLallo asked the name of her abuser, she named Father Chet Warren, who had been expelled from the priesthood six years earlier after numerous complaints of sexual abuse.

When DiLallo pointed out that Warren was an Oblate of St. Francis de Sales—a religious community regionally headquartered in Toledo and not part of the diocese—she countered that he could only have served as a Toledo priest with Bishop Hoffman's approval. DiLallo promised to investigate and get back to her.

For four months she waited for a reply, finally calling DiLallo, requesting another meeting. This time she came armed with a detailed medication statement from her pharmacist, as well as a letter from her mother superior, asking the diocese to pay compensation.

At the second meeting, DiLallo promised a diocesan representative would meet an oblates' representative to discuss her demands.

But after months of waiting, Sister Annie Louise became increasingly frustrated by the diocese's apparent lack of interest, feeling no one was taking her seriously.

Then she heard about a national victims' advocacy group called SNAP (Survivors Network of those Abused by Priests) and placed a call to their Toledo office.

IRONICALLY SNAP HAD BEEN FOUNDED IN 1989 BY A LOCAL Toledo woman named Barbara Blaine, as a direct result of Father Chet Warren's sexual abuse. She was a 13-year-old devout Catholic schoolgirl at Toledo's St. Pius X School in 1969 when Father Warren, then 42 and the school's assistant pastor, invited her to Sunday dinner with the priests.

After the meal she found herself alone with Warren, who molested her for the first time and would continue to do so for the next four years. She never told anyone about her abuse, but her school grades suffered and she became estranged from her family.

For the next ten years she suffered post-traumatic stress syndrome, but in 1985, after reading about a priest who'd abused altar boys, Blaine, then 29, finally told her family what had happened. Then she formally complained to the Oblates of St. Francis de Sales, who put Father Warren on leave, eventually expelling him from the order.

In 1989, Blaine moved to south Chicago, where she founded SNAP, an organization designed to reach out to victims of clerical abuse. Its first meetings were in a homeless shelter, using word of mouth to attract abuse victims.

"We spent so many years thinking we were the only ones," Blaine said. "It was really affirming and consoling once we found other people."

In late 1992, her story was featured on *The Oprah Winfrey Show*, putting the organization on the map. Over the next ten years, membership increased to 6,000, driven by a string of clergy sex abuse scandals.

In summer 2002, Claudia Vercellotti, the SNAP organizer in Toledo, herself a one-time victim of clerical sexual abuse, with a background in criminal justice and social work, began receiving a series of desperate calls from Sister Annie Louise.

"She contacted me because she felt stymied," remembered Vercellotti. "She contacted me repeatedly about the process with the diocese. That it wasn't going very well and she wanted to see it through. But I don't think she was aware of just how many other victims there were of Chet Warren."

Vercellotti then met Sister Annie Louise, finding her highly credible, and agreed to help her.

On August 20, 2002, under increasing community pressure, the Toledo diocese signed a special agreement with the Lucas County Prosecutor's office. It agreed to turn over all files relating to priests who might be prosecuted for child sexual abuse.

"This was at a time," explained Lucas County Prosecutor Julia Bates, "when the Church was reexamining and reevaluating policies and procedures and what they had to tell us about. We were in kind of a deal with them where we said, 'Look, we want to see your files. We want to make sure there's nothing there that couldn't still be prosecuted.'"

Soon after it was formally signed, the diocese invited Sister Annie Louise to testify before a newly appointed Church review board, consisting of six Catholic laypersons hearing abuse allegations. Later she would claim Frank DiLallo had assured her the diocese would pay for her therapy if the review board found her credible.

On June 11, 2003, Sister Annie Louise, now in daily contact with Claudia Vercellotti, appeared before the review board. At the hearing she gave each member a four-page single-spaced typed statement she had written the day before, outlining her sexual abuse and mentioning Father Gerald Robinson by name.

"This report is written for the Diocesan Review Board members," it began, "to chronicle the severe abuse I experienced beginning at age 2."

Then, in harrowing detail, she outlined her allegations of how the nightmare had begun with Father Chet Warren molesting her at her home, while her mother was upstairs resting. The statement included graphic descriptions of the horrendous abuse she'd suffered over the next few years and recruitment into a Satanic cult, including several members of her own family.

"The rituals were horrifying and sadistic," she wrote. "Designed to break our wills and internalize whatever core programmed message they wished to use to further our powerlessness."

She outlined several horrifying incidents when she was 5 years old that had permanently scarred her. One had occurred soon after her pet Labrador Smoky died, when her father told her one night that he was taking her and her sister to see their beloved pet.

"We arrived at an old house," she wrote, "and down in the basement was a large table on which Smoky was lying."

Then her father and the other adults present in the basement had changed into black robes, preparing for a ceremony.

"My sister," she continued, "was given a meat cleaver and she began to hack Smoky apart. The priest told me that because I was such a bad girl, [my sister] had to hurt Smoky like that."

The priest then told her that she could bring Smoky back to life, if she really loved her pet.

She was then taken to Calvary Cemetery, the largest Catholic cemetery in Toledo, and placed in a coffin.

"Cockroaches were released into the box," she wrote. "I thought I was going crazy. They told me the bugs were marking me for Satan."

She described another incident a year later when cult members sexually initiated her to the slow beat of a drum.

"[A priest] carried me to a table," she wrote, "and vaginally raped me."

She wrote of being penetrated by a snake "to consecrate these orifices to Satan," and claimed to have been forced to eat an eyeball at the age of 11, before witnessing the murder of a young child.

"They wanted me to know they were always watching me," she wrote in the letter to the diocese. "After the eyeball incident they killed a little girl who was about three. I don't know who she was or where she was from."

Sister Annie Louise wrote of being left alone with the

little girl's mutilated body for hours in "a sea of blood and stench."

She only managed to survive by sitting atop an old flattened cardboard box for hours, pretending it was a little island of safety.

"I told myself if I stayed on the cardboard, I wouldn't go crazy," she wrote. "I wished I had died."

When she was 14, she alleged, Father Warren had pimped her out to men for sadomasochistic sexual liaisons.

"One of these S&M perpetrators was Father Gerald Robinson, a diocesan priest," who paid for at least one encounter at St. Vincent Hospital, she wrote. "I do not know who the others were."

At the end of her highly emotional interview with the review board, Sister Annie Louise walked out of the room, feeling that at least several of the members had shown compassion and believed her.

AS SOON AS SISTER ANNIE LOUISE LEFT THE ROOM AT THE Catholic Center, board review member Dr. Robert Cooley, a psychologist who counsels sexual abuse victims, and the only non-Catholic on the six-person board, demanded that her allegations be brought to the police immediately.

But apparently Dr. Cooley was the only review board member who found Sister Annie Louise's allegations credible, and after he was defeated in a vote, the meeting was adjourned.

"We suspect that this was in an effort to 'contain' the information . . . on Robinson," said Claudia Vercellotti. "The Toledo Catholic Diocese should have laced up their gym shoes and sprinted over to the prosecutor's office. But they didn't."

Reportedly, review board chairman Frank DiLallo then went upstairs to see Father Michael Billian, the chancellor and Episcopal vicar of the Toledo diocese, responsible for its day-to-day operations. DiLallo showed Father Billian the nun's four-page statement, informing him that Dr. Cooley was demanding it be given to the police.

Father Billian then contacted the Toledo diocesan law firm of Shumaker, Loop & Kendrick, asking if he had a "professional obligation" to report the allegations. Within hours, the diocese's counsel, Thomas G. Pletz, had responded with a letter to Frank DiLallo marked "Privileged and Confidential," with copies also going to Reverend Billian and another diocesan attorney, John F. Hayward:

> I appreciate that [the Diocesan Review Board] members are taking their responsibilities very seriously. I also know that they are aware of the sensitivity of this information, which they must hold closely as privileged, with no disclosure except as required by law.

He also claimed that a year earlier, the diocese had given Sister Annie Louise's file to the Lucas County Prosecutor's office.

> Its contents thus have already been reported to the proper legal authorities, who decide whether to prosecute persons for criminal offenses in this county.

Pletz also cited a five-page legal opinion by the Ohio Attorney General, finding that professional counselors and licensed social workers don't have to report child sexual abuse after the victim becomes an adult.

The letter also maintained that review board members did not act in "an official or professional capacity," and were not there to provide any counseling or advice."

On June 12, SNAP's Claudia Vercellotti was leaked a copy of the letter. She viewed it as a ploy to intimidate Dr. Cooley and stop him from bringing Father Robinson's name to the attention of law enforcement again.

"It was a veiled threat," she contended, "saying cease and desist. It didn't pass the smell test and flew in the face of the August 20, 2002, agreement between the diocese and the prosecutor."

A few days after the legal letter, Dr. Cooley and Vercellotti met with Sister Annie Louise, urging her to go to the prosecutor's office herself. She declined, saying that she wanted to carry on pursuing her case through the diocese, without involving law enforcement.

On June 27, Thomas Pletz sent a second confidential letter to the Chairman of the Diocese of Toledo Review Board, with copies also going to Father Billian and Frank DiLallo. In the letter Pletz expressed "concern" about whether the review board believed it should report the nun's allegations to the Toledo Police Department or the Lucas County Prosecutor. He wrote that the diocese was in "continuing contact" with the prosecutor, who had already carried out a "detailed review" of the victim's file.

"A follow-up report on that victim's latest reports has already been made to the Lucas County Prosecutor's Office," wrote the diocesan attorney. "These actions are above and beyond any statutory requirement."

When Vercellotti was leaked the second letter, she realized that the diocese had no intentions of reporting the allegations. Soon afterward, Dr. Cooley discreetly warned Sister Annie Louise not to place her faith in the diocese, as it did not have her interests at heart.

Finally, at the repeated urging of Vercellotti and Dr. Cooley, Sister Annie Louise agreed to allow them to take her complaint naming Father Robinson to the Ohio Office of the Attorney General in Bowling Green.

ON JULY 23, 2003, THE DIOCESE INITIATED ITS OWN INVESTIGATION into Sister Annie Louise's allegations, hiring John Connors and Lawrence Knannlein, two retired Toledo Police Department detectives. Case Manager Frank DiLallo personally briefed the two veteran investigators, who were also devout Catholics, both in their sixties.

Several years later, Connors would speak candidly about the special relationship between the Toledo Police Department and the Catholic Diocese.

"I can tell you there was always somebody the diocese could go to in the police department," he admitted to the

Toledo *Blade*. "And I can tell you that, at one time, I was that man."

Over the next nine months, the two investigators interviewed more than forty-five people, including nuns, priests and other members of the clergy. They spent more than seventeen hours alone with Sister Annie Louise, who tearfully described her years of sexual abuse in graphic detail, including her encounter as a teenager with Father Robinson.

Investigator Connors would later tell the Toledo *Blade* that he had been stunned by her allegations.

"I had conducted a lot of different investigations for the diocese going back a lot of years," he said. "But this was the first time I had ever heard these kinds of stories."

EARLY ONE FRIDAY MORNING IN SEPTEMBER 2003, CLAUDIA Vercellotti collected Dr. Robert Cooley in her old battered Toyota, driving twenty miles south to Bowling Green for a 7.30 a.m. meeting at the Ohio Office of the Attorney General. They were both very nervous about what they were about to do, realizing the implications.

"I didn't sleep the night before," remembered Vercellotti. "We were looking over our shoulders the whole way there. I knew that this was big, but didn't really appreciate how big."

Earlier the two had discussed how they would handle the meeting, which Sister Annie Louise did not attend. As a psychologist, Dr. Cooley felt bound by his role on the review board and breaching patient confidentiality.

"I had Sister Annie Louise's permission, and could represent what she was trying to say," said Vercellotti. "So we kind of made a whole person."

At the attorney general's office, they spent more than an hour with Special Agent Phil Lucas, who had agreed to review Sister Annie Louise's charges.

"We showed him her letter and discussed the allegations," said Vercellotti. "The systematic cover-up issues that were going on in this diocese."

Father Gerald Robinson's name was also mentioned at the meeting.

"He was always rumored in the survivor community to be the priest [who] got away with it," said Vercellotti. "So here's Sister alleging abuse at the hands of Father Robinson in a systematic way."

Soon after the meeting, Dr. Robert Cooley was fired by the diocese review board for breaching confidentiality. It was a damaging accusation that could irrevocably jeopardize his career as a psychologist.

"I think there were some issues," Father Billian told *The Blade*, "of his doing that work confidentially."

SNAP's Vercellotti was shocked that the review board would fire the only qualified psychologist who was a member, with more than ten years' experience in treating victims of sexual abuse.

"Between the two cease-and-desist letters and Cooley's firing, it just screamed," she said. "Methinks thou do protest too much. None of this made any sense. So there had to be something more to this."

Over the next few weeks, Vercellotti paid several more visits to the attorney general's office, providing copies of the nun's statement and the two confidential letters from the diocesan attorneys. By now, Special Agent Lucas was treating Sister Annie Louise's allegations seriously, but wanted additional information before officially asking the Lucas County Prosecutor's office to launch an investigation.

IN OCTOBER 2003, JOHN CONNORS AND LAWRENCE KNANNLEIN reported progress in their ongoing investigation to Frank DiLallo, at the Catholic Diocese's downtown Toledo headquarters.

"She came across well," Connors reportedly told the diocese case manager. "She seemed to make a real effort to be honest and accurate. I have no reason not to believe her."

In his written report Knannlein agreed there was "little doubt" that the sister believed she had been abused by Father Gerald Robinson, Chet Warren and others.

"I think we need to find some evidence that would corroborate her allegations," he advised.

CHAPTER TWENTY-ONE

Reopening the Case

ON TUESDAY, DECEMBER 2, 2003, THE TOLEDO COLD CASE squad held its regular monthly meeting at the Lucas County Coroner's office. During the meeting Cassandra Agnosti, the DNA expert for the Ohio Bureau of Criminal Investigation (BCI), who had tested Father Gerald Robinson's letter for blood several years earlier, casually asked Sergeant Steve Forrester if he had received investigator Phil Lucas's letter. After Forrester said he had not, Agnosti told the cold case squad about Sister Annie Louise's disturbing allegations involving Father Gerald Robinson.

"It was a name well known," said Detective Tom Ross, 58, who attended the meeting and had worked on the investigation into Sister Margaret Ann Pahl's murder.

As soon as Sergeant Forrester and Detective Ross returned to the Toledo Police Department, they called Lucas, asking him to fax the letter straight over.

"Tom Ross was with me when I received the fax," remembered Forrester, "and we decided, just by [Father Robinson's] name triggering it, why don't we open this case up?"

And when they showed Sister Annie Louise's letter to Lucas County Prosecutor Julia Bates, who well remembered the Mercy Hospital murder, she immediately agreed to reopen the case.

"The nun's letter talked about abuses," explained Bates. "Father Robinson's name was mentioned, and of course, it was an open case that we had never forgotten."

The next day Sergeant Forrester telephoned Investigator

Lucas, asking who had written the letter. The investigator said he did not know, but told him to talk to Dr. Robert Cooley, who had brought it in. Forrester called the psychologist, who told him more about the circumstances surrounding the letter that had prompted him to take it to law enforcement.

After putting down the phone, Sergeant Forrester briefed Detective Ross, and they discussed the best way of reopening the case, which had lain dormant for almost a quarter of a century.

TWO DAYS LATER, DETECTIVE ROSS AND SERGEANT FORrester officially reopened the investigation into Sister Margaret Ann Pahl's murder by first reviewing the old 1980 case reports and notes.

"There's a protocol we follow on the cold case squad," explained Detective Ross. "We decided to physically look at the evidence to make sure everything was still there and available."

Since the early 1980s, all evidence had been stored in the property room, deep in the basement of the Toledo Police Department headquarters, where it had been collecting dust. The two investigators had it brought up to the department's Scientific Investigations Unit, so they could personally inspect it.

"Our policy has been to actually touch the evidence," explained 50-year-old Sergeant Forrester, a twenty-seven-year veteran of the Toledo P.D. "Go get it. See if it's there. Two pieces of property in particular caught our attention—the altar cloth and the dagger-shaped letter opener."

The detectives first donned surgical gloves before laying out sheets of brown paper over the top of a large conference table. Then they carefully removed the yellowing white linen altar cloth, ten feet long by two-and-a-half feet wide. They next brought out the smaller altar cloth, which Sister Madelyn Marie had picked up before finding Sister Margaret Ann Pahl's body. Then Father Robinson's letter opener was taken out of a sealed white envelope, still bearing Detective Art Marx's typed evidence tag.

They then unpacked the rest of the evidence, including a pair of black-and-white rubber-soled shoes, Sister Margaret Ann Pahl's bloodstained clothing, a bottle of Valium prescribed to Father Robinson the day of her death and various bodily samples, including fingernails, hair and swabs.

There was also a file folder containing police reports and statements, black-and-white crime-scene photographs and the late Dr. Renate Fazekas' autopsy report.

Once the evidence was laid out on the table, they were joined by Keefe Snyder, who was in charge of the Scientific Investigations Unit. They first turned their attention to the large altar cloth, which had been found wrapped around Sister Margaret Ann's right arm. It had not seen the light of day since Detective Marx had checked it in to the property room two days after the murder and ten days before Father Robinson's letter opener had been found.

Ross and Forrester carefully unfolded it, laying it out the length of the conference table. They immediately noticed a long, thin dried bloodstain, bearing the unmistakable sweeping curve of a dagger.

Then they took a hard look at Father Robinson's letter opener, noting the gentle turn of the blade and the finger guard—and to their astonishment, saw it was almost a perfect mirror image of the bloodstain.

"We were stunned," said Forrester. "We just looked at each other and we were just shocked. You can see this finger guard on this dagger-shaped letter opener matches this [stain], and the blade matches this one. Obviously we are not experts, but we can see there's great similarities there."

Although Sergeant Forrester had often worked with blood transfer patterns, he had never encountered anything like this. At that moment he knew Sister Margaret Ann's own blood could finally bring her murderer to justice.

"So we wanted to know what we could do further to verify what we were seeing," said the cold case detective. "It more than got our attention."

Keefe Snyder suggested having a forensic expert at the BCI office in Bowling Green examine the altar cloth. So

Sergeant Forrester called BCI's Casey Agnosti, who suggested Dan Davison, a forensic scientist and blood-spatter expert.

The next day, Forrester took the altar cloth and the letter opener to Davison at the Ohio Bureau of Investigation. But after spending a day and a half examining them, he was unable to say for certain if the letter opener had made the bloodstains or punctures on the altar cloth.

"I cannot include or exclude the letter opener as the potential weapon," he wrote in his report.

On Monday, December 8, Forrester and Ross interviewed Sister Annie Louise, the first of several meetings they would have with her over the next three weeks. The two detectives found her a highly credible witness and, although she knew little about Sister Margaret Ann Pahl's homicide, she advised them to look for a specific sign of Satanic ritual defilement.

"She said one thing that was significant," Sergeant Forrester later testified. "That we should be looking for an upside-down cross on the victim's chest."

Later that day, Ross and Forrester questioned Claudia Vercellotti, who provided additional background information, including all correspondence between Sister Annie Louise and the diocese.

"I think they originally interviewed her dismissively," said Vercellotti. "It was Sister Annie Louise [who] said, 'Was she stabbed in the shape of an upside-down cross? Was she penetrated?' These were details that she could never have known."

THE BIGGEST HURDLE TO REOPENING THE CASE WAS THAT some of the key Toledo Police Department reports had disappeared. Nothing on paper existed about Father Robinson's two 1980 interrogations or the interview with Father Swiatecki, who had died of a massive stroke in the mid-1990s.

Later there would be allegations of a cover-up by Deputy Chief Ray Vetter, who would vehemently deny them. In 1986 Vetter had retired from the Toledo Police Department, calling Sister Margaret Ann Pahl's unsolved homicide the biggest disappointment of his thirty-four-year career in law enforcement.

So Detective Ross and Sergeant Forrester knew much depended on what the long-retired homicide detectives who had worked the original investigation could still remember after so many years.

"One of the things that we thought was important," explained Sergeant Forrester, "was to go back to some of the old-timers, and see what they knew outside of the reports and what their memories were like.

On December 10, Detective Tom Ross called his old Toledo Police Department colleagues Bill Kina and Art Marx, informing them that Sister Margaret Ann Pahl's case had been reopened, and asking for their help. Ross had started his career in law enforcement under Kina, considering him a mentor.

"Tom Ross from the cold case squad called me about the nun's homicide and wanted to interview me," remembered Kina, now in his eighties and in good health. "They still didn't know whether they had a case."

A week later, Ross and Forrester visited Kina at his house in the northern suburbs of Toledo.

"They asked me details about the case," said Kina. "At that time it was thrown at me cold. I mean, I didn't draw a complete blank, but a lot of it was blank."

To try to jog his memory, the detectives laid out photographs of the sacristy murder scene, the bloodstained altar cloth and the dagger letter opener on his kitchen table.

"They showed me a blood smudge on the altar cloth," said Kina, "with the letter opener laying right below it. And it showed the distinct sign of the handle beneath it. The smudge and the opener appeared to be a perfect match."

Over the next few weeks, Ross and Forrester regularly visited Kina, discussing the case and asking questions about their prime suspect, Father Robinson. Gradually he began to remember details of his original investigation.

"All these reports were missing," said Kina. "So we

didn't have anything to go on as far as the priest's involvement in this, other than our memories."

Ross and Forrester also visited the original lead detective, Art Marx. Now in his late seventies, Marx had recently remarried and ran a part-time polygraph test business.

"We talked to him," said Forrester. "Some of these early meetings were just introductions. Just to tell them what we're doing and what we're about. See what they remember."

When his old boss Bill Kina telephoned to compare notes, Marx admitted that his memories of the investigation were sketchy.

Over the next few weeks, the two cold case investigators spoke almost daily to the two elderly detectives, gleaning more and more details of the thwarted investigation.

But when Kina talked to Tom Ross on January 15, 2004, he voiced concerns that Marx was still unable to remember details.

Four days later, Kina telephoned his old colleague to see if he could help fill in the gaps.

"I further discussed the case with him," said Kina. "He could not remember physically sitting at a typewriter making reports."

Eventually the prosecutor's office initiated roundtable discussions, where Marx, Kina and a prosecutor's representative regularly met face-to-face to discuss the case and review old reports together.

"And that was the only way it was resurrected," said Kina. "It brought all this stuff back."

ON DECEMBER 15, 2003, FORRESTER AND ROSS MET WITH FATHER Michael Billian, in his fourth-floor office at the Catholic Center at 1933 Spielbusch Avenue, in downtown Toledo. The Diocese had been in transition since Bishop James Hoffman's death in February 2003. Father Billian had served as acting bishop until eleven days ago, when Bishop Leonard Blair had been officially installed.

Now Father Billian held the powerful position of Episcopal vicar of the Toledo diocese, coordinating the diocese's day-to-day activities and supervising the Catholic Center. He also advised the bishop on all parish matters, as well as examining allegations of clerical abuse of minors.

The two cold case detectives informed Father Billian that they had reopened the investigation into the murder of Sister Margaret Ann Pahl, and Father Gerald Robinson was the main suspect. They requested all Father Robinson's diocesan personal records immediately, in case they contained any information relevant to the case.

Father Billian then left the room for a few minutes, returning with a file. He handed it to the detectives, saying it was all the diocese had on Father Robinson.

Sergeant Forrester later wrote in a search warrant:

> The file was substantially devoid of any information concerning Father Robinson's service in ministry. His performance evaluations (or their equivalent), and/or any internal (canonical) investigation(s) conducted by the Catholic Diocese of Toledo into the death of Sister Margaret Ann Pahl or Father Robinson's fitness to serve in ministry.
>
> In short, the Catholic Diocese of Toledo provided information concerning Father Robinson, which included his picture, brief biographical information, his date of ordination and bare-bones information concerning his service in ministry.

Forrester then told Father Billian how Sister Annie Louise had suggested they look for signs of an upside-down cross, and any penetration of the sister's body.

"We asked him if he had any resources here locally," explained Forrester. "And if there was any significance to the upside-down cross. He guided us by telling us that the appropriate resources would be in Chicago, and that we should contact the archdiocese."

Father Billian then gave the detectives the phone number of the Archdiocese of Chicago's expert on exorcism, ritualism and the occult, Jeffrey Grob. As soon as they returned to the Safety Building, they contacted Reverend Grob and made an appointment.

Three days before Christmas, Ross and Forrester had a three-way telephone interview with Grob. During the two-hour conversation they briefed him about the case, making plans to visit him in Chicago and show him the case file.

"We didn't expect any instant answers," explained Forrester. "We just told him what we had."

CHAPTER TWENTY-TWO
CSI Toledo

AT THE REGULAR JANUARY MEETING OF THE COLD CASE squad, Casey Agnosti of BCI agreed to forensically examine the evidence for traces of DNA. But, she warned, it was so old, any DNA present could have degraded over time and from exposure to natural elements. Another problem, she pointed out, was that anyone coming into contact with Sister Margaret Ann Pahl's body in the original investigation could have contaminated it.

At the end of January, Agnosti brought the sister's underwear to the BCI laboratory in London, Ohio, where she tested four different areas for traces of DNA. Over the next few months Agnosti would conduct further DNA tests on other items of evidence, with varying degrees of success.

By its February meeting, the cold case investigation was gaining momentum. Forrester and Ross now asked Lucas County Deputy Coroner Dr. Diane Scala-Barnett to study Dr. Renate Fazekas' original autopsy report and the crime-scene photographs, and advise them how to proceed.

"By this time we were getting together as a group and going over this stuff," explained Forrester. "Dr. Barnett had given us some opinions she thought were important, and helped guide us in our investigation."

Dr. Scala-Barnett, who had been a resident at the Lucas County Coroner's office in 1980 and a pupil of Dr. Fazekas, was familiar with the altar cloth and the letter opener, which she had already inspected. Now she was asked if she felt Sister Margaret Ann Pahl's flesh wounds were consistent with

Father Robinson's letter opener, or if another weapon had caused them.

"We were trying to be convinced at this point that [the letter opener] is the cause of these marks," explained Forrester. "We asked her about knives, scissors and blades. She didn't think scissors could do it in the skin."

Later, Dr. Scala-Barnett would testify that she believed the dagger-shaped letter opener was the murder weapon.

"It was my conclusion," she said, "based on my experience, my knowledge, my training, that this weapon caused these injuries. Or a weapon exactly like it."

Now armed with Dr. Scala-Barnett's findings, the investigators asked Detective Terry Cousino, an evidence technician for the Toledo Police Department's Scientific Investigations Unit, to take a closer look at the altar cloth.

An eighteen-year veteran of the Toledo Police Department, the boyish-looking detective was reputed to have "an artist's eye" for his composite sketches of suspects from witness descriptions. He had been in high school at the time of Sister Margaret Ann Pahl's murder, knowing little about the case.

On Friday, February 27, Sergeant Forrester walked into Cousino's office carrying the altar cloth and letter opener, along with a white envelope containing the Capitol building medallion that Josh Franks had pried off in 1980.

"He explained that he was reopening this investigation into Sister Margaret Ann's murder," remembered Cousino, "and asked me to examine the letter opener and the altar cloth to see if any bloodstains were consistent with the letter opener."

After Sergeant Forrester left the office, Detective Cousino, who had blood-spatter training, started photographing, measuring and documenting all the evidence. He then placed the letter opener alongside some of the stains, taking photographs of the comparisons. One particular transfer pattern on the cloth jumped out at him.

"I felt that this transfer pattern was consistent with the curve and the shape of the tip of the blade," he would later testify. "Another separate transfer pattern again has a similar curve and similar size and shape consistent with the letter opener."

Even more startling was his observation that the mirror image of the distinct ribbing on the opener handle could be seen on the altar cloth in dried blood.

"This was a definite transfer pattern," explained Cousino, "that had a ribbed design to it."

He found another large transfer bloodstain pattern like an acorn, that clearly matched the decorative knob at the end of the handle. And he was particularly interested in a bloodstain at one end of the altar cloth, with a distinct lack of blood in the middle.

"And that could have been caused by that recessed area of the letter opener," he explained, "where the medallion was."

He then turned his attention to the eighteen stab holes at the center of the altar cloth. Initially the punctures appeared randomly placed, a clump of nine on the left and nine on the right. But as Detective Cousino looked closer, he noticed there was a clear pattern to the holes. Suddenly it all made sense.

"As soon as I started to look at them," he later explained, "it was pretty easy to observe that this cloth was folded, and there were actually only nine puncture defects through a folded cloth."

When Cousino folded the altar cloth, the eighteen holes lined up perfectly with each other, as did the bloodstains. As the right side of the cloth was bloodier than the left, Cousino reasoned that the left side would have been folded over and set closer to the sister's body.

He then took another look at the nine puncture wounds and noticed a definite symmetry. Six of the holes were in a parallel row of three, almost exactly six inches apart. Two more were spaced farther apart, forming a line slicing horizontally through the rows. There was one stray puncture at the bottom.

When Cousino connected the dots, he realized the holes

The Pahl family house on the rural farm where Sister Margaret Ann Pahl grew up. *Credit: The Pahl family*

The Pahl family sisters in 1941, several years after Sister Margaret Ann first joined Mercy Hospital, Toledo. From left to right: Sister Margaret Ann, Evelyn, Mary, Catherine and Sister Laura Marie. *Credit: The Pahl family*

As a young nun, Sister Margaret Ann was always known by her religious name: Sister Mary Annunciata. It wouldn't be until the 1960s that she could use her real name. *Credit: The Pahl family*

Sister Laura Marie (left) on a religious retreat with Sister Margaret Ann, soon after they entered holy orders. *Credit: The Pahl family*

As a young priest, Father Gerald Robinson was highly regarded in the Toledo Polish community. *Credit: Lucas County Prosecutor's Office*

In the 1970s, Father Robinson served at several Catholic Toledo parishes. There were rumors he was involved with a Satanic group of renegade priests who dressed in drag, known as the Sisters of Assumed Mercy. *Credit: Lucas County Prosecutor's Office*

Mercy Hospital in downtown Toledo, where Father Robinson was sent in the early 1970s to be a chaplain. *Credit: John Glatt*

Father Robinson took mass daily in Mercy Hospital Chapel.
Credit: Lucas County Prosecutor's Office

A few months before her murder, Sister Margaret Ann looked forward to her well-earned retirement. *Credit: Lucas County Prosecutor's Office*

Det. Art Marx was the lead investigator for the 1980 homicide investigation. He interrogated Father Robinson twice before his superior interceded. *Credit: John Glatt*

Homicide Lieutenant Bill Kina was in charge of the 1980 investigation, but became disillusioned after he saw his prime suspect being let off the hook, taking early retirement. *Credit: John Glatt*

Lieutenant Bill Kina's own diary of events in the April 1980 investigation. *Credit: John Glatt*

Lucas County Prosecutor Julia Bates founded the cold case squad, which reopened the murder case in late 2003, 23 years after the original murder. *Credit: John Glatt*

Assistant Lucas County Prosecutor Dean Mandross led the State's case against Father Robinson. *Credit: John Glatt*

Father Robinson's house on Nebraska Avenue, Toledo, where he was finally arrested on April 23, 2004. Inside, detectives found many occult reference books and numerous photographs of dead bodies in coffins. *Credit: John Glatt*

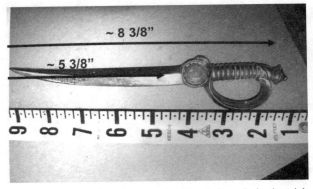

Father Robinson's letter opener played a major role in the trial. *Credit: Lucas County Prosecutor's Office*

that had been stabbed through the cloth and into Sister Margaret Ann's chest formed a perfect cross, except for one badly aimed stab at the bottom.

"Not only did it fit the form of a cross," he later noted, "the symmetry and the precision of it would suggest to me that something was used as a template to put down on the cloth and stab around."

The detective then placed the altar cloth on Sister Margaret Ann's habit, finding that the holes perfectly matched up on the left side, forming an upside-down cross.

ON MONDAY MORNING, MARCH 1, THE COLD CASE TASK force held a special meeting. "He [Detective Cousino] wanted to examine the large altar cloth in front of us," said Sergeant Forrester, "because he said he'd found something of great significance." There was much expectation, with everyone hoping this would be the big breakthrough in the case.

The meeting was held in a large office in the Safety Building. Lucas County Prosecutor Julia Bates attended, along with her two assistant prosecutors, Dean Mandross and J. Christopher Anderson.

Detective Cousino began by laying the folded altar cloth out on the large conference table. He then placed a sheet of paper over it, marking nine little stars directly over the puncture holes. Then he placed a crucifix between the stars, clearly demonstrating an inverted cross.

"It was a passionate day," Prosecutor Bates remembered. "They came here with the stuff and said, 'Wait till you see this. Boy, have we got something to show you.' It was very, very dramatic."

After the demonstration the cold case squad trooped down into the basement to view the altar cloth under different light.

"We had decided to use an alternate light source after he discovered a pattern in that altar cloth," remembered Detective Ross. "He took precise measurements of those puncture holes and concluded in our presence that this was not random jabbing of this altar cloth. That this appeared to be very precise, as though it was around a template."

When Detective Cousino, who had carefully photographed the demonstration, suggested hiring a blood-spatter expert to confirm his findings, Prosecutor Bates immediately agreed.

"We said, 'Go ahead. Go work it,'" she said. "Find an expert. Find someone to tell us what this is. We can see it. I can see it. Find out about this upside-down cross. What does it mean?'"

The following day, Detective Cousino telephoned T. Paulette Sutton, the director of investigations and an associate professor at the University of Tennessee, and one of only five experts in the world certified in bloodstain-pattern transfer analysis. Dr. Sutton agreed to review the altar cloth, letter opener and other evidence, and give her expert opinion.

TWO DAYS LATER, DETECTIVE TOM ROSS AND SERGEANT Steve Forrester paid the first of two visits to the St. Bernardine retirement home in Fremont, Ohio, to interview Sisters Phyllis Ann Gerold and Madelyn Marie Gordon.

The former CEO of Mercy Hospital was now in her eighties, but in good health and as astute as ever. She well remembered the day of Sister Margaret Ann Pahl's murder, telling the detectives how she had called Father Robinson's room when he'd failed to appear after the murder.

They then interviewed Sister Madelyn Marie, now frail but still lucid. The elderly nun became highly emotional, reliving her terrible ordeal after finding Sister Margaret Ann dead in the sacristy.

The following day the cold case investigators interviewed Wardell Langston, who had heard the running footsteps overhead about the time of the murder. They also talked to former Mercy Hospital housekeeper Shirley Lucas, who recounted how Sister Margaret Ann had been so distraught the day before her murder, after Good Friday service had been cut short.

The next witness interviewed was Josh Franks, the now-retired Toledo Police Department criminologist, who described testing the letter opener medallion and getting a presumptive finding for blood.

That afternoon, retired Detective Dave Weinbrecht gave Tom Ross a tour of Mercy Hospital, walking him through the murder scene and the two-room apartment Father Robinson had once occupied. He carefully pointed out where Margaret Warren had heard the "frantic" running footsteps ending up outside Father Robinson's quarters.

"I had not thought about the case since 1980," Weinbrecht said.

Ross asked Weinbrecht his impressions of their primary suspect.

"[He] described Father Robinson as a very meek and mild individual," Ross later wrote in his report. "He hardly spoke unless asked a question while he was in Weinbrecht's presence."

Detective Ross also contacted the diocese's investigators, John Connors and Lawrence Knannlein, requesting they stop their investigation. The cold case detectives were concerned that the diocesan probe might impede theirs, and worse still, tip off Father Robinson that he was under suspicion.

Now 66 and virtually retired, Father Robinson looked the part of an elderly pious man of the cloth, with his craggy features and wispy white hair. Since 1997 he had not been affiliated with any particular Toledo church, but was still revered by the Polish community, and his sermons in Polish still drew crowds.

His parents had died some years earlier and he now lived in their modest home at 2401 Nebraska Avenue, which he and his brother Thomas had inherited. But outside the church, the always-reclusive priest was almost invisible, tottering around in his garden wearing his blue jeans and plaid shirt.

ON FRIDAY, MARCH 5, DETECTIVE TERRY COUSINO RESTAGED Josh Franks' presumptive blood test on Father Robinson's letter opener in his office. Sergeant Forrester and Detective Ross watched as Detective Cousino sprayed some luminol onto the empty spot on the handle, which had once held the medallion. It was the same place where Franks had found a reaction twenty-four years earlier.

"We were in a completely darkened room," explained Detective Cousino. "And when I sprayed the luminol on, there was a very, very tiny reaction. It fluoresced blue. It was no bigger than a pinhead . . . it was maybe thirty seconds."

Forrester and Ross both witnessed the positive reaction for blood, asking Cousino to conduct a second test and take photographs. Cousino told them that although the reaction was probably too small to photograph, he would try anyway.

"I did spray it again," he said, "and I did not get a reaction on the second attempt."

Six days later, Sergeant Forrester and Detective Cousino flew to Memphis, Tennessee, with the letter opener, the stained altar cloth and the Capitol building medallion. They had a 9:00 a.m. meeting the following morning with T. Paulette Sutton, the first expert they would hire.

An unassuming gray-haired woman in her fifties, Sutton is a world-renowned expert in bloodstain pattern analysis. She is also co-author of her esoteric field's definitive book, *Principles of Bloodstain Pattern Analysis: Theory and Practice*, published in May 2005.

At an initial meeting, Sutton laid out the evidence on her examination table for a cursory look. She drew the detectives' attention to several transfer patterns on the altar cloth that she felt could have been made by the letter opener.

"She seemed to be pretty impressed with what we had," remembered Cousino.

Sutton asked if they could leave the evidence with her, so she could do more detailed analysis. It was agreed that Cousino would collect it a few weeks later, when he was scheduled to attend her seminar on bloodstain interpretation in Dearborn, Michigan.

Later that day, after the two detectives left for Toledo, Sutton thoroughly examined the three key items of evidence.

"I tried to follow scientific methodology," she explained. "I was asked a question and I had to devise a method by which I was going to follow to try to reach my conclusions."

In her well-respected bloodstain analysis seminars, Sutton defines a transfer as a bloodstain pattern created when a wet bloody surface comes into contact with a second surface.

"It's sort of like a rubber stamp," she explained. "If I put ink on a rubber stamp and I then impress that on a second surface, what you come away with is what was on the stamp."

She first carefully studied the size, shape and characteristics of each of the stains on the altar cloth. Then, following bloodstain analysis protocol, she tried to eliminate the letter opener as the source of the transfer patterns, as it would be easier to exclude it.

Taking a clean white linen cloth—provided by the detectives—she wrapped the letter opener in saran wrap, before dipping it in stage blood and making a new set of transfers.

"It's good practice to take that object and actually make known transfer stains," she said.

"I tried to eliminate the dagger from being the object that made the stains on the altar cloth," she later wrote in her report. "Instead I found it was consistent with the patterns made."

Sutton examined a total of eighteen bloodstains believed to have been caused by various parts of the letter opener. But there was one particular stain that got her attention. It was a small circle-like mark, and under a magnifying glass she could clearly see a rectangular-shaped outline, which appeared to be a mirror image of the embossed U.S. Capitol building figure in the letter opener's medallion.

"I did a rubbing [of the medallion]," Sutton later testified, "like you probably did as a child."

She laid a piece of paper over the medallion and rubbed a pencil across it, transferring the Capitol building image onto the paper. Then she placed the rubbing directly over the corresponding bloodstain on the altar cloth, and they were a perfect match.

Later when she scanned photographs of the bloodstain and the medallion into her computer, digitally superimposing them on each other, she discovered six specific points that matched perfectly.

In addition to the three pieces of evidence, the detectives also left eighty black-and-white crime-scene photographs. Sutton was specifically asked if a small round bloodstain on Sister Margaret Ann's forehead could have been made by a circular part of the opener between the handle and the blade, which they suspected was some kind of ritual anointing.

"First I physically looked at it," said Sutton, "and said, 'Yes, it's a semicircular-type pattern on her forehead, and that is consistent with being made by one side of a circular object.'"

Sutton's problem was that she had nothing to scale the pattern on Sister Margaret Ann's forehead to the raised surface of the dagger she suspected had caused it. So she took another look and found that if she compared the stain to the width of the cross arm on the dagger, she could determine the stain's diameter.

And it was such a perfect match to the circular part of the dagger, she could even see the embossed stars from the bloody letter opener on the sister's forehead, meaning that her killer had pressed the handle down hard.

The next day Sutton wrote a preliminary report, finding that the transfer stains on the altar cloth were consistent with the letter opener.

"If it wasn't this letter opener," she wrote, "then the stains were made by an instrument of the same shape, same size, and same configuration."

CHAPTER TWENTY-THREE

"An Effrontery to God"

ON TUESDAY, APRIL 20, DETECTIVE TOM ROSS AND SERGEANT Steve Forrester went to Chicago for a meeting with Father Jeffrey Grob, the archdiocese's exorcist and occult expert. Since their telephone conversation two weeks earlier, the detectives had sent him detailed background case material, along with photographs of Sister Margaret Ann Pahl's defiled body in the sacristy.

"We were there to get the results of what he had learned from his studies," explained Forrester. "How he interpreted this information."

The intense bespectacled priest told the detectives that he believed there were strong Satanic elements to the sister's murder.

"Here you have a good woman," he explained. "I'm sure she had her faults—she's human, thank God—but she was violated in the most violent kind of way. It's reprehensible."

He found it deeply significant that the sister had been viciously stabbed through the same cloth that would have graced the altar later at Holy Saturday service.

"It covers the place where the sacrifice is going to take place," he would later testify. "This is now placed over a dying or deceased person, and something is used to stab the person multiple times. In a sense, it's an image of penetration. You're stabbing something through the sacred. Blood is involved. So it is an effrontery to the altar."

The symbolism of the upside-down cross, he told them, dated back to the story of St. Peter, who, feeling unworthy of dying on a cross like Jesus Christ, asked to be executed on an inverted one.

"It's been part of Catholic tradition," he said. "Unfortunately, for many centuries now, that image has been usurped and is used in Satanic worship as an effrontery to the sacred. We look at it as an effrontery to God. You're taking someone that's dedicated to God, and violating every aspect you can."

Grob said only a killer well versed in religious ritualism, like a priest, would have staged the murder on Holy Saturday, while the Holy Eucharist—the flesh and blood of Christ—was temporarily housed in the sacristy.

"One's decorum while in the sacristy is that of genuflection," he explained. "The Blessed Sacrament there is paramount to making that space holy. In a sense, it's been shifted from the chapel proper to the sacristy. One more affront. Some kind of ritual activity has taken place in front of it."

Another revealing aspect to the murder was that the victim was a devout nun.

"She wears a wedding band," he explained. "She believes she's consecrated to God. To God alone."

After viewing the photographs of Sister Margaret Ann Pahl's body, Father Grob observed that the murderer had actually anointed her dead body with her own blood by pressing the bloody murder weapon across her forehead.

But the ultimate act of degradation, he told the detectives, had come at the end when the murderer had hoisted the sister's dress up to her chest, pulling down her panties to reveal her nakedness to the world. Then, as she lay by the Holy Eucharist, her killer had penetrated her with a crucifix.

"These aren't random acts," he explained, "at least in any understanding of ritual. The nature of ritual, be it Catholic ritual or any other religious tradition, is the conglomerate. Putting all those things together. It defines ritual. It's a series of practices that are put together to effect some kind of end."

The detectives then asked how much ritualistic knowledge the murderer would have required to have committed such an act.

"Some specialized knowledge," said Father Grob. "A religious sister would have that knowledge. Certainly a priest . . . possibly a seminarian. All these things have deep symbolic meanings."

Finally the investigators asked the consequences of a Roman Catholic priest ever revealing any details of a confession, as Father Robinson had done in his first police interrogation in 1980.

"The priest is a representative of God," answered Father Grob, "in that context for the forgiveness of sins."

Under Canon Law, he told them, the sacramental seal of confession can never be violated, the automatic penalty being excommunication.

"It's absolute," he declared. "It's not required that a judge impose it. A judge of the Church or due practice. It happens. Once the crime is committed, the excommunication takes place. Period."

BACK IN TOLEDO, SERGEANT FORRESTER AND DETECTIVE Ross were now certain that Father Gerald Robinson had murdered Sister Margaret Ann Pahl. They began to discuss the best ways of bringing him to justice.

"We narrowed our pool of suspects," Sergeant Forrester later testified. "We were now more than definitely focused on Father Robinson."

The cold case detectives reasoned that the killer had had a brief window of opportunity to commit the murder, eliminating a lot of potential suspects. Also, the 1980 investigation had accounted for everyone at the hospital at the time of the murder—with the exception of Father Robinson.

"We were considering all the people in the religious order," explained Forrester. "We wanted to eliminate all of them, because of what Father Grob had told us, and he had his opinion on what had happened. Father Swiatecki was in the cafeteria and [we] were able to account for the times for all the sisters."

The case against Father Robinson was also bolstered by Margaret Warren and Wardell Langston having heard frenzied running footsteps, finishing at Father Robinson's quarters.

"We had this footstep issue," said Forrester. "There were two witnesses [who heard] footsteps, and there were detectives [who] did a footstep experiment. So this was in our mind."

They also ruled out robbery or sexual assault as possible motives.

"It had no characteristics of a robbery," Forrester observed. "And if this was a sexual assault, it certainly wasn't a normal sexual assault. It wasn't a typical rape."

The cold case task force felt certain the killer had known his victim, because of the frenzied intensity of the murder.

"This is overkill, which is typical of someone who knows the victim," said Forrester. "A lot more stabbing than was necessary to kill someone. If someone's coming in to kill someone, they kill them and leave. Kill them or take something, or whatever their objective is."

The cold case squad now decided to place the elderly priest under round-the-clock surveillance before moving in to arrest him.

"We were watching him," Sergeant Forrester later admitted. "We had intended at some point to do a search warrant on his house. But we didn't know what his office situation was or where he actually went during the day, so we were doing a little surveillance on him.

Several times a week, a detective would sneak up to Father Robinson's house in the dead of night, exchanging his garbage bag with one full of rolled-up newspapers. Later, back at the detectives' bureau, an investigator would carefully sift through his garbage, mainly consisting of empty liquor bottles.

The cold case squad's biggest fear was that Father Robinson would find out he was under investigation, and get rid of the crucifix used in the murder.

"We had talked to people at the diocese," said Forrester. "We feared that information may get back to him."

But as the cold case task force methodically plotted its next move, fate intervened to change everything.

CHAPTER TWENTY-FOUR

The Arrest

AT 5:30 A.M. ON FRIDAY, APRIL 23, 2004, SERGEANT STEVE FORRESTER was woken up by a telephone call. A detective who was keeping Father Gerald Robinson's home under surveillance informed Forrester that the media had apparently found out about the investigation. Several reporters were now cruising the priest's modest house.

Forrester immediately alerted Lucas County Prosecutor Julia Bates, who called an emergency meeting of the cold case task force for 8:00 a.m.

The meeting, in her office on the third floor of the Lucas County Courthouse, was chaired by Prosecutor Bates and attended by Sergeant Forrester and Detective Tom Ross, as well as Assistant Prosecutors J. Christopher Anderson and Dean Mandross.

Bates immediately ordered the cold case detectives to apply for a search warrant for Father Robinson's home. At that time they did not intend to make an arrest, but only interview the priest and search his house.

"We had to do the search warrant that day," Forrester said. "If there was evidence at his home [and] he [had] gotten word we were looking at him, possibly he would have gotten rid of evidence. That was our fear."

After the meeting, Sergeant Forrester typed up an official request for a search warrant, taking it to Lucas County Common Pleas Judge Robert Christiansen, who duly signed it.

At about 3:30 that afternoon, Ross and Forrester arrived at Father Robinson's corner house at 2401 Nebraska Avenue.

During the short drive over, they had decided to take a non-confrontational approach with the father. It was agreed that Forrester would first engage him in casual conversation to relax him, before gently broaching the subject of Sister Margaret Ann Pahl's murder. Then Detective Ross—nicknamed "Father Confessor" for his knack in getting confessions—would take over and confront him with the damning new evidence.

Armed with the search warrant, the two detectives walked up his driveway, knocking on his screen door. It was several minutes before the elderly priest appeared, casually dressed in blue jeans and a plaid shirt.

"We introduced ourselves," Sergeant Forrester later testified. "We said we were with the cold case squad and that we had reopened the case of Sister Margaret. We wanted to know if we could come in and clarify some statements with him."

Father Robinson led them into the living room, where a faded painting of Jesus Christ was hanging on a wall. The two detectives gave the father business cards before sitting down, with Forrester facing Father Robinson and Ross to his right.

"We told him what we were there for," said Forrester. "We wanted to talk about the old case and then we asked him a series of questions."

The 66-year-old priest said he remembered Sister Margaret Ann Pahl's death on Holy Saturday in 1980. After some prodding, he outlined his movements around the time of the murder.

"He said he was in his room until after the murder," said Sergeant Forrester, "when he received a call from Sister Phyllis Ann [and] went to the sacristy."

Then, to the investigators' amazement, Father Robinson, who had been evasive up until then, suddenly volunteered how Father Swiatecki had publicly accused him of killing Sister Margaret Ann while administering the last rites in the sacristy.

"He said Father Swiatecki looked at him and said, 'You killed her. Why did you kill her?'" said Sergeant Forrester.

The astonished detectives immediately asked why Father Swiatecki would possibly say that.

"We kept asking him why," remembered Forrester, "but he didn't respond."

Forrester then asked about his first 1980 interrogation with Detective Art Marx and Lieutenant Kina, where he'd made the claim that he had taken a confession from Sister Margaret Ann's killer, and then retracted it.

"He did admit he said that back then," said Forrester, "but he offered no explanation."

He was then asked about his dagger-shaped letter opener, seized in 1980 from his office desk. The priest replied that he had never loaned it out or cut himself with it. When questioned as to whether he had always locked the door to his Mercy Hospital apartment, he said it was secured.

The investigator followed up, asking if he'd had a key to the sacristy at the time of the sister's murder. The priest answered that he had not, as he never went in there.

"That was curious to me," said Forrester, who, as a Catholic and a former altar boy, knew that the father would have to use the sacristy every time he conducted Mass. "I thought I didn't hear him right, so I asked him over and over again, 'Did you have a key to the sacristy?' And he said 'No,' he had no reason to go in the sacristy. I mean, it's called the *priest*'s sacristy, it's like where he came for Mass."

The two detectives knew Father Robinson was lying, as Sister Phyllis Ann Gerold and several other nuns had already told them Father Robinson had a key to the sacristy, where he'd been seen on numerous occasions.

At this point, about forty-five minutes after arriving, Detective Ross announced that he had brought some photographs for the father to look at, suggesting they move into the kitchen and lay them out on the table. Father Robinson and Detective Ross went into the kitchen, while Forrester remained in the living room, where he could hear everything.

ONCE THEY WERE ALONE IN THE KITCHEN, ROSS BECAME more confrontational. The 58-year-old white-haired "Father

Confessor" now presented Robinson with the incriminating new evidence.

He first laid out photographs of the bloodstained altar cloth and the letter opener on the large kitchen table, as the priest looked on uncomfortably.

"I advised Father Robinson," Ross later testified, "that the puncture holes and the shape of that blade were consistent with one another. That those puncture holes were caused by that knife or a knife like it."

Father Robinson did not reply, staring blankly at him without a trace of emotion. Detective Ross then informed him experts had found that the blood transfer patterns on the altar cloth matched his letter opener, even down to a perfect imprint of the Capitol dome medallion.

His voice getting louder with each point, Ross said he knew Art Marx had taken the letter opener from the father's desk in 1980. He said the police had an altar cloth with patterns in Sister Margaret Ann's blood, caused by his letter opener.

"And I asked him to explain to me," said Ross, "those mirror images being placed on that altar cloth. [He did not] have an explanation."

The cold case investigator then laid out several eight-by-ten black-and-white crime-scene photographs, showing gruesome close-ups of Sister Margaret Ann Pahl's body. She looked asleep with her eyes closed, but there was blood on her nose and forehead, and numerous stab wounds littering her face, neck and chest.

Father Robinson peered at the photos, as Ross asked if he knew this woman. And for the first time, the priest's face registered annoyance, as he identified her as Sister Margaret Ann Pahl.

Then Ross asked who could have done this to her, and after a long pause the priest replied that he did not know.

Finally at about 4:45 p.m., after showing the father a succession of murder scene photos, culminating in one particularly horrific one of the nun's exposed body, Detective Ross informed Father Robinson that he was under arrest for the murder of Sister Margaret Ann.

Detective Ross then read him his Miranda rights, showing him the search warrant, and said that the priest would be taken into custody, while Sergeant Forrester remained behind to search his house.

Father Robinson put on a black jacket over his checked shirt, walking slowly toward his front door. Ross thought it unnecessary to handcuff him, escorting him out of his house onto Nebraska Avenue for the three-block walk to the Toledo police district station at Scott Park, to give a formal statement.

Almost exactly twenty-four years after Sister Margaret Ann Pahl's savage murder, Father Gerald Robinson was finally in police custody—the first time that a Roman Catholic priest had ever been charged with killing a nun.

AS SOON AS DETECTIVE ROSS AND FATHER ROBINSON HAD left, Sergeant Forrester began searching the house. He was soon joined by Detective Terry Cousino and another officer. The modest house, which Father Robinson's parents had lived in before their deaths, seemed rooted in the past. The furniture dated back to the 1950s, and everything harked back to a bygone age.

Sergeant Forrester started in the kitchen, going through drawers and cabinets without finding anything. He was especially looking for a crucifix matching the one detectives believed the murderer had used as a template in the stabbing of Sister Margaret Ann.

Proceeding to the living room, he found nothing of interest and went into Father Robinson's bedroom. It was sparsely furnished with a bed, a couple of chairs, a nineteen-inch color television and a radio alarm clock. There were a couple of bookshelves lining a wall, and a few CDs of ethnic Polish folk songs.

In a wardrobe he found the priest's clerical black jackets and cassocks, along with a few layman's street clothes.

Then, on an overhead shelf, he spotted a large brown cardboard box. Hoisting it down and placing it on the bed, Forrester found that it contained hundreds of photographs of corpses in coffins, some dating back more than a hundred years, and others relatively new. All the dead bodies were clothed, and many seemed European.

Sergeant Forrester looked through them, fascinated by the implications. Did they have something to do with Satanic ritual, tying in with other aspects of the case? He asked himself what kind of person would possibly keep so many photos of dead people.

He then turned his attention to Father Robinson's book collection, scouring the shelves for anything of interest. There were books on church history and liturgy, and many in Polish. But one particular pamphlet stood out, entitled "The Occult."

It had been published before the murder in the 1970s by a Catholic group, and looked well-thumbed-through. Many passages had been underlined or highlighted in yellow marker, and he noted the chapter on "The Black Mass," a Satanic parody of the Catholic Mass. Among several items underlined in that chapter was a paragraph describing a black Mass where "an innocent" is used as an altar. It advised that the human sacrifice be tortured, sexually abused or even murdered for Satanic empowerment.

When he had finished the search, without finding a crucifix, Sergeant Forrester locked up Father Robinson's house. He then brought the box of dead people's photographs and the occult book to the Scott Park District Station, where his partner Detective Ross was now in the midst of interrogating Father Gerald Robinson.

CHAPTER TWENTY-FIVE
Tripping Up

AT 5:50 P.M., DETECTIVE TOM ROSS SWITCHED ON A VIDEO camera, mounted on the ceiling of a small 8'×8' white-walled interrogation room. It was focused on Father Gerald Robinson, who sat across a round table from Detective Ross. But the interrogator and his subject would occupy just the bottom left-hand quarter of the low-quality video.

"Father," began Detective Ross in his casual Midwestern drawl, "you've been placed under arrest with the charge of murder. OK?"

The priest just stared blankly at the investigator, who then read him his Miranda rights, informing him that he had the right to have a lawyer present.

"Do you understand?" asked Ross.

"OK," mumbled the priest.

"We went over a lot of things at your house, didn't we?" continued Ross. "A lot of things that we discussed, correct?"

When there was no reply, he asked when Father Robinson's parents had purchased his house on Nebraska Avenue.

"Two or three years before I was ordained," replied the priest in a raspy whisper. "1966–1967."

Slowly the detective steered the subject to Mercy Hospital, asking what Sister Margaret Ann Pahl had done there.

"Well, she helped out with pastoral care, visiting," replied Father Robinson. "And she also was predominately sacristan."

When asked if she had been in charge of the sacristy, Father Robinson shrugged his shoulders.

"I don't know," he said wearily. "The sisters made all the assignments. I had nothing to do with it."

Ross then asked about his duties, as one of the two hospital chaplains.

"I went out there visiting with the people," replied the priest. "Saying Mass. I visited rooms. That was my work."

But when the detective mentioned Father Jerome Swiatecki, the priest suddenly became animated.

"He was an alcoholic," he declared. "He came to [Mercy Hospital] as a last resort because he couldn't be in a parish anymore because of his drinking. He would go to retreats and give talks on alcoholism."

Changing tack, Ross deftly steered the conversation to the time around the murder, asking if the father had been busy with the holy season.

"Well, not so much as usually," replied the priest. "We only had one service."

Ross then asked about Father Robinson's residence at Mercy Hospital.

"There was a door to your residence, correct?"

"Yes," replied the priest, clasping his hands together and beginning to fidget.

"And there was a key utilized?" Ross continued. "I assume you kept that residence locked. Is that true?"

This seemed to take Father Robinson by surprise. He began looking around the interrogation room, as if searching for an answer. For the next eleven seconds he pondered the simple question.

"I don't know," he mumbled eventually. "I didn't keep mine locked."

The seasoned detective's ears perked up at this, as less than an hour earlier, at his home, Father Robinson had said he'd always kept his door locked.

"You did not keep your door locked?" asked Ross, seizing the advantage.

"I don't know," replied Father Robinson shakily.

"Father," declared Ross, looking the priest straight in the

eye, "prior to the conversation we're having now, we had a conversation at your home, correct?"

"Yes," said the priest.

"And when I asked you that question at your home, you said you kept your door locked and you utilized the key to enter and exit, [and kept] that locked to safeguard your residence. Is that not the truth?"

"Yes," replied Robinson unsteadily. "I think I only had it for the cleaning lady."

"I mean, we all try and maintain some sort of privacy, correct? Was not your residence locked?"

"It could be," agreed Father Robinson, "because [Lieutenant Kina and Detective Marx] had to knock when they came in that evening."

Ross then pointed out that the father had lived there more than six years, so he must remember how he'd gained access.

"Probably with the key," he conceded.

"So your residence is locked? It takes a key to enter?"

"Yes," mumbled the priest. "I think the cleaning lady had a key."

Asked who his cleaner was in 1980, Father Robinson replied that she was long dead.

Then Detective Ross placed the father's National Historical Wax Museum letter opener on the desk, asking if it was the same one taken from his residence in 1980. Father Robinson agreed that it was, and the detective asked him where it had been kept.

"No," replied the priest, apparently not hearing the question, "I hadn't used that letter opener since I got it. I just didn't have a reason."

When asked if he'd used it to open mail, the priest cut him off mid-sentence.

"I never used that letter opener!" he snapped.

Then the veteran interrogator asked about his movements on the morning of Holy Saturday 1980, and how he had heard about the murder.

Father Robinson said he had just gotten out of the shower when Sister Phyllis Ann Gerold telephoned, informing him that Sister Margaret Ann had been killed.

"The phone call said, 'We need you immediately,' " he related.

"OK," continued Ross methodically. "You'd gotten out of the shower. Do you remember if you had dressed yet?"

"No," replied the priest. "Because I was just drying off."

"You might even have had a towel around you," reasoned Ross.

"Yes, I did when I went to the phone. And when Sister said what happened then, I just quickly dressed up. Didn't finish anything else and ran. I put the cassock on and ran."

Father Robinson said he had gone straight to the chapel, where he'd seen a policeman. Then he'd gone into the sacristy, where Father Swiatecki had just finished administering the last rites.

Sister Phyllis Ann then told him that the sister had been murdered, but he claimed not to have seen the body, as there were so many people there.

"I stayed with the sisters for quite a while in the chapel," he explained.

"By the way," segued the detective, "do you remember what time you may have gone to bed Good Friday night?"

"No, I don't," he replied testily.

"Father," continued Ross, becoming more conversational, "I'm kind of a creature of habit. I go to bed about the same time every night. And I'm kind of an early bird [as I get] older. So that night you couldn't estimate when you may have gone to bed?"

"I get calls all the time," said the priest, shifting uncomfortably in his chair. "Sometimes I get calls in the middle of the night."

When Detective Ross asked what time he had woken up on Holy Saturday morning, there was a long silence as Father Robinson clasped and unclasped his hands.

"Well," said Ross, "were you up very long before you took a shower?"

"No, I just got out of bed and into the shower."

Detective Ross then asked when he'd first been questioned by detectives.

"Neither of them talked to me that first day," he said, "because they were talking with Father Swiatecki, who had come in and found her there."

But a few days after the murder, he was finally interviewed.

"I got this call and they came to the hospital," he said. "The two of them came and asked me to come to the police station."

He said Lieutenant Bill Kina and Detective Art Marx had questioned him two days in a row, estimating that each session had lasted eight hours.

"Well, the police wanted to interrogate Father Swiatecki," he suddenly informed Ross. "I know they talked to him, because he found a lawyer immediately."

Ignoring that, Detective Ross asked what kind of questions they had asked him during the two interrogations.

"They said they had bits, and the odd facts about something or other," he replied. "They didn't have any facts, which I think was proven later with a lawyer."

Ross then asked if Kina and Marx had mentioned Margaret Warren and Wardell Langston hearing running footsteps going toward his second-floor residence.

"They said I had run out," replied Father Robinson, "and the lawyer then checked it out, and he said [it] could have been anyone."

"Father," said Ross, "it's Holy Saturday morning when Sister was murdered. That was an unusual day at the hospital, was it not?"

"Not really," sighed the priest. "It was just like any other."

The detective then pointed out that most student nurses had left for Easter vacation, leaving him the only resident on the second floor of the hospital.

"Now I'm sure the detectives told you all along," reasoned the detective, "the receptionist and the janitor heard those footsteps?"

"There were no footsteps," said the priest, clasping his hands together. "And [the] lawyer said, 'No.'"

Ross then asked if his 1980 interrogators had told him that Warren and Langston had carefully listened for the sound of someone leaving through the fire exit, but heard nothing.

"No, no," said the priest, "nobody said anything about closing and opening . . ."

Circling his prey, Ross asked if he could think of anyone else, apart from himself, who might have been running along the hallways.

"Well," replied the priest, "people walk up to the bathroom."

"Right, Father," said Ross, his voice rising. "We just said it's Holy Saturday, and quiet. There's no students. They've gone home. The night janitor was working downstairs. I'm telling you right now, he's one of the people down there that heard these footsteps. I'm telling you right here and now the receptionist is the other person who heard these footsteps. She is downstairs. What do you think of that? It wasn't you running?"

"I had a cassock on," he mumbled. "I couldn't be running in that."

Then Ross seized on Father Robinson contradicting himself, just minutes after claiming he had run to the chapel after receiving the telephone call.

"I wasn't running," he conceded, "but I was going very quickly."

"I'm sorry," said Ross with more than a hint of condescension. "I don't mean to put words in your mouth. So you were walking in a rapid fashion?"

"I had a cassock on, so I can't run."

"OK. I understand. That's long. That comes down to your ankles?"

"Yes."

Moving on, he asked if Kina and Marx had explained anything else apart from the footsteps. "Apparently they had some concerns, correct?" declared Ross.

"I guess, from what Father [Swiatecki] was telling them,"

replied Father Robinson, becoming agitated again. "Father Swiatecki was talking to them for quite a while."

"Do you take it that they gleaned a lot of this information from Father Swiatecki?"

"I presume they did," replied the priest, "because they mentioned him."

"Did you like each other?" asked the detective.

"Yes," replied Father Robinson. "He had his own agenda and I had my own agenda. We'd eat in the same dining room."

"Like ships passing in the night," observed Ross.

"That's all it was, yeah."

Ross then asked what Father Swiatecki could have told Kina and Marx to arouse their suspicions.

"That's what I didn't understand," replied the priest, "'cause Father Swiatecki didn't know me much."

"Did [their questions] become accusative toward you?"

"Remarkably forceful," he agreed.

"At any time did any of those detectives say, 'Father, you did it'?" asked the detective.

"They may have."

"How did you respond to that?"

"I was dumbfounded. They said I wasn't acting like a person who would respond that way and holler for a lawyer. I told [them] I answered what they wanted to know, and after eight hours . . . then I went back to the hospital."

Father Robinson said he'd sought the advice of Sister Phyllis Ann Gerold the next day.

"I just told her that the detectives were talking to me about it," he explained. "That I didn't understand what they were getting at."

He said she had expressed "surprise," telling him to co-operate fully with detectives.

Ross then asked about the Toledo police polygraph test that he had failed before his second 1980 interrogation.

"You were on Valium?" asked Ross. "You had administered Valium to yourself. Do you recall when you obtained that Valium and why?"

"I think it was a doctor," replied the priest. "He gave it to me after Sister was murdered. I had it filled in the hospital."

He said a doctor had prescribed him Valium for a headache on the morning of the murder. Although the tranquilizer had relaxed him, he maintained it had not affected his polygraph test results.

Then Detective Ross asked about the second interrogation, cut short by Deputy Chief Ray Vetter and Monsignor Schmit.

"It was the same questions from the night before," said Father Robinson.

"And you were upset?" asked the detective.

"I wasn't upset. I was just a bit tired. Then the lawyer, Henry Herschel, came in."

Suddenly, Ross confronted the priest with his earlier admission, that Father Swiatecki had publicly accused him of killing Sister Margaret Ann.

"At any time," asked Ross, "did Father Swiatecki become forceful with you, and accusatory?"

There was a long silence, as the priest started to fidget again.

"Didn't Father get in your face," asked Ross, his voice rising with each syllable, "and say, 'You know you did that'?"

"It was in the sacristy when I first came in, I think," he replied meekly.

"In front of everybody?"

"The sisters and everybody else who was there."

"He says, 'You did this'?" asked the detective.

"And I just looked at him, because it's the first I'm seeing Sister [Margaret Ann],—and to say something like that . . . I had no idea what he was talking about."

"Holy cow!" declared Ross, throwing his hands back in amazement. "Didn't you say, 'Father, what are you saying?' "

"But I'm not one to answer," replied the priest. "I'm a calm and not a forceful person. That's my choice."

"What!" shouted Ross across the table. "Are you going to stand there and take it?"

"Well," the priest replied, "I took a lot."

Detective Ross then asked why Father Swiatecki thought he had killed Sister Margaret Ann.

"I couldn't answer that," he replied. "I had no idea why."

And he said Father Swiatecki had never again raised the subject during the remaining year they worked together at Mercy Hospital.

TOWARD THE END OF THE INTERROGATION, DETECTIVE Ross confronted Father Robinson with the cold case task force's new evidence. Reaching into his briefcase, he drew out photographs of the bloodstained altar cloth and the father's letter opener, spreading them out on the round table between them.

Again, as he had done in Father Robinson's kitchen, the detective explained how experts had proven that the murderer had repeatedly stabbed Sister Margaret Ann through the altar cloth, using an inverted crucifix as a template.

"You can see the holes for yourself here," he declared. "Can you see?"

Father Robinson clasped his hands and remained silent.

"We were told by several experts," continued Ross, "that it's very consistent with the blade of that instrument that was taken from your room. This ornamental piece under your desk in your office—you signed a waiver of search, and those officers took that. What else did they take?"

"A cassock," answered the priest.

"What you call a ceremonial cassock that you wear during Mass?"

"I wore it all the time."

He said detectives had tested a stain on the sleeve, which later turned out to be gravy.

"Now did they ever show you the altar cloth back then?" asked Detective Ross, pointing to the photographs on the table.

"No."

"So they weren't privy to this information about the holes and these transfer stains from this ornamental knife onto that altar cloth?" said Ross. "In other words, what these experts are telling us is that this knife caused those punctures. This knife caused not only this stain, but numerous other stains—bloodstains—on that altar cloth found next to Sister's body. How do we explain that, Father?"

"I don't know," he mumbled.

Now with his prey firmly in his sights, Detective Tom Ross leaned over toward the priest, recapping his version of what had happened Holy Saturday morning.

"OK. You're in there taking a shower when Sister calls and says, 'My Lord, we've found Sister Margaret. She's been killed down there in the chapel.' You dry off. You get dressed. You put on your cassock and you run down— I'm sorry, you *walk quickly* down to the chapel.

"Father, you're in the sacristy," continued Ross, jabbing his finger at the petrified priest. "Next to Sister is this altar cloth with these puncture wounds through it. With the blood transfer from this knife to that altar cloth.

"You had to have had that knife down there, and you had to have killed Sister with this knife."

At this point Father Robinson broke into a nervous smile.

"Father," shouted Detective Ross, angrily rising to his feet, "why do you smirk at me! I mean, this is serious."

"I'm not smirking at you," replied Father Robinson. "Because I don't know how you know all this stuff. The fact is [the letter opener] was not there. I was not there."

"Father," continued Ross in a calmer voice, "how do we explain this knife causing those puncture wounds and leaving those transfer marks on the altar cloth? She's stabbed through that altar cloth with a perfect crucifix [cross] on the chest, upside-down—the long part of it under her chin and the short part of the cross towards the middle of her abdomen. What's that all about?"

"That, I don't know," said the priest, regaining composure. "I really don't. I never heard that they thought of it as Satanic."

"Whatever it is," Ross told him, "Satanic, ceremonial or whatever, what *was* going on?"

"There was nothing going on."

"Well, something went on. Somebody decided to take this woman's life. And it comes back to the knife in your room, on your desk, Father. What's going on? And here's Father Swiatecki, turns around in the sacristy and points, 'Why did you do this?' Swiatecki knew something."

"Well, if he did," mumbled Father Robinson, "I didn't know it."

"You had to be blown away by that. Didn't you think later, 'What the heck is that all about?' "

"No, I didn't."

"As we sit here in 2004, Father, what do you think that was all about?"

"I wish he would have talked to me about it."

Then Ross asked if Father Swiatecki had a key to his room, and had ever unlocked his door to gain access.

"I don't know," shrugged the priest.

"This is your knife!" declared Ross, jabbing his finger at the photograph of the letter opener. "Your ceremonial souvenir. It is exclusively yours. You have exclusive control over this souvenir. How does it end up leaving its shadow in blood? Leaving the outline of this blade through this altar cloth, and you can't be involved?"

There was a long silence, as Father Robinson searched for an answer.

"I was not involved," he finally said. "I wasn't. I don't know. I wasn't involved."

Then the detective asked about his relationship with Sister Margaret Ann, and if they had ever had a disagreement.

"Sister was quiet," he told Ross, adding that they never argued. "She just did her job. Nothing extraordinary. The sisters and me had a good relationship. We even went out for picnics."

"Sister had thirty-one stab wounds," declared Ross. "That is an act of rage. That's somebody that's angry. Did she ever make you angry, Father?"

"No, she did not," he said wearily.

Detective Ross again asked if he had a key to the sacristy,

which was always kept locked. And once again the priest maintained he had never had one, borrowing a key from one of the sisters whenever he needed access.

"They had keys to everything," he snorted. "The sister would unlock [doors] and took care of the hospital. I just worked there."

Finally the detective asked who he thought the murderer was.

"Did you ever suspect anyone?" said Ross.

"I really didn't. And the sisters didn't either."

Then, eighty-two minutes after the interrogation had started, Detective Ross asked if there was anything else he wanted to add, and Father Robinson said no.

"Father," he said in a friendlier tone of voice, "would you care for anything to drink? We have water, we have pop, we have bottled water. Would you like me to make coffee? Anything to eat?"

"No," said Father Robinson forlornly. "I just want to make a couple of calls."

Detective Ross walked out of the interrogation room, announcing he'd be back shortly.

LEFT ALONE, FATHER ROBINSON, UNAWARE HE WAS STILL being videotaped, dropped his face into his hands and bent down over the table.

Looking close to tears, he began to mumble incomprehensibly and grunt to himself in despair.

"Oh, my Jesus," he suddenly whispered. "Sister, won't you come through for me? Please. Won't you?"

CHAPTER TWENTY-SIX

"I'll Be Damned"

AT 10:15 P.M., FATHER GERALD ROBINSON WAS FORMALLY
charged with the murder of Sister Margaret Ann Pahl—
twenty-four years and eighteen days after the killing. Detective Tom Ross then handcuffed the bewildered 64-year-old
priest, driving him to Lucas County jail, where he would remain until his Monday morning arraignment at Toledo
Municipal Court.

The arrest warrant, signed by Sergeant Steve Forrester,
read:

> The defendant, Gerald J. Robinson, caused the death of the
> victim, Sister Margaret Ann Pahl, with the cause of death
> being strangulation. Sister Margaret Ann Pahl was found to
> have numerous post-mortem cuts on her body and an instrument, with unique characteristics associated with Sister
> Margaret Ann Pahl's post-mortem cuts, was found to be in
> Gerald Robinson's possession.

On arrival at Toledo downtown jail, Father Robinson was
given a regulation brown prison jumpsuit to wear, before being fingerprinted and photographed. He then handed over
his rosary beads, a set of keys and $4.80 in cash.

An hour later, Toledo Police Chief Mike Navarre held a
press conference, announcing Father Robinson's arrest for
the murder, crediting "new technology" for the breakthrough
in the case.

"We received full cooperation from the Toledo Catholic

Diocese through this investigation," he told reporters, refusing to provide any further details.

The Reverend Michael Billian, Episcopal vicar of the Diocese of Toledo, told the Toledo *Blade* that Bishop Leonard Blair was praying for Father Robinson.

"It certainly saddens the diocese that any of its ministers would be in this situation," he said. "Whenever this kind of event happens, it's a blow to the Church."

When a reporter reached Ray Vetter, the retired Deputy Chief appeared genuinely surprised at the news, declaring, "I'll be damned."

As a Catholic, he said he had "mixed feelings" about a priest's arrest for murder, but would be "happy" if he turned out to be guilty.

"If he's the right man," said Vetter, now 82, "I hope they get a conviction. I hope they have more evidence than we had."

THE ARREST MADE THE ELEVEN O'CLOCK NEWS ON ALL four local network affiliates. Perhaps the most baffling murder in city history, the killing had haunted Toledo for more than a quarter of a century.

Among the thousands of viewers who watched the TV coverage was Jean Marlow, now 41. She instantly recognized the pictures of the white-haired Father Robinson, in clerical garb, as one of the members of the "Sisters of Assumed Mary" group that had allegedly tortured and raped her as a young girl.

"[I] recognized and identified Robinson as one of the abusers," she would later claim in a civil action, "and further recognized him as 'Mary-Jerry' from the basement and the woods."

ON SATURDAY MORNING THE TOLEDO *BLADE* DEVOTED ITS whole front page to Father Gerald Robinson's arrest, with a huge headline, "Priest accused of murdering nun in 1980." The story—accompanied by head shots of the accused killer and his victim—comprehensively recapped the 1980 homicide, describing Sister Margaret Ann Pahl's murder as "part of a ritual slaying," where her body had been "posed" after death.

When the Polish community learned that one of its most respected priests was accused of murder, there was outrage and disbelief. Jack Sparagowski, president of St. Anthony's Church pastoral council, and a close friend of Father Robinson's for more than twenty years, was on his computer when a committee member called him with the news.

"I was absolutely stunned," he said. "In all the years that I've known him, I've never even heard him raise his voice."

And Father Paul Kwiatkowski, who had lived with Father Robinson at St. Hedwig for four years in the 1990s, refused to believe he was a murderer.

"The Polish community was outraged at the accusations," said Father Kwiatkowski. "No one believed he could do it. He's a very shy and quiet person. I mean, there's no way he could have done that murder. He literally wouldn't hurt a fly."

When Sister Margaret Ann Pahl's family learned of his arrest, it reopened all the old wounds, as reporters and television news crews descended on Edgerton, seeking interviews.

"We had people knocking on our doors, and telephone calls," said Mary Casebere, now 88, "wanting to come for stories."

Sister Margaret Ann's only other surviving sister, Catherine Flegal, who had just turned 90, had mixed feelings about the arrest.

"It doesn't bring my sister back," she said. "It's been so many years ago."

Lee Pahl, Sister Margaret Ann's nephew, soon became Pahl family spokesman, saying that he'd had no idea the case had been reopened.

"It was just pretty shocking that this ever came up again," he said. "It was hard to open the old wounds again, going back to when it first happened. You didn't really know how to feel, because obviously we didn't know for sure at that point whether he was guilty or not."

One person not surprised by the arrest was Dave Davison, the first law enforcement officer at the murder scene. Over the years, Davison had tirelessly campaigned to reopen the case, writing letters to the FBI, the Pope, the Justice Department and even TV's *Unsolved Mysteries*.

Under the Freedom of Information Act, he had managed to obtain more than 200 pages of police reports covering the original investigation. Now he felt vindicated by the arrest.

"There were people [who] thought I was a nut," said Davison. "I was laughing when I heard. There's no cold case about this. No one ever believed me all these years. When I heard, I called my brother in Baltimore and said, 'Turn on CNN and you'll see I was telling the truth. The priest did do it.'"

But when Sister Annie Louise—whose original accusations against Father Robinson had led to the case being reopened—heard the news, she was traumatized.

"She went into hiding," explained Claudia Vercellotti of SNAP. "It was horrible, and there were a lot of emotions. She was afraid, concerned and overwhelmed. So when he was arrested, she went away for a little while. I mean, we were all scared. It was a very, very scary time."

THAT AFTERNOON, DETECTIVE TOM ROSS AND SERGEANT Steve Forrester held a press conference at the detectives' bureau. They cryptically told reporters that Sister Margaret Ann Pahl had been murdered as part of a "ceremony," refusing to elaborate. They said the homicide investigation had been reopened five months earlier, after the old evidence had been brought out of storage for another look.

"We noticed something that was startling," explained Sergeant Forrester, adding that blood transfer patterns had conclusively placed the murder weapon at the scene of the homicide.

The investigators told reporters how Sister Annie Louise, who they did not identify, had prepared a detailed exposé, outlining years of sexual abuse by several priests, including Father Robinson.

Later that afternoon, Toledo defense attorney John Thebes, after being contacted by Father Robinson's brother Thomas the previous night, agreed to represent the priest. A devout Catholic, Thebes had first met his new client as a young boy thirty years earlier, when Robinson was associate pastor of Christ the King Parish.

After a brief jailhouse meeting with his new client, Thebes told reporters that Father Robinson had barely slept since his arrest, but was holding up well under the circumstances.

"Like anybody who's in that spot," explained the attorney, "he's in a certain amount of shock."

He told reporters he had handled two other cold cases in his career, both ending in acquittal.

"There's a reason these cases are cold and sit for twenty-four years," he said. "Because the evidence is not good to begin with."

A few hours later, Lucas County Assistant Prosecutor Gary Cook, who had been assigned the case, countered Thebes' comments.

"New sets of eyes saw something that hadn't been seen before," he explained. "That's what these detectives do. That's why we have cold case units."

ON SUNDAY, APRIL 25, SISTER PHYLLIS ANN GEROLD TOOK part in an annual celebration at the Pines. But Sister Margaret Ann Pahl, buried in the scenic grounds of the convent, was on everyone's mind. The former CEO of Mercy Hospital at the time of the murder, Sister Phyllis Ann described Father Robinson's arrest as "so painful" and a huge shock.

"Going through this once was devastating," she told a reporter. "In a sense, we're reliving it again."

At that morning's service the nuns and priests had said special prayers for Father Robinson.

Now, Sister Phyllis Ann drew a parallel between the murder and the newly released blockbuster movie *The Passion of the Christ*.

"Isn't it something that Mel Gibson's movie is so big

right now when this [crime] comes back to us?" she asked. "The movie reminds us that we are all sinners and need God's mercy. It's almost a clarion call to recognize God's love.

"The terrible hate inflicted upon Sister Margaret Ann is beyond comprehension. Yet we pray for the truth, for the priests, for all of us."

CHAPTER TWENTY-SEVEN

A Leave of Absence

FATHER GERALD ROBINSON'S ARREST THREATENED TO plunge the Toledo diocese and the police department into deep scandal, as retired Toledo police officer Dave Davison went public with allegations of a well-orchestrated cover-up twenty-four years earlier. In a front-page article in the Toledo *Blade*, the former cop revealed that the priest had always been the prime suspect, demanding to know why it had taken so long to arrest him.

"My department and the diocese colluded to cover this up," declared Davison. "When I was talking to people at the hospital after the murder to get statements, they all said Robinson did it."

Deputy Chief Ray Vetter angrily hit back, denying any cover-up.

"We just wouldn't do it," he told *The Blade*. "I can't believe anyone with any sense, who knows us as investigators and us as people, [would say] that we could cover this up."

After Sunday Mass, the Bishop of Toledo, Leonard Blair, 54, just four months after becoming spiritual leader of the diocese's 314,000-strong Catholic community, held a press conference, distancing it from Father Robinson.

"Now that Father Robinson has been arrested," he declared, "I'm as shocked and troubled as anyone. I'm shocked that anyone would commit such a crime. If it's one of your own, that's troubling."

The bishop's apparent lack of support for Father Robinson was met with anger by the Polish community, who still held him in high regard. But it was not totally unexpected. The Father Robinson affair was the latest in a long line of scandals, resulting in a dozen lawsuits against the diocese.

In the 1990s, as several child sexual abuse incidents involving priests made headlines all over America, Bishop James Hoffman smugly denied that Toledo had a problem. But all that changed in June 2002, when former Toledo priest Father Leo Welch admitted sexually abusing small boys in the 1950s, when he was at the Immaculate Conception church in Bellevue, Ohio.

The fallen priest revealed how, in 1961, after he had been caught, his Church superiors sent him home to his parents, without calling the police. Three months later, Father Welch had been transferred to the Christ the King Parish in Toledo—where Father Robinson would later serve three years as associate pastor—his new congregation being told nothing of his history of abuse.

Years later, two of his victims filed a lawsuit against the diocese, drawing national attention. They revealed that between 1956 and 1961, dozens of altar boys had been brought to the priest's cottage outside Toledo, and sexually abused in his bedroom.

The resulting publicity prompted many other Toledo victims of clerical abuse to come forward and tell their stories, to the embarrassment of the diocese.

"It was like the floodgates opened," explained Claudia Vercellotti of SNAP. "People felt they could now talk without being afraid."

A victim of clerical sexual abuse herself as a young girl, in 1996, at the age of 26, Vercellotti had taken her case to Bishop Hoffman.

"I sat down and told him everything that had happened to me," she remembered. "He told me to pray for the man who had done these sex crimes to me. Then he got very angry with me and we did not part on good terms."

Perhaps the most high-profile Toledo diocese scandal prior to Father Robinson's arrest concerned the Reverend Dennis Gray, whose story would later be told in the acclaimed 2005

Oscar-nominated HBO documentary *Twist of Faith*. The popular Toledo priest, known for helping troubled youths, was accused of enticing young boys to his summer cottage and raping them.

Even after other priests warned a Toledo police officer about Father Gray, no action was taken. Gray, who finally left the priesthood to become a probation officer, has never admitted any wrongdoing. But according to a local newspaper report, a later investigation by the Toledo diocese found the claims against him "credible" and "substantiated."

Now in 2004, with the national spotlight focused on the widespread clergy abuse of children, a priest accused of murdering a nun was a potential nuclear bomb for the diocese.

BY MONDAY MORNING, NEWS REPORTS OF FATHER GERALD Robinson's arrest were making headlines around the world. *The New York Times* featured the story prominently, as did England's *Daily Telegraph* and France's *Le Monde*. It also made all three network morning shows, with Toledo Police Chief Mike Navarre and Dave Davison giving exclusive interviews to NBC's *Today* show and CBS's *Early Show* respectively.

A little after 9:00 a.m., a haggard-looking Father Robinson, cuffed and dressed in a brown regulation jail jumpsuit, was brought through an underground tunnel from his jail cell into Toledo Municipal Court. He was greeted by a barrage of reporters shouting questions on his arrival, but refused to say anything.

Inside the packed courtroom more than twenty of his supporters sat in the public gallery. It was an emotionally charged moment as he took his place at the defense table, next to his new attorney, John Thebes.

In a brief three-minute hearing, where no plea was entered, Judge Mary Trimboli set bail for $200,000, despite Thebes' plea for a far lower figure. The defense attorney asked the judge to take into consideration Robinson's clean record and his position as a priest.

A preliminary hearing was scheduled the following

Monday, with a Lucas County Grand Jury convening later that week to hear evidence, before considering an indictment.

The 66-year-old priest was returned to his jail cell without uttering a single word.

Outside Municipal Court, Claudia Vercellotti and other leaders of SNAP, including founder Barbara Blaine, staged an impromptu protest. They demanded to know why the diocese had not placed Father Robinson on leave ten months earlier, after Sister Annie Louise's accusations.

"Father Robinson has been on the radar for over a year," Vercellotti told reporters. "Given the seriousness of the allegations, why was he still saying Mass as late as last week?"

A few hours later, diocese spokeswoman Sally Oberski maintained that there were no credible allegations against Father Robinson prior to his arrest.

"[He is] a pretty low-key guy and is very revered," Oberski told *New York Times* reporter Stephen Kinzer, adding that the diocese would not be paying his legal fees, as it was "something that happened outside the Church."

She then referred all further questions as to why Father Robinson had not been placed on earlier leave to Reverend Michael Billian, who did not return reporters' calls.

After the arraignment, John Thebes said his client was now over the initial shock of being arrested for murder.

"He thought the whole thing was behind him in 1980," said the defender, "when he cooperated fully."

Thebes predicted prosecutors would have an uphill battle presenting a credible case so long after the murder.

"Witnesses die," he explained. "Memories become faded over time. Twenty-four years is a heck of a long time. It's difficult to ascertain who was where, who said what. There are many, many issues that have to be delved into."

LATER THAT DAY, JACK SPARAGOWSKI AND A GROUP OF Father Robinson's supporters from St. Anthony's church announced a defense fund to raise bond money at a local bank. For the priest to make the $200,000 bail, they would need to post $400,000. Father Paul Kwiatkowski and his mother took up a small collection from the congregation at St. Hedwig, as did many other local Polish churches.

"I later sent the money to him," said Father Kwiatkowski, "and received a very nice handwritten thank-you note."

The Nebraska Avenue home that he co-owned with his brother Thomas was put up toward the bond. His brother also agreed to put his own home up, as did three of the priest's closest friends—Dorothy Sieja and Gary and Kathleen Glowski.

ON TUESDAY AFTERNOON, BISHOP LEONARD BLAIR VISITED Father Robinson in jail, placing him on a leave of absence. It would later be claimed that the decision to suspend Father Robinson was the direct result of a secret canonical penal process at the bishop's direction.

In a dramatic five-minute face-to-face meeting at Lucas County jail, Bishop Blair told Father Robinson that from now on, he could only celebrate Mass alone.

Straight after the meeting, the Catholic Diocese of Toledo issued a terse press release on its website, headlined "Bishop Leonard Blair Places Father Gerald Robinson on Leave of Absence."

> April 27—Toledo, Ohio
>
> Bishop Leonard Blair made a pastoral visit to Father Gerald Robinson this afternoon in the Lucas County jail. Bishop Blair and Father Robinson discussed Father's canonical status given the allegations against him in the 1980 murder of Sister Margaret Ann Pahl. Bishop Blair has placed Father Robinson on leave of absence with the following restrictions: namely, that he is excluded from public ministry; may only celebrate Mass alone with no one present; may not celebrate the other sacraments.
>
> Father Robinson has accepted these restrictions effective today."

Later, Jack Sparagowski said Father Robinson had been disappointed at the lack of support from Bishop Blair and the diocese.

"The Bishop went to jail," said Sparagowski, "and spent about five minutes, if that, with him. And in effect told him, 'You're suspended. You're no longer to perform public Mass.' And that was it. [Bishop Blair] never had any other contact with him."

A few hours before their meeting, Bishop Blair had issued a statement, outlining the Toledo diocese's version of the events, leading up to Father Robinson's arrest and why it had not placed him on leave earlier. In it, he pledged to "revisit" Sister Annie Louise's original allegations against Father Robinson.

April 27—Toledo, Ohio

In the spring of 2003, the Oblates of St. Francis in Toledo asked that the Diocese of Toledo's Review Board review an accusation regarding clerical sexual abuse allegations involving Oblate priests. The Oblates made this request of the diocese because they did not have a review board of their own.

The diocese's Review Board met on June 11, 2003, where members were addressed by Sister Annie Louise and given her written statement. It contained shocking allegations of satanic cult activity and sexual abuse, naming Father Gerald Robinson among others.

The Board decided her allegations should be thoroughly investigated, appointing two professional investigators to "this difficult and complex case." Now, after receiving the investigator's results, the Review Board will "revisit" Sister's allegations.

"In the course of our investigator's work," continued the statement, "the Lucas County Prosecutors' office specifically asked them not to contact Father Robinson, because the Prosecutors' office had opened its own investigation with regard to the murder of Sister Margaret Ann Pahl. The Diocese was also advised in confidence that the Prosecutors' Office had reopened its murder investigation. It should be noted that this murder was not mentioned in what had been presented to the Review Board by the alleged sexual abuse victim.

The steps that have been outlined above are entirely consistent with the sexual abuse policy of the Diocese of Toledo. Once an allegation against a cleric is deemed credible by the Bishop upon the recommendation of the Review Board, then the appropriate measures are taken in accordance with the policy. Because of the wide-ranging nature and scope of the allegations against many individuals in this case, and the need for a thorough investigation, a determination of credibility has yet to be made regarding an accusation of sexual abuse by Father Robinson."

IN A HARD-HITTING EDITORIAL A COUPLE OF DAYS LATER, THE Toledo *Blade* castigated the Diocese of Toledo for its handling of Father Robinson's arrest, following in the wake of the Church's problem with pedophile priests:

> The diocese invites more public bruising, more disdain from communicants, and worsening assessments of its credibility by keeping bad behaviors secret until it becomes public in a shocking manner. The arrest of Father Robinson by Toledo police makes that point.
>
> Forthrightness and good citizenship are necessary if the diocese doesn't want to keep conveying the impressions of subterfuge, cover-up, and irresponsibility that have plagued Roman Catholicism here and in Western Europe for nearly two decades of sex scandals.

THE MORNING AFTER HIS JAILHOUSE MEETING WITH FATHER Robinson, Bishop Leonard Blair flew to the Vatican for an audience with Pope John Paul II. Some would later speculate as to whether the Father Robinson affair was on their agenda, and whether the Pope had issued any instructions on how to handle it.

ON WEDNESDAY, LUCAS COUNTY PROSECUTOR JULIA BATES placed a gag order on the Father Robinson case, saying that her office would no longer comment on it. She then issued a statement, warning that a national media "frenzy" could poison a future jury pool, jeopardizing the defendant's right to a fair trial.

"It's unfair to him," she explained, "and it's unfair to us."

That morning, Bill Kina drove to Art Marx's house to discuss the original investigation, attempting to come up with something new to bolster the prosecution's case. The two elderly detectives had not seen each other for years. Marx told his old friend how he had gone through a seven-year divorce case and now had a new family. Marx complained that the new career he had started as a polygraph operator after retiring did not pay enough, saying he planned to write a book about the case when it was all over.

"We talked about the case," remembered Kina. "But again, he didn't remember anything about it or the missing reports."

Later that day, veteran Toledo defense attorney Alan Konop joined John Thebes on Father Robinson's defense team. The 69-year-old graduate of the University of Toledo's College of Law had been a defender for forty-three years, and was considered one of the best in the city.

The thin, balding attorney with a snow-white beard had handled several major local cases over his career, including winning an acquittal for Kim Anderson, who had been accused of shooting her husband to death in self-defense in Wyandot County. He also defended Kelly Jagodzinski, a 22-year-old mother accused of leaving her dead baby in a wooden box behind a Sylvania, Ohio, ice-skating rink in 2000. She could have been sentenced to 10 years in a state prison, but only received 6 months' jail time and 5 years' community service.

The defense attorney was known for his deceptively folksy manner, always wearing a pair of reading glasses perched on the end of his nose.

Within a few days they were joined by 84-year-old defense attorney John Callahan and 28-year-old Nicole Khoury, who completed Father Robinson's defense team. They had all agreed to take the case pro bono, as everything Father

Robinson and his family owned would be needed to provide collateral to free him on bond.

On Friday, April 30, a Lucas County Grand Jury was convened to hear the prosecution's case for indicting Father Robinson. Behind closed doors, assistant Lucas County Prosecutors J. Christopher Anderson and Tim Braun presented the evidence against Father Robinson.

The secret panel had been asked to consider whether to indict the priest on murder or aggravated murder, as he could only be indicted on one of the counts. An aggravated murder charge allows parole after 20 years served, whereas a murder charge allows it after only 15. Father Robinson would not face the death penalty, as capital punishment had not been in force in 1980 when the murder was committed.

After the two prosecutors presented evidence, a vote was taken, but the grand jury's decision would remain a closely guarded secret over the weekend.

CHAPTER TWENTY-EIGHT

A Celebratory Party

ON MONDAY, MAY 3, 2004, FATHER GERALD ROBINSON WAS indicted by the grand jury for the aggravated murder of Sister Margaret Ann Pahl, the first time in U.S. history that a Roman Catholic priest had ever been charged with murdering a nun.

The indictment, signed by Lucas County Prosecutor Julia Bates, read:

> The Jurors of the Grand Jury of the State of Ohio, within or for Lucas County, on their oaths, in the name and by the authority of the State of Ohio, do find and present that GERALD ROBINSON, on or about the 5th day of April, 1980, in Lucas County, Ohio, did purposely, and with prior calculation and design, cause the death of another, in violation of #2903.01 (A) of the Ohio Revised Code, Aggravated Murder, contrary to the form of the statute in such case made and provided, and against the peace and dignity of the State of Ohio.

Prosecutor Bates would later say she had no hesitation indicting a priest for murder.

"I saw him as a man who killed a woman," she explained. "And so he happened to be a man wearing a collar, and she was a woman wearing a habit. It was a crime. We didn't look too much beyond that to say, 'Gee whiz, we better not do this, because after all, he's a priest.'"

She said the real issue was whether a Toledo jury would

ever convict a man of the cloth, something inconceivable twenty years earlier.

"That was tricky," she admitted. "Will people be willing to convict a priest in the face of what we think is significant evidence?"

A few hours later, Father Robinson was in Lucas County Common Pleas Court for a bond hearing. The $400,000 property bond, required to meet the $200,000 cash one set by Judge Mary Trimboli, would comprise 2401 Nebraska Avenue, as well as his brother Thomas' house in Maumee, Ohio. The priest's close friends Gary and Kathleen Glowski of Sylvania, Ohio, and Dorothy Sieja of south Toledo, had all put up their homes, making up the shortfall to help him post bond.

Although the bail bond had no conditions, if he failed to attend court dates, prosecutors could start foreclosure proceedings to evict the homeowners.

At the end of the hearing, Judge Ruth Ann Franks, who had randomly drawn the Father Robinson case, recused herself. She cited a potential conflict of interest, having been an assistant prosecutor in 1980 at the time of the murder. The case was then reassigned to Judge Patrick Foley.

One hour after the hearing, Father Robinson was released from the Toledo jail, wearing a black suit and clerical collar. The frail-looking priest, who had spent 10 days behind bars, left through a back door, carrying a bag and an envelope. He was greeted by friends, family members and about a dozen supporters who had been waiting for him.

Reporters and TV news crews were also there in force, screaming questions at him. But Father Robinson smiled and said nothing, as he locked arms with his attorney, John Callahan, and sister-in-law Barbara Robinson, who escorted him to a waiting SUV.

Then, despite his attorney's pleas not to follow the priest, several TV crews jumped in their cars, tailing him back to his brother Thomas' house in Maumee.

Later John Thebes castigated the media, saying that members of the Robinson family were "angry" that their privacy had not been respected.

That evening, seventy Father Robinson supporters held a party to celebrate his release at the Scott Park Banquet Room on Nebraska Avenue, just a short walk from his home. They welcomed Father Robinson like a conquering hero, patting him on the back and proclaiming his innocence, as they sipped drinks and ate finger foods. Then there was a collection to raise funds for the beleaguered priest's defense.

Father Robinson seemed overwhelmed by this show of support, politely thanking everyone for coming.

Then, as the party was winding down, a middle-aged woman burst into the banquet hall, carrying a doll dressed like a nun, screaming "Sinners!" at the top of her voice.

"I'm here for Sister Margaret!" yelled the blonde-haired woman, later identified as Pauline Garcia Cleveland of south Toledo. "She is the one who suffered! Justice for Sister Margaret!"

On her way out of the hall, Cleveland hit Father Robinson supporter Rick Napierala with her nun doll. When he grabbed the doll, she attacked him, grabbing his jacket and ripping his shirt, before scratching his face and knocking off his spectacles. When he ran back into the hall, she followed, throwing a pitcher of water at his head, before seizing the doll and leaving.

"We came here and had a very peaceful press conference," Napierala told reporters, saying he would file a police complaint. "And I think she got mad because we ignored her."

Later Cleveland told reporters she was prepared go to jail to honor Sister Margaret Ann Pahl.

ON FRIDAY MORNING, MAY 7, FATHER GERALD ROBINSON was back in Lucas County Common Pleas Court, where he pleaded not guilty to the aggravated murder of Sister Margaret Ann Pahl. The media was there in force, as the priest, wearing his clerical collar, entered with his defense team through a private area to the side of the courtroom. Several of his supporters sat in the public gallery, including his brother Thomas and sister-in-law Barbara.

For the entire five-minute hearing in front of Judge

Patrick Foley, the ashen-looking priest stood, resting his hand on a chair for support. He spoke just once, when he officially waived his right to appear at a May 24 pre-trial hearing.

After the brief hearing, no one was allowed to leave the courtroom, as sheriff's deputies escorted Father Robinson out through a jury area, to avoid reporters and TV news crews.

Outside the courtroom, defense attorney Alan Konop told reporters he would not be making any comments until the trial.

"Through the course of this proceeding," he declared, peering at the cameras through his reading glasses, "there will be no statements coming from the defense counsel on any personal information concerning Father Robinson."

The veteran defender said the evidence in the case would only emerge in court proceedings, ensuring his client received a fair trial.

"We have got a long road to go down," he said. "It will come out step by step."

Since his release from jail, Father Robinson had moved into Thomas and Barbara Robinson's home on Cranbrook Drive, in Maumee. He kept a low profile, seldom leaving the house, except to attend Mass and other Church functions.

"He wasn't active in the Church," said Jack Sparagowski. "Even when he attended some Masses he would sit in the back of the church. I saw him at maybe four or five Masses over that period, as well as two funerals, where he said the eulogy."

Over the next few months, Father Robinson would occasionally be spotted in local restaurants, having dinner with his family and supporters. The fact that he always wore his clerical garb and collar in public drew much criticism.

"What does it say when Bishop Blair puts Robinson out of ministry but lets him wear clerics?" SNAP's Claudia Vercellotti told the *Toledo City Paper*. "Not only is Robinson accused of sexually abusing a minor, he's been indicted for the ritual murder of an old nun, as a direct result of the sexual allegations. Aside from helping Robinson's PR campaign, why would Bishop Blair sanction him to dress as a priest?"

With the extraordinary publicity generated by the case, Father Robinson became a constant target for local reporters and photographers, who would stalk him for photographs. Producers from network primetime news shows, including CBS-TV's *48 Hours* and *Dateline NBC*, had expressed interest in covering his case.

Former Toledo cop Dave Davison said he'd received numerous calls from the media in the days after Father Robinson's arrest. He was even contacted by a California producer, offering him $100,000 for the movie rights to his story. He initially signed the contract, but then had second thoughts, canceling the agreement.

"I tell them, 'This is blood money,' " he explained. "If I want that kind of money, I'll go to the blood bank [and] get twenty-five bucks. I do not want to make money in this fashion."

CHAPTER TWENTY-NINE

The Exhumation

ON WEDNESDAY, MAY 19, 2004, LUCAS COUNTY PROSECUTOR Julia Bates issued an order of disinterment, to exhume the body of Sister Margaret Ann Pahl. With her family's consent, prosecutors wanted a coroner to perform a second autopsy, in order to obtain DNA samples and other standards from the victim's body.

"We wanted to see if any of the puncture wounds to her flesh would uncover any markings to her skeletal remains," explained Assistant Prosecutor Dean Mandross. "Perhaps this would firm up our theory that the letter opener was the murder weapon."

Early the next morning, Lucas County Deputy Coroner Dr. Diane Scala-Barnett arrived at the St. Bernardine cemetery in Fremont to supervise the exhumation. It was unusually warm and muggy as Detectives Tom Ross and Terry Cousino, Assistant Prosecutor Tim Braun, and Bob Keller from the Lucas County Coroner's office, gathered around the grave to witness the solemn exhumation. Also present was Sister Marjorie Rudemiller, president of the Toledo Sisters of Mercy. There were no representatives from Father Robinson's defense team, as they had not been informed.

As cemetery workers began digging up her grave, the retired nuns from the Pines convent, most of whom had known Sister Margaret Ann, gathered in the nearby chapel to pray.

Then a crane slowly raised up Sister Margaret Ann's pine casket from the vault, where it had lain for more than twenty-four years. The only sound breaking the silence was the click of Detective Cousino's camera, recording the event.

The waterlogged coffin, which was disintegrating, was then placed in a transport van, and driven forty miles north to the Lucas County Coroner's office.

On Friday morning, Dr. Scala-Barnett conducted Sister Margaret Ann Pahl's second autopsy—almost a quarter of a century after the first one, performed by her mentor Dr. Renate Fazekas. Once again Detective Cousino was taking photographs to fully document it.

Prior to the autopsy, Dr. Scala-Barnett had reacquainted herself with the crime-scene evidence, rereading Dr. Fazekas' original report.

"When we first took her out of the disintegrating casket," remembered Dr. Scala-Barnett, "I was really worried about the condition that the body was going to be in. She had been down about twenty-four years, so basically I didn't know what I was going to find [or] if the body was going to be helpful. But once we got her here in good light, we saw that she was actually better preserved than I had anticipated."

Dr. Scala-Barnett began her postmortem with an external visual examination of the body, which had been laid out on a surgical table. Many of the wounds documented by Dr. Fazekas so many years earlier were still clearly visible.

"[I wanted] to look at the injuries myself," she would later testify. "Believe it or not, twenty-four years later, you could still see many of the stab wounds in the actual skin and in the soft tissue.

"Some weren't as pristine," she elaborated. "The skin is more shriveled now, and darker, but you could still see the stab wounds in the neck and chest area. That made me pretty excited, as I didn't think we were going to be able to see that."

Dr. Scala-Barnett then re-opened Dr. Fazekas' 'Y' incision, stretching from the shoulders to the breastbone, and extending down from the sternum to the pubic bone. Then she conducted an examination of the remains of the internal organs.

"The first thing that I noticed when we took back the skin flaps," she said, "was in the soft tissues over the chest area. There, still preserved, was this triangular-shaped defect from one of the stab wounds in the chest. And after twenty-four years, it had stayed pretty good."

Then, because Dr. Fazekas had documented some slight injuries to the bone caused by the murder weapon, Dr. Scala-Barnett collected small pieces of bone, placing them in a body bag for later inspection by the Lucas County Coroner's director of the Forensic Anthropology Laboratory, Julie Saul, who was out of town.

Dr. Scala-Barnett then turned her attention to obtaining a DNA sample from the body.

"We extracted teeth from the mandible," she explained, "because they are an excellent source of DNA. And we also took a scalp hair standard and a section of femur bone."

In order to remove several teeth, the deputy coroner had to saw through a two-inch portion of mandible or lower jaw, which she placed with the other bone samples in a body bag.

Three days later, Julie Saul returned to the coroner's office. The silver-haired forensic anthropologist worked closely with Dr. Frank Saul, her professional partner and husband since 1964.

The Sauls specialize in the reconstruction of life history through skeletal bones. After 9/11, Julie Saul spent a month working at Ground Zero at the remains of the World Trade Center. She has also traveled all over the world, working with human remains in the wake of many air disasters.

Dr. Scala-Barnett had requested that Julie Saul examine the bone samples collected during the second autopsy. "My role was to examine underlying bone and look for marks," she later testified. "The stab wounds were all tightly clustered, and there's underlying bone. So we wanted to try and see if we could learn more about the weapon involved by looking at the bone."

As human bone is very hard, it retains marks or scratches better than soft tissue, and far longer.

"We call it a weapon signature," Saul explained. "So we have a little more information about the weapon there."

First Dr. Scala-Barnett brought out Sister Margaret Ann's body, pointing out areas of importance. The deputy coroner showed Saul a diamond-shaped defect right above the right second rib in the soft tissue.

"I could see the rib cartilage underneath was fractured," she said. "And there's a little grooved area here, and then a piece that's missing . . . like a small pointed object had pierced, punctured it and the force of that had fractured the cartilage. So the force of the stab punctured the cartilage and fractured it."

Dr. Scala-Barnett then showed her the manubrium—the upper part of the sternum—where there was another diamond-shaped puncture.

"So I began to formulate more about the kind of instrument involved," she said.

The experienced forensic anthropologist noted that the puncture wound had been made prior to burial—the inside of it was brown, like the rest of the bones that had been stained brown over the years by body and embalming fluids.

There was also chipping and fracturing the whole width of the left fourth rib cartilage, splitting it in two. And instead of a puncture, there was a tiny piece missing.

"We call that a percussion chip," explained Saul. "If you wanted to split an ice cube with an ice pick and you hit it, you get little chips as well as the fracturing."

She then moved to the neck vertebrae, dating various fractures and markings by their degree of brown staining, to see if they had been made before or after burial. She found one rough diamond-shaped puncture on the seventh neck vertebra, clearly demonstrating the sheer force of the stab wound.

"To stab through and puncture the front of the vertebra, it has to go a fair distance," she later testified. "It has to go through the trachea and the esophagus in front of it."

Earlier, when Saul had looked at the original autopsy photographs, she had seen a number of stab wounds to the left side of the sister's face. So she wanted to examine the underlying bone for any clues about the murder weapon. She reasoned that, as the mandible was very "hard and dense," it would preserve a weapon signature better than other bones.

But then she realized, to her horror, that a section of the left mandible was missing, having been removed by Dr. Barnett for DNA. So she started looking for it around the coroner's office.

Julie Saul eventually found it at the bottom of a body bag and pulled it out, immediately noticing a "stellar diamond-shaped" defect made by one of the stab wounds. She then rinsed off the mandible section, studying the puncture. She noted that it went downward at a slight angle to the chin, meaning the blade did not go straight in.

"It was a very distinctive, well-defined diamond-shaped puncture in the mandible," said Saul. "So I formed an opinion of what the weapon might look like, or at least the tip. I knew that it had to have a point. I knew it had to be fairly sturdy in order to puncture this really hard, dense bone. And it had a rounded, flattened diamond shape at the tip cross-section."

When Julie Saul told the cold case squad of her findings, there was great excitement that Sister Margaret Ann Pahl's mandible bone was the smoking gun, proving conclusively that Father Gerald Robinson's letter opener was the murder weapon.

LATER THAT DAY, LUCAS COUNTY PROSECUTORS GAVE THE defense 107 pages of discovery documents, along with a videotape of Father Robinson's interrogation by Detective Ross the night of his arrest. At a brief pre-trial hearing, Assistant Prosecutor Gary Cook told Judge Patrick Foley that his office would not be ready for trial until 2005. The judge set another hearing for July 13, to arrive at a trial date.

A few days later, the Diocese of Toledo asked Sister Annie Louise to undergo psychiatric evaluation as part of its ongoing probe. When she refused, the diocese shut down the investigation.

"My question back to them," an angry Sister Annie Louise told the Toledo *Blade*, "was, 'Why don't they tell the priest who abused me to undergo psychiatric tests?' Do hospitals ask rape victims to have psychiatric evaluations?'"

The sister said she had cooperated with the diocese in allowing investigators John Connors and Lawrence Knannlein to interview her therapist and members of her family.

After the Church probe was closed, the two detectives prepared a thirty-nine-page report, presenting it at a final meeting with the diocesan case manager. But the two investigators were split, with Connors finding Sister Annie Louise credible, while Knannlein did not.

"I just felt that if we had kept going," Connors said, "we could have corroborated at least some of her story."

CHAPTER THIRTY

"A Perfect Fit"

ON TUESDAY, JUNE 1, 2004, SISTER MARGARET ANN PAHL'S RE-
mains were returned to the Pines and reburied in a private
ceremony. Three days later, Detective Terry Cousino flew to
Memphis to collect the letter opener from T. Paulette Sutton,
bringing it back to Toledo, so its blade could be compared to
the tiny hole in the mandible.

The following Monday, Cousino brought it to the Lucas
County Coroner's office, where Julie Saul and Dr. Diane
Scala-Barnett had devised an experiment to see if they
matched.

Detective Ross, Sergeant Forrester and a representative
from the prosecutor's office were there as observers. Dr.
Frank Saul also attended to offer his expert advice.

Julie Saul first examined the tip of the letter opener, seeing if it matched the small hole in the mandible.

"I saw that this blade has a ridge on each side," she later
testified, "that runs the length of the blade. And that ridge
pulls it up into a diamond shape. And I saw the point. I saw
that it was a fairly sturdy blade. And it appeared to be consistent with what I'd been seeing in the bone."

It was then decided to gently stab a lump of clay with the
letter opener, and see what weapon signature it would make.
The only available clay in her laboratory was a facial reconstruction that she and her husband were currently working
on. So Dr. Frank Saul sliced off a disk from the back of the
head for the experiment.

Then, as Detective Cousino took photographs, Julie Saul plunged the letter opener into the raw clay.

"We compared the shape of the defect in the clay with that in the bone," she stated. "And they were very consistent with each other."

Dr. Scala-Barnett then decided to take the experiment further, telephoning Assistant Prosecutor Gary Cook for permission to fit the tip of the opener into the actual section of Sister Margaret Pahl's mandible.

"We felt it would be best to go on with what is the normal procedure," said Julie Saul. "It's very common to do this. It's something that's done with great care."

After obtaining permission, on the understanding that every possible precaution would be taken not to damage the bone, everyone gathered around to watch.

"And so we proceeded," said Dr. Scala-Barnett. "Julie had removed any soft tissue that still clung to the bone, and I took the letter opener and inserted it into the defect. It was a perfect fit.

"It was my conclusion, based on my experience, my knowledge, my training, that this weapon caused these injuries, or a weapon exactly like this."

The next day, Julie Saul wrote her report of the successful experiment, but doubted Detective Cousino's photographs would do it justice.

"It's very difficult to photograph because it's so tiny," she would later explain. "But it's potentially very, very important."

At the next meeting of the cold case task force, she suggested calling in a bone expert to restage the fit test for a second opinion, documenting it with more sophisticated photography equipment. Prosecutor Julia Bates immediately agreed, realizing that this could be key evidence at trial to prove Father Robinson's guilt beyond a reasonable doubt.

ON THURSDAY, JULY 8, THE TOLEDO *BLADE* REVEALED THAT Sister Margaret Ann Pahl's body had been exhumed a month earlier, for a second autopsy. Sergeant Steve Forrester said that the Pahl family had given permission, refusing to say whether any new evidence had been recovered.

At a pre-trial motions hearing the following Tuesday, Father Robinson's defense attorney Alan Konop lashed out at prosecutors for exhuming the nun's body without telling them. He expressed "surprise" and "concern" that the defense team had only been informed about the exhumation six or seven weeks after the fact, not allowing them to have a representative present.

Father Robinson did not attend the hearing, avoiding the television cameras in the courtroom. But in his absence his attorneys waived his right to a speedy trial, allowing both sides more time to prepare.

Prosecutors also told Judge Foley they had now handed over about ninety percent of discovery evidence to the defense, although they would still have to share any DNA or other test results.

A few miles away in Bowling Green, cold case task force DNA expert Casey Agnosti had already started testing evidence against a standard of Sister Margaret Ann's DNA.

"It was a tooth," Agnosti would later testify. "And I had also received a standard from Gerald Robinson."

Agnosti tested the altar cloth, and Sister Margaret Ann's underwear and other clothing, using the standard PCR (polymerase chain reaction) test, which makes millions of exact DNA copies from a single biological sample. PCR amplification allows scientists to analyze minute samples, as small as a few skin cells, but great care must be taken to prevent contamination by other foreign materials.

Agnosti discovered DNA on the victim's underwear that did not belong to her. But when she compared it to the standard from Father Robinson, she excluded him.

"He could not have left the DNA," she explained, adding that it could have come from anyone in the sacristy on the day of the murder.

And when she examined the altar cloth, she found a partial

profile that matched Sister Margaret Ann, but nothing else of any significance, as the DNA had become so degraded over the years.

A few days later, Lucas County prosecutors subpoenaed tissue samples from Father Jerome Swiatecki and former coroner Dr. Steven Fazekas, both deceased, refusing to reveal how it related to their case.

ON FRIDAY, JULY 23, DETECTIVE TERRY COUSINO AND DRS. Frank and Julie Saul drove Sister Margaret Ann's mandible bone and the letter opener to Erie, Pennsylvania, for a meeting with Dr. Steven Symes at Mercyhurst College. The renowned board-certified forensic anthropologist specializes in sharp trauma, and has state-of-the-art photography equipment in his laboratory.

"The Sauls had called me because I'd known them for many years," he remembered. "They told me about the case, saying they'd like me to look at it hands-on."

Julie Saul briefed Dr. Symes, explaining how they had performed a fit test on a segment of mandible bone.

"They talked about finding the defect," said Dr. Symes. "They talked about testing the fit. And I thought it seemed like they'd covered it. And I said, 'That's interesting,' and we discussed it for a day."

That night Detective Cousino and the Sauls returned to Toledo with the mandible and the letter opener. It would be another six months until Dr. Symes next reviewed the evidence and did his own scientific testing.

ON AUGUST 5, LUCAS COUNTY COMMON PLEAS COURT JUDGE Patrick Foley announced that Father Gerald Robinson would stand trial for the aggravated murder of Sister Margaret Ann Pahl on February 22, 2005.

"As far as I'm concerned, that is a firm date," he said at a pre-trial hearing.

Assistant Prosecutor Gary Cook told the judge that the DNA tests should be completed in six weeks.

"It's an appropriate trial date," he told reporters outside the courtroom, "considering the facts and circumstances."

Three weeks later, Cook and Detective Terry Cousino drove 160 miles south to Kettering, Ohio, to recruit Dr. Henry Lee, the legendary forensic pathologist, who had worked on many celebrated cases, including those of O. J. Simpson, JonBenet Ramsey and Scott Peterson. Dr. Lee was delivering a lecture, and Cook and Cousino waited patiently at the back of the hall until he had finished.

"They brought me some crime-scene photographs and some forensic reports," remembered Dr. Lee, who has investigated more than 6,000 cases during his forty-year career. "They asked me to look at it."

After a cursory examination, Dr. Lee agreed to join the prosecution team as a paid expert, coming to Toledo later in the year to stage a complete crime-scene reconstruction of Sister Margaret Ann Pahl's murder.

CHAPTER THIRTY-ONE

Canon Law

ON MONDAY, AUGUST 30, 2004, SERGEANT STEVE FORRESTER learned that the Catholic Diocese of Toledo kept a top secret archive at its Spielbusch Avenue headquarters. His informant told him that since 1917, all the sensitive diocesan files had been stored in a special area, entirely separate from the standard personnel documents and other routine files.

The cold case investigator reasoned that as Father Gerald Robinson had been the prime suspect in Sister Margaret Ann Pahl's 1980 murder, there must have been an internal diocese investigation with official records. He'd long suspected that the three-page file of Father Robinson's Church assignments, given to him in April by Father Michael Billian, was far from complete.

A trained lawyer, Forrester started doing his own research into the Code of Canon Law, the supreme law of the Catholic Church that transcends secular law and is sacrosanct, containing some of the Church's most sensitive secrets.

For the next two weeks, Forrester and Lucas County Assistant Prosecutor Thomas Aquinas Matuszak researched Catholic Church Canon Law, as it related to Diocesan secret archives. They read an English translation of *Codex Juris Canonici*, the Roman Catholic Church's official source of canonical law, which mandates how bishops and other diocesan leaders handle sensitive subjects, such as pedophile priests, to prevent Church scandals.

They learned that under Canon Law, the Toledo diocese had been compelled to investigate Father Robinson, seeing if he had caused Sister Margaret Ann's death. This investigation by diocesan officers would be fully documented, with the findings kept locked in a safe.

Canon 489 reads:

> There is also to be a secret archives in the diocesan curia or at least a safe or file in the ordinary archives, completely closed and locked which cannot be removed from the place, and in which documents to be kept are to be protected most securely.

Canon 490 dictates: "Only the bishop may have the key to the secret archives." And the safe containing secret archives can only be opened by the diocesan administrator. "Documents are not to be removed from the secret archives or safe," it commands.

The Bishop must also ensure that all documents in the secret archive be "diligently preserved," and make duplicates of inventories or catalogues, with one being kept in the Church's own archive and the other in the diocesan one. If, after ten years, the file was destroyed, the diocese was required to keep a written summary of the investigation.

Reads Canon 1719:

> The acts of the investigation, the decrees of the ordinary which initiated and concluded the investigation, and everything which preceded the investigation are to be kept in the secret archive of the curia if they are not necessary for the penal process.

And Canon 1722 rules that at any stage of the investigation— "to prevent scandals"—the accused can be excluded "from the sacred ministry . . . or even can prohibit public participation in the Most Holy Eucharist"—as was the case with Father Robinson since his arrest.

Sergeant Forrester learned that diocesan officials were expressly forbidden by Canon Law from giving police access to any files in the secret archive.

"Canon Law supersedes civil legal authority," noted Sergeant Forrester.

On September 15, the detective took unprecedented action, applying for a search and seizure warrant for the Catholic Diocese of Toledo. In a twenty-page affidavit, Forrester accused Bishop Blair and Father Billian of concealing the diocesan secret archives. It demanded the Toledo diocese hand over all secret archive records, documents or photographs relating to Fathers Robinson and Swiatecki, and Sister Margaret Ann Pahl from 1980 to the present.

The affidavit read:

> This Affiant has reason to believe that the Catholic Diocese of Toledo was aware of the allegations of secular criminal misconduct as early as April of 1980, specifically that Father Robinson was suspected of the murder of Sister Margaret Ann Pahl. This Affiant has reason to believe, based upon a review of Canon Law, that the murder of a nun by a priest constitutes a violation of canon law (e.g. Thou Shalt Not Kill), thereby making the act an act of canonical misconduct.

Sergeant Forrester wrote that under Canon Law, the diocesan bishop in 1980 had to "initiate a canonical penal process" to determine if Father Robinson, or anyone else affiliated with the diocese, was involved in the sister's murder.

"Canon Law requires that such an inquiry," he wrote, "be memorialized in written form and those documents and/or materials be placed in the diocesan secret archives."

That afternoon, after Lucas County Common Pleas Court Judge Robert Christiansen signed the search warrant, Sergeant Forrester and Detective Tom Ross arrived at 1933 Spielbusch Avenue to serve it. The two investigators took the elevator to the fourth-floor chancery, asking to see Bishop Blair.

Sergeant Forrester then served the search warrant on the bishop, demanding access to the diocesan secret archive.

The bishop replied that the diocese did not keep a secret archive and the material they wanted did not exist.

Bishop Blair then put diocesan Episcopal Vicar Father Michael Billian on speakerphone to explain further.

Father Billian said that files on priests were either kept in the document room outside Bishop Blair's office, or in the chancellor's office. The bishop then telephoned the diocesan attorney Thomas Pletz, informing him of the search warrant.

A few minutes later Pletz arrived, taking the detectives into the documents room, giving them Father Swiatecki and Monsignor Schmit's files. Pletz then left the room, returning several minutes later carrying a thick folder with 148 documents relating to Father Robinson.

Back at the Safety Building, the two investigators studied the files, finding little of interest about Father Robinson.

So two days later, Sergeant Forrester prepared a second search warrant, this time to search Father Billian's office.

"It appears that Father Billian," Forrester wrote in his affidavit to Judge Christiansen, "in contravention of Canon Law, maintains records separate and apart from the general archives and/or the secret archives."

Judge Christansen signed the search warrant, as well as an order to seal it. The two detectives then returned to Spielbusch Avenue and searched Father Billian's office, leaving empty-handed after finding no files about Father Robinson.

Later it was reported that the detectives did find files marked "privileged," containing sensitive information about child sexual abuse accusations against Toledo priests.

IN THAT NOVEMBER'S LOCAL ELECTIONS, JUDGE PATRICK Foley lost his seat at the Lucas County Common Pleas Court to Assistant Prosecutor Gary Cook, running on the Democratic ticket. Normally Cook would have taken over as judge in the Father Robinson case, but he stepped down, as he'd investigated it and was to have been the lead prosecutor.

The high-profile case was then assigned to Judge Thomas Osowik, a Roman Catholic who had also won a seat at the

Common Pleas Court after serving fifteen years as a municipal court judge.

Soon after the election, Lucas County Prosecutor Julia Bates gave Dean Mandross, one of her most experienced deputy prosecutors, an interesting proposition.

"Dean," she said, "I have a little case for you to do, OK? Did I mention to you that it was twenty-five years old? Did I mention that? OK. Did I mention to you that many of the witnesses have died and have disappeared? But OK. No problem. Because you're good and you can handle it.

"Did I mention to you that many of the police reports in this case have disappeared as well, and cannot ever be located? Oh by the way, Dean, did I mention to you that someone else's DNA has been located at the crime scene on the altar cloth and on the nun's girdle?

"Oh, yes. The other thing I wanted to mention to you, Dean, did I tell you that the defendant is a priest? OK. Now go and do the case!"

Mandross immediately agreed, and Bates' unusual pitch later became a running gag in the prosecutor's office.

The 52-year-old chief of the Lucas County Criminal Division already knew the case inside and out, having attended many of the cold case task force meetings. At the time of Sister Margaret Ann Pahl's murder, Mandross was in his last year at the University of Toledo College of Law, working part-time at the prosecutor's office.

He well remembered the murder, as he and his sister had just bought an old Victorian house on Collingwood Boulevard, near Mercy Hospital.

"Ironically, I was very close to where it happened," remembered the tall, elegant prosecutor with graying full beard and glasses. "Everyone in that area was on guard because a homicide had occurred, and no one had been arrested for it."

A few months after the murder, Mandross graduated, starting full-time with the Lucas County Prosecutor's office.

During his twenty-four-year career as a prosecutor, Mandross had worked on many homicide cases, including the successful prosecutions of serial killers Anthony and Nathaniel Cook, which had led to the creation of the cold case task force.

He had also prosecuted several other high-profile murder cases, including Douglas Coley and Joseph Green, convicted of abducting and then executing 21-year-old Samar El-Okdi near the Toledo Museum of Art in 1997.

The disarmingly low-key prosecutor had also crossed swords with John Thebes, Father Robinson's defense attorney, on several occasions. In 1996 he had come out on top, gaining a conviction of a young man named Jamie Madrigal, who had murdered high school student Misty Fisher at a Toledo KFC restaurant.

Now Mandross faced perhaps *the* most difficult case of his career, and threw himself into preparing for the upcoming trial. One of the first things he did was buy a copy of *Catholicism for Dummies*, reading it cover-to-cover.

"I had to educate myself," explained Mandross, who is of Greek descent and not Catholic. "That was a barrier, because a lot of the case obviously had religious overtones and aspects to it. I like to joke and say it took me almost a year to understand that the Eucharist and the Blessed Sacrament were one and the same thing."

Married with two teenage children, Mandross dropped one 'S' from the spelling of his surname several years ago after his daughter told him it was more authentic, although he still has not gotten around to updating his business cards. He also took lessons from one of the Catholic prosecutors, as well as Reverend Jeffrey Grob, the prosecution's expert witness for occult ritual.

"There were a lot of things to consider," said Mandross. "You don't want to be tilting at windmills."

Unlike his previous homicide cases, this one was so old, it took him some time to find a direct connection with the victim, as he likes to do. He spoke with Sister Margaret Ann Pahl's nephew Lee, as well as her surviving sisters Mary Casebere and Catherine Flegal. But not until a visit to the Pines in Fremont to meet the now-retired Sisters of Mercy nuns who had known her, did he begin to get an idea of what she had been like.

"Through them I got to know Sister Margaret Ann Pahl," he reflected. "She was a very interesting woman. I learned this religious order actually owned and ran the hospital, and I never in my naïveté fully appreciated that. This particular order at one time owned up to nine hospitals and these women ran them, managing multi-million-dollar budgets. They hired and fired and kept things going seven days a week, twenty-four hours a day."

Over the next few months, Mandross regularly visited the Pines, preparing Sisters Phyllis Ann Gerold and Madelyn Marie Gordon for the ordeal of testifying against Father Gerald Robinson at his upcoming trial.

TOWARD THE END OF 2004, FATHER ROBINSON QUIETLY moved back into his house on Nebraska Avenue. Up until then he had been living with his brother Thomas Robinson and sister-in-law Barbara, but wanted to be back in his own home. He had also been diagnosed with the early stages of Parkinson's disease.

"Little by little he would go back into the house," said his good friend and supporter Jack Sparagowski. "Then he did reside at his house."

During this time, Sparagowski, along with several other supporters, organized occasional fundraising dinners or Masses for Father Robinson's defense.

"We spread the word about the community that we were raising money," recalled Sparagowski. "We had a pretty strong database of about 1,600 names. And we notified them we were supporting Father and we'd appreciate any donations that they'd care to make to his defense fund."

Regular collections were also taken up at Mass in Polish churches, and a local television station even broadcast an appeal.

Although the four defense attorneys worked pro bono, they had hired several expensive high-profile expert witnesses. Their star expert was former forensic anthropologist, now best-selling author, Kathy Reichs, the inspiration for the Fox TV prime-time hit *Bones*.

"The expert witnesses were paid out of the defense fund," said Sparagowski. "And Reichs didn't come cheap."

Since his arrest, there were indications that Father Robinson had started drinking heavily, as he sat alone night after night, contemplating his upcoming trial.

"He pretty much stayed in," said Sparagowski. "He read or just watched television and whatever else he did. He also met with his lawyers during the course of that time, helping them prepare his case."

Many close to him were concerned about his mental health, with all the pressure he was now under. But outwardly the priest seemed remarkably calm and even philosophical about his plight.

CHAPTER THIRTY-TWO

Dr. Henry Lee

THREE DAYS AFTER CHRISTMAS, DR. HENRY LEE FLEW TO Toledo, to conduct a crime-scene reconstruction of the murder of Sister Margaret Ann Pahl. The internationally renowned forensic expert first went to Dean Mandross' office, where he was shown black-and-white photographs of the murder scene, studying them with his ever-present magnifying glass.

He was then driven to Mercy Hospital by the lead prosecutor, where they were joined in the chapel by Detectives Tom Ross and Terry Cousino, and Sergeant Steve Forrester. Lying on the sacristy floor was a realistic life-size mannequin, representing Sister Margaret Ann Pahl, dressed in clothing similar to hers on the day of her murder.

Referencing the old crime-scene photos, the detectives had previously arranged the mannequin in the same position the sister had been found in. The limbs had been carefully straightened out, the bra raised and panties lowered for the reconstruction.

The mannequin would later play a crucial role for the prosecution at trial, when Mandross would use it as a powerfully dramatic visual tool.

Dr. Lee's protocol employs three levels of crime-scene reconstructions, using pattern evidence, conditional evidence and transfer evidence.

"The first level," he explained, "is the so-called complete crime-scene reconstruction. If they call me right away and the scene's still intact, I can reconstruct it in a more complete fashion."

The second tier is a partial reconstruction, which Dr. Lee does in his office at the University of New Haven in West Haven, Connecticut.

"This particular case," Dr. Lee later testified, "I will classify as a limited reconstruction. Not a complete scene reconstruction."

Lee began by photographing and measuring the floor, to help him piece together how the sister had been murdered. As he began closely studying the sacristy floor and the 1980 photographs, he was particularly concerned with the pattern of bloodstains.

Then he sat by the sacristy window, taking a long, hard look at the terrazzo floor.

"I compared this floorboard with the photograph," he later explained. "There are a couple of blood spatters and I did not see any blood dripping down."

Dr. Lee observed from photographs that the altar cloth had been wrapped around the sister's right arm, noting a bloodstain on her left shoulder. He also saw it was far more "saturated with blood" than the bloodstains on the left side of her chest and shoulder. From this he deduced that the first nine stab wounds had been through the altar cloth, which the killer had then removed, before stabbing her a further twenty-two times.

A particularly revealing photograph showed a large bloodstain by her neck area. Later, when he looked at her dress, he saw the same bloodstain, but with very little dripping.

"She wasn't standing up," he explained. "If she was standing up, we should see some vertical blood drops. We should see some blood running down along the dress. So based on that, I reach a tentative conclusion: she's probably disabled or knocked down pretty quickly on the floor."

Then Dr. Lee moved on to the thirty-two stab wounds all over her body.

"That's a lot of wounds," he observed. "These wounds are more commonly associated with a frenzied type of killing."

Lee noted far less blood on the floor than would have

been expected from such a brutal attack, making him think that Sister Margaret Ann had died prior to being stabbed.

"She either was immobilized," he said, "or [it was] some quick attack. [She's lying] on the floor—most of the stabbing is, in fact, afterwards."

Dr. Lee did not think the sister had struggled or tried to fight off her attacker.

"It was a passive scene," he said. "In an active scene we usually see furniture knocked down. This [sacristy] is a preparation room. We have a lot of little knick knacks, objects all over the place. I did not see . . . a big struggle."

Dr. Lee then considered whether the killer had posed the sister's body to stage a murder scene, trying to mislead detectives into thinking the crime was sexually motivated.

"Sometimes the suspect tries to alter the scene," he explained. "This does have some indication [it] could be [a] staged scene. Her undergarment was removed, but based on [the] autopsy report, laboratory report, no semen was found. So this removal of her undergarment is not related to sexual assault."

The next morning, Dr. Lee went to the Lucas County Coroner's Office, where he viewed the altar cloth, the letter opener and the remaining physical evidence. He also wanted to reexamine the altar cloth, using a special reagent to enhance the bloodstain transfer patterns.

In the twenty-four years since the murder, the bloodstains on the white linen altar cloth had turned brown from oxidization. So Dr. Lee wanted to test it with a chemical reagent called tetramethylbenzidine (TMB), which would turn the transfer patterns a greenish-blue, and make them far easier to see.

As Dean Mandross and the other cold case squad investigators looked on, he began spraying the left-hand side of the altar cloth.

"We start seeing this parallel line pattern more defined [than] before," said Dr. Lee.

Under the chemical, the image of the curved letter opener outlined in Sister Margaret Ann's blood became even more dynamic.

Then Dr. Lee sprayed another blood transfer on the cloth, clearly demonstrating to the investigators how the murder weapon had glanced across it.

"You can actually see something move along the altar cloth," he declared. "Like a swipe pattern. A bloody object contacts this surface with a motion—creates a pattern."

Dr. Lee sprayed the cloth a third time, discovering what he called "definitive lines" in a one-inch area. From this he deduced that a bloody object with parallel lines had come into contact with it, noting that some lines were longer than others. This led him to believe that the object had been in motion when making contact.

Later, Dr. Lee was asked if the distinctive Capitol building medallion on the handle could have been one of the transfer patterns on the altar cloth. He carefully measured the medallion to see if he could exclude it as the cause of the stain.

"The size is similar," he explained. "The shape is similar. The diameter is similar. So those are class characteristics."

Dr. Lee was especially interested in a distinctive rectangular pattern in one bloodstain, like the one on the medallion. It even had a little curvature, matching the dome at the top of the Capitol building.

At the end of his two days in Toledo, Dr. Lee said that the blood transfer patterns could have been made by Father Robinson's letter opener or a similar instrument.

"I cannot exclude it," he said. "It is similar. I cannot tell you this pattern is produced exactly [by the letter opener]. I can only say similar."

ALTHOUGH THE LUCAS COUNTY COLD CASE TASK FORCE WAS still investigating Sister Margaret Ann Pahl's murder, the Toledo Police Department now launched its own investigation into Sister Annie Louise's allegations of rape, torture and murder. They searched Sister Annie Louise's "House of Blood," an abandoned wooden farmhouse on Raab Road, a few miles outside Toledo. But after a thorough investigation, detectives came up empty-handed, unable to find any evidence.

Detectives also interviewed a 43-year-old woman named Teresa Bombrys, who had made similar allegations about clerical ritual abuse. Although the two women had never met, Bombrys told detectives that she too had been sexually abused in the late 1960s by a cult of priests in a farmhouse, although she did not mention Father Robinson.

In April 2002, Bombrys had filed a civil lawsuit against Father Chet Warren—the same ex-priest accused by Sister Annie Louise—reportedly reaching settlement with the Toledo diocese and the oblates.

"I know it's hard for people to really understand this," she told the Toledo *Blade*, "but it was real. It happened, and I've lived with it for most of my life."

Father Robinson's friend Jerry Mazuchowski was also interviewed about the Sisters of Assumed Mary. He denied that the group he had founded had any sinister overtones, claiming it was merely a camp Halloween joke for parties and bars.

"We did nun drag," he declared, denying that Father Robinson was ever a member. "We gave each other nuns' names. It was nothing but absolute fun."

There has never been any finding of criminal activity by Mazuchowski in connection with the SAM group.

CHAPTER THIRTY-THREE

"A Church in Crisis"

ON FRIDAY, JANUARY 28, 2005, A COLD CASE TASK FORCE IN-
vestigator brought Sister Margaret Ann Pahl's mandible
bone back to Erie, Pennsylvania, for more exhaustive testing
by Dr. Steven Symes.

"I was somewhat skeptical when I started," he later admitted. "I put in a little more scrutiny."

Dr. Symes first placed the slice of jawbone under a high-
powered microscope and photographed it, using a state-of-
the-art Nikon camera. He then carefully measured the tiny
indentation in the bone from different angles to one one-
hundredth of an inch, defining the blade trajectory. He found
it to be "unusually small," at less than a tenth of an inch.

He then measured the thickness of the very tip of the letter opener's flattened blade.

"This blade is a replica of a sword or a saber," he said. "The
point on this is actually of interest [and] to me is important."

He then had his assistant cast a mold of the slice of
mandible, to avoid physically testing the real one with the
dagger blade.

"I make my comparisons using a molding technique," he
explained. "I've never stuck something into something. I
feel better that way."

He then made casts of the mandible, the letter opener and
the tiny wound in the bone.

Finally, Dr. Symes positioned the cast of the mandible to
the angle it would be in the body, before gently inserting the
tip of the blade.

"There's one way in which it slips in and fits," he said. "I think very, very well. You're looking at a defect two millimeters in diameter [but] it's a nice fit. I feel these tests indicate that the mandible defect was created by a tool similar in size and shape to the tip of the suspected letter opener."

THE NEXT MORNING, FATHER GERALD ROBINSON'S TRIAL WAS postponed eight months, until October 17. In open court, newly appointed Judge Thomas Osowik explained that the defense needed more time to prepare its case, as it was "complex."

Outside the courtroom, Lead Prosecutor Dean Mandross refused to discuss any aspects of the case, citing the gag order. But he pledged that he would be ready to go to trial in October.

The following Wednesday, February 2, the Toledo *Blade* lodged a motion in the Lucas County Common Pleas Court to unseal the search warrant affidavits served on the diocese four months earlier. At a hearing on February 24, Father Robinson told the court he had no problem with making them public, and Judge Osowik agreed to unseal them.

Earlier, Assistant Lucas County Prosecutor John Weglian had argued against *The Blade*'s motion.

"Those documents . . . should not be released to the public," he told the judge.

Fritz Byers, an attorney for *The Blade*, disagreed, saying that the public had a right to know what was in the warrants. Judge Osowik ruled that the warrants would be unsealed within a couple of days, although certain "sensitive information" would be redacted.

Claudia Vercellotti of SNAP welcomed the judge's decision. She immediately wrote to the Lucas County Prosecutor's office, demanding it stage a third raid on the diocese, seizing more files.

"We think the information contained in the files that were not seized," she told *The Blade*, "could possibly unearth the magnitude of cover-up, concealment and secrecy this diocese continues to operate under."

On Monday, February 28, the diocesan search warrants were made public, with portions redacted. The explosive documents revealed for the first time that Father Gerald Robinson had "failed" a lie-detector test on April 18, 1980, administered by the Toledo Police Department.

"[He scored] 'deception indicated' on relevant questions concerning the murder of Sister Margaret Ann Pahl," read Sergeant Forrester's search warrant. "The results indicated that Father Robinson was involved in the murder."

The warrants also made public that the second polygraph test several days later in Dearborn had proven "inconclusive."

Also revealed was the fact that detectives believed the Toledo diocese was "obstructing justice," by withholding "secret files" that might have incriminated Father Robinson.

Within hours of their release, a clearly embarrassed Diocese of Toledo issued a statement to the local media, defending itself:

> Reports have been circulated in the media implying that the Diocese of Toledo has not been forthright or had withheld information concerning the Rev. Gerald Robinson case. This is based on the claim that the Church's Code of Cannon Law says the dioceses should maintain a "secret archive" for certain confidential matters, and therefore the Diocese of Toledo must have such a "secret" archive which it has hidden from the public authorities.
>
> The fact is that the Diocese of Toledo has no separate "secret archive" to which "only the bishop may have the key." There is no indication that one might have existed in the past, and there is certainly none in the present.
>
> The fact that the Diocese of Toledo has no "secret archive" was explained to the police on Sept. 15, 2004, and nothing has been found to the contrary for the simple reason that there is nothing to find.
>
> All the diocese's information concerning Rev. Robinson, including what would be called confidential information, is filed in the records that are now in the custody of the prosecutor's office and the police. It is further alleged that

> *because Bishop Leonard Blair placed Rev. Robinson on*
> *leave at the time of his arrest, the bishop must know that*
> *Rev. Robinson is guilty. This is utterly false.*
>
> *Since murder is a crime in church law as well as civil*
> *law, the bishop was obliged to place Rev. Robinson on leave*
> *once he was arrested. The diocese has agreed to cooperate*
> *with the ongoing investigation by the civil authorities.*
>
> *All decisions regarding Rev. Robinson's status within the*
> *diocese will be made after the conclusion of the pending*
> *criminal proceedings.*

After reading the statement, SNAP's Claudia Vercellotti remained unimpressed.

"We may never know what happened to Sister Pahl," she told a local television station. "But what we do know is that the Toledo Catholic Diocese had the most information at its hands again, and failed to do the right thing with it. In fact, they went to great lengths to stymie the discovery of that information and to great lengths to conceal that information."

A day after the search warrants went public, lead defender Alan Konop called a press conference, where Father Robinson's former attorney Henry Herschel disputed that he had ever failed a polygraph test. Dressed in a baggy tee-shirt, Herschel explained to reporters that Father Robinson had been under great stress after being subjected to two six-to eight-hour police interrogations.

He vehemently denied that the polygraph examiner, Detective James Weigand, had ever used the word "failed" in his report. He then read out a portion of it, saying Father Robinson "needs to relax" and be in "a calmer state," after his previous night's questioning, which had lasted until 2:00 a.m.

He maintained that the second out-of-state lie-detector test, which he'd arranged, had been far more accurate.

SEVERAL DAYS AFTER THE TOLEDO DIOCESAN STATEMENT, Bishop Leonard Blair took the unprecedented step of issuing a public apology to hundreds of parishioners at Pius X

church in western Toledo. He said he regretted the behavior
of Chet Warren, now 77, the former priest accused by Sister
Annie Louise of sexually abusing her, along with Father
Robinson.

Bishop Blair's *mea culpa* letter was sent to all parishioners as part of the diocese and parish's legal settlement
with Teresa Bombrys, who had accused Warren of molestation while attending the parish's grade school.

"On behalf of the Diocese of Toledo and Saint Pius X
Parish," wrote Bishop Blair, "I apologize to Teresa Bombrys
for the harm she suffered. I continue to pray for her and all
the other innocent victims of sexual abuse and ask your
prayers as well as those who have been harmed."

Responding to Bishop Blair's apology, the Toledo *Blade*
ran a scathing editorial entitled, "A Church in Crisis."

"This is a tough time to be Catholic in Toledo," it began.
"Sexual abuse by priests has rocked the church to its founda-
tion, nationally and locally. Another priest is charged with
murdering a nun in a bizarre ritualistic crime 25 years ago at
a local hospital."

The editorial criticized the Toledo diocese for only aggra-
vating the "substantial public relations damage" already
done, by being "less than forthcoming" in the Father Robinson homicide investigation.

"It is lamentable," it opined, "that Toledo Police detectives felt they had to take the extraordinary step of seeking
two search warrants, two days apart, to get information bearing on the Robinson case. Certainly it can be fairly inferred
that their earlier requests for all relevant materials had not
been met."

The following Sunday, Bishop Blair went to Pius X
church to personally apologize to Teresa Bombrys and more
than 200 parishioners, victims and supporters. At the end of
the morning's 8:00 a.m. Mass, Bishop Blair, wearing Lenten
vestments, addressed Bombrys and the other abuse victims.

"I want to apologize to you, Teresa," he declared, "in person and publicly as the Bishop of Toledo, for the harm you
have suffered. And my apology goes to anyone who has

been abused, whether at this parish, or anywhere in the diocese of Toledo."

ON APRIL 20, 2005, JEAN MARLOW AND HER HUSBAND SUED Father Robinson in civil court, accusing him of torturing and raping her as a young girl in the basement of St. Adalbert's church. Also named in the civil suit were Gerald Mazuchowski, the Diocese of Toledo, St. Adalbert Parish and School and the Oblates of St. Francis de Sales, Inc.

Filing under the name Jane Doe and Spouse Doe, the suit, seeking in excess of $25,000, alleged that Marlow, now 43, recognized Father Robinson as one of her abusers, after seeing his photo on a TV newscast after his arrest. Then, in February, she'd recognized Mazuchowski after seeing his picture, accompanying a Toledo *Blade* investigation into clergy ritual abuse, mentioning the Sisters of Assumed Mary.

"Until that time," said her attorney, Mark A. Davis, "she didn't know that one of her abusers was Father Robinson."

In her fifteen-count lawsuit, filed in the Lucas County Common Pleas Court, Marlow graphically listed the abuse she claimed to have suffered from 1968 to 1975.

"When [the] plaintiff was approximately five to thirteen," read the suit, "Defendants Robinson and Mazuchowski intentionally engaged in illegal, harmful, and offensive sexual abuse and exploitation of her."

It accused the "vile priests" of touching her, as well as "hitting, spanking, cutting, beating and burning" her body.

"Said Defendants also intentionally engaged in sexual attacks and offensive touches upon her person, including, but not limited to, raping her with a dead snake, raping her with their penises (vaginally and sodomy) or other objects, and or jamming their penises into her mouth and throat."

She claimed her abusers often dressed up in nuns' clothing, chanting Satanic verses as they abused her. And she accused Fathers Robinson and Mazuchowski of threatening to kill her if she ever told a soul.

Father Robinson's attorney Alan Konop refused to comment on the allegations.

"We do not believe that the allegations deserve the dignity of a reply," he said.

The openly gay Mazuchowski, now a retired public schoolteacher, laughed off the accusations, saying that he had never "been, in any shape or form, involved with a woman."

Two months later, attorney Thomas Pletz, representing the Toledo diocese, St. Adalbert's Parish and the oblates, lodged a motion demanding Jean Marlow's civil suit be dismissed, as it had been filed after the statute of limitations had expired. Labeling it "stale," "vague and unspecific," the diocese claimed it was outside the court's jurisdiction.

"In the end," concluded the motion, "Plaintiff's Complaint is so fatally flawed, and incapable of curative amendment, it must be dismissed . . . under controlling Ohio law."

On July 11, attorney Mark Davis countered with a twenty-four-page motion. It included no less than forty-three pages of Jean Marlow's rambling, childlike, often incoherent regression poems and drawings illustrating her alleged abuse at the hands of Father Robinson and others, which Davis had made a point of copyrighting.

IN LATE SEPTEMBER, A FEW WEEKS BEFORE FATHER ROBINson's murder trial was due to begin, his defense team requested a further postponement, saying it needed more time. In a brief hearing on September 29, Judge Osowik agreed, moving the trial date to April 17, 2006.

"I am going to emphasize that this is the final trial date," he told the attorneys. "So this will be a firm date."

A COUPLE OF WEEKS EARLIER, CLAUDIA VERCELLOTTI'S apartment building mysteriously burned down, destroying everything she owned, and the complete records for the Toledo branch of SNAP. The Toledo fire brigade investigated, but were unable to come up with a cause, although Vercellotti did not believe it to be accidental.

CHAPTER THIRTY-FOUR
"It Is Hurtful to Catholics"

OVER THE NEXT FEW WEEKS, SEVERAL NEW WITNESSES CAME forward, greatly strengthening the prosecution's case against Father Robinson. On October 28, Leslie Ann Kerner called the Lucas County Prosecutor's office with important new information regarding the case. Eighteen months earlier she had seen a report of Father Robinson's arrest on *Good Morning America*, but hesitated in coming forward, not wanting to get involved. The former Mercy Hospital EKG technician now lived in Missouri, and was going through a divorce, while bringing up a young child.

On Holy Saturday morning in 1980, Leslie Kerr, as she was known then, had been on duty in the coronary care unit, punching the time clock at 6:50 a.m. to start her shift.

At about 7:00 a.m. she had come out of her office and looked down the hallway leading to the chapel. There, she told a cold case investigator, she had seen Father Robinson standing by the chapel doors, wearing his collar and black cassock. She said she had immediately recognized him, but never thought any more about it until she heard screams coming from the chapel an hour and a quarter later.

A week after the murder, when interviewed by detectives, she had not mentioned seeing Father Robinson standing near the chapel doors.

Now her estranged husband had finally persuaded her that it was her duty to tell investigators how she had seen Father Robinson at the chapel at the time he had claimed to be still in his room.

On October 28, a middle-aged disabled woman named Grace Jones telephoned the Toledo Safety Building, saying that she had important information. Immediately connected with Detective Forrester, she also told of seeing Father Robinson in the vicinity of the chapel at the time of the murder.

In her deep Southern drawl, Jones told a detective how she had been working the 4:00 a.m. shift in the Mercy Hospital laboratory. A little after 7:00 a.m. she had gone to buy a Toledo *Blade* newspaper, taking the elevator from the ground floor up one level to Madison Avenue. After getting a newspaper from a machine, she returned and was waiting for an elevator, when she saw Father Robinson coming out of the chapel, wearing a black cassock and hat and carrying a duffle bag. She said he had walked right past her, and they had exchanged nods, before she took the elevator back to the laboratory.

A short time later, Jones heard the "Mr. Swift" call, and discovered that Sister Margaret Ann had been murdered. Later that morning she told her superior about seeing Father Robinson coming out of the chapel, but according to her testimony at trial she was told to keep that to herself or lose her job.

For twenty-five years, she had never told a soul about seeing the priest hurrying out of the chapel that morning. On hearing the news of his arrest, her first thought had been, "Thank you, Jesus!"

IN OCTOBER, PROSECUTORS CONSIDERED THE POSSIBILITY OF calling Sister Annie Louise as a witness. Her name appeared in court documents, among more than one hundred potential witnesses for both sides.

Assistant Prosecutor Dean Mandross refused to elaborate on the nun's connection to the Father Robinson case, but papers lodged in Lucas County Common Pleas Court said she would challenge any defense claim of the defendant's "good character."

On December 9, the defense filed a motion demanding

a tape recording it believed existed of Father Robinson's original 1980 interrogation. It also wanted any existing notes, reports or summaries covering the two interrogations with Lieutenant Bill Kina and Detective Art Marx.

"The recordings have disappeared," read the motion.

Dean Mandross quickly responded, claiming that no such tape ever existed.

"Recordings were never done," wrote Mandross, "and, as a result never existed."

Later, Bill Kina explained that the Toledo Police Department had never taped suspect interviews in those days, in case it made the suspect uncomfortable.

On Friday, December 30, just before leaving his office for the New Year's holiday, Dean Mandross filed papers to reduce the charge against Father Robinson from "Aggravated Murder" to "Murder." He also backed off of the prosecution's original contention that Sister Margaret Ann Pahl's murder had been premeditated, dropping the words "with prior calculation and design," from the grand jury indictment.

Later Mandross would explain that it was a strategic move to prevent having to prove premeditation.

"The only thing we would get out of that," he told Toledo *Blade* religion editor David Yonke, "is a sentence of 20 to life instead of 15 to life . . . and with a 68-year-old man, what's the point?"

ON FRIDAY, FEBRUARY 3, 2006, FATHER GERALD ROBINSON WAS back in court for a dramatic five-hour pre-trial hearing. His defense attorneys had filed a motion for the case to be dismissed, and in the event it was not, they wanted the videotape of Father Robinson's 2004 interrogation deemed inadmissible at trial, as he'd never been read his Miranda rights. The defense also wanted to clarify if tape recordings or reports still existed from the two 1980 police interrogations.

At the hearing, Detective Tom Ross was called as a witness. He revealed that in his first interrogation in 1980,

Father Robinson had claimed to have taken the confession of Sister Margaret Ann's killer, before quickly recanting.

"He lied about that," Detective Ross told Judge Thomas Osowik. "Nobody confessed."

Ross then read out a document from the 1980 investigation, with Detective Art Marx's incredulous response to the priest's claim.

" 'I find it hard to believe, Father,' " he read, " 'inasmuch as somebody confesses to you, you would not be telling me here and now, because you are a priest. You are bound by certain oaths.' "

Then Detective Ross said that the defendant had readily admitted lying about the confession in his April 2004 interrogation.

Detective Marx then took the stand for some tough questioning by lead defender Alan Konop, who asked if he remembered taking notes during the two interrogations.

"I cannot specifically recall," answered Marx. "But I am sure I did."

Six weeks later, just a month before the trial was due to begin, Judge Osowik gave prosecutors a major victory, ruling that Father Robinson's damning videotaped interrogation could be played to the jury. In a pre-trial status meeting not attended by Father Robinson, Judge Osowik found that the priest had not been under arrest at the time of the interview, and was voluntarily answering Detective Ross's questions.

In another setback for the defense, the judge ruled that lack of documentation from the 1980 interrogations did not mean Toledo police had acted in bad faith. Even if they did exist, the defense had failed to prove them of any value to its case.

So this cleared the way for Lieutenant Kina and Detective Marx to testify about their two interrogations with the defendant.

Judge Osowik also announced that, as all remaining pre-trial issues had been resolved, jury selection would begin on April 17.

"We have sufficiently moved this case along," he told the hearing. "We have narrowed the issues down."

BY THE BEGINNING OF APRIL, THERE WERE SO MANY MEDIA requests to cover the trial, Judge Osowik moved it to a larger courtroom. He had been planning to use his regular thirty-seat court, with just ten seats for journalists. But after Court TV announced it would be broadcasting the entire trial gavel-to-gavel, it was transferred to Courtroom 5, the largest available in the building.

Plans were hastily drawn up for an outside media center to cater to the overflow of reporters.

"This probably is the highest-profile case we've ever done," said Lucas County Common Pleas Court Security Supervisor Mark Lair, in charge of security for more than twenty years.

The Lucas County Prosecutor's office had spared no expense, utilizing a $6,000 state-of-the-art computerized "SMART Board." This would allow the prosecution to present its complicated case using graphics and photographs to highlight the evidence.

"It's like a remote control computer," proudly explained Lead Prosecutor Dean Mandross. "You can run your computer off the SMART Board."

With the upcoming blockbuster movie *The Da Vinci Code* scheduled for release on May 19, there was tremendous media interest in the Father Gerald Robinson trial, with its allegations of a cover-up from the very top of the Catholic Church.

As jury selection drew nearer, many were concerned that the defendant would wear his clerical collar at his trial, unduly influencing the jury. On April 9, Toledo SNAP activists Claudia Vercellotti and Jon Schoonmaker arrived at the Catholic Center to hand deliver a protest letter to Bishop Blair. Refused entry at the front door, they handed it to the building's manager, who promised to give it to the Bishop.

"We fear that allowing Father Robinson to dress in clerical garb may unduly bias the proceedings," read the letter.

"It is hurtful to Catholics," it read. "And sends a mixed message to the community. In 2004, you placed Father Robinson on [a] leave of absence. Why would you still allow him to appear in his Roman collar now?"

The Toledo chapter of SNAP vowed to attend each day of the trial, protesting the diocese's handling of the Father Robinson case.

"We know that this is a trial about murder," Vercellotti told the *Toledo Free Press*. "But the cover-up can't be ignored."

ON HOLY SATURDAY — APRIL 15 — HUNDREDS OF TOLEDO Catholic parishioners celebrated Easter Vigil Mass, and Father Gerald Robinson was on everyone's mind. It was the day after his 68th birthday, one day before jury selection, and many of his former parishioners were praying for him.

"It's a very sad thing," said Eric Hite, a former parishioner of the recently closed St. Anthony's Parish, where Father Robinson had served in the 1980s. "I just hope with all the coverage and bias, he does get a fair trial and justice is served."

Long-time friend and fundraiser Jack Sparagowski, who had by now raised $12,000 for the defense fund, said that Father Robinson was optimistic and ready for trial.

"I had dinner with him a week ago," said Sparagowski. "He is very upbeat. But then, he has always been upbeat about this and his chances."

CHAPTER THIRTY-FIVE

His Day in Court

AT 9:00 A.M. ON MONDAY, APRIL 17, JURY SELECTION BE-
gan. Summonses had already been sent out to 250 citizens,
to be whittled down to twelve panelists and four alternates.
By the time the first batch of prospective jurors streamed
into Courtroom 5 on the fourth floor of the Lucas County
Courthouse, almost half had been excused for a variety of
reasons.

The public gallery and the twenty-seat press bench were
full.

Court TV had already set up camera and sound equipment at the back of the courtroom, and outside, in the street,
had parked a large truck containing a well-equipped television studio. Although nothing would be broadcast until
opening arguments, it was already supplying a live feed to
all local television stations and its paid subscriber service
Court TV Extra.

There was heavy security in the courthouse, and although
everyone entering the building had gone through a metal detector, several armed deputies patrolled the courtroom.

At about 9:15 a.m. Father Robinson, wearing his clerical
collar and black suit, entered the courtroom with his four
attorneys, Alan Konop, John Thebes, John Callahan and
Nicole Khoury. He had visibly aged since his arrest. The defendant, his face a blank slate, walked slowly past the public
gallery toward the two defense tables, as if carrying a great
weight on his slender shoulders, and took his place across
from the jury box.

At the prosecution table sat Lucas County Criminal Division Chief Dean Mandross, flanked by Assistant Prosecutors J. Christopher Anderson and Larry Kiroff. Behind them was jury psychologist Lucia Hinojosa, to assess potential jurors, discreetly reporting her observations to Mandross via handwritten notes.

Then Judge Thomas Osowik entered, wearing his black judicial robe, and addressed the prospective jurors. He told them the trial could last up to a month. They were then given a questionnaire to fill in, with questions ranging from their religion to whether they had "strong opinions" on the Roman Catholic Church or members of the clergy.

The jurors were then questioned individually by Judge Osowik and attorneys from both sides. Nine of the first ten prospectives were Catholic, and the prosecution faced a daunting task in finding a jury prepared to convict a priest, as a quarter of Toledo's 300,000 residents were Catholic.

Lead prosecutor Dean Mandross was under no illusions about the hurdles he faced.

"Part of the strategy in jury selection," he later explained, "is to get those jurors to understand that priests are human beings. They're subject to the same emotions and feelings as everyone else. In 1980 I doubt that you could have got[ten] twelve people who would say, 'Oh yeah, I think a priest could kill.' So things have changed, and those priestly vows aren't viewed the same now."

Throughout the questioning the defendant sat between Konop and Thebes, listening intently and occasionally closing his eyes, his chin resting in his hands. The only sign of any emotion was when he suddenly chuckled, after a prospective female juror asked whether, if selected, she would still be able to read the *Garfield* comic strip.

By 5:15 p.m., when Judge Osowik adjourned for the day, just thirty had been interviewed and three excused.

The next day a further thirty-seven prospective jurors were questioned. Out of these, eighteen were excused, including a Catholic man in his twenties who said he could not possibly stand in judgment of a priest.

At the close on Wednesday, a total of 103 prospective jurors had been interviewed, out of which forty-four had been dismissed, leaving fifty-nine to be questioned. That morning prosecutors had objected to Father Robinson sitting at the defense table, directly facing potential jurors. Judge Osowik ordered him to turn his chair toward the bench.

Just after 2:30 on Thursday afternoon a jury was finally seated, with both sides agreeing to the final twelve jurors and four alternates. The seven-woman, five-man jury selected to judge Father Robinson included four Catholics.

AT PRECISELY 9:00 A.M. ON FRIDAY, APRIL 21, DEAN MANDROSS rose from the prosecution bench to deliver his opening statement. Thomas and Barbara Robinson sat behind the prosecution table in the public gallery, along with a few of Father Robinson's friends and supporters. Across the courtroom was Sister Margaret Ann Pahl's nephew Lee, representing the family. He would attend trial every day, dutifully reporting back to his relatives in Edgerton.

Perhaps the only person there who appeared totally unaffected was Father Robinson, who arrived with his defense team looking as if he was about to conduct Mass. As a photographer took pictures, the priest turned to his supporters in the public gallery and smirked.

But as soon as the jury filed in and took their places, his whole demeanor changed. During the trial many observers would note that whenever the jury was out of the courtroom, the defendant appeared in good spirits, chatting with his supporters. But as soon as they returned he would blankly stare ahead, as if lost in thought.

"At the front of most Catholic churches and chapels," began Mandross softly, the jury hanging on his every word, "there's a small room called the sacristy. It's a place used by the priest to don his vestments, and also a place to store religious items of the church."

He then described how the sacristy takes on a whole new aspect on Good Friday, when the Eucharist is stored there until Holy Saturday evening.

"And it was in the sacristy of the chapel," continued Mandross, using his hands to emphasize each point, "located at Mercy Hospital here in Toledo, on April fifth, 1980, Sister Margaret Ann Pahl was brutally murdered. Someone choked the sister around the neck to the very edge of death and then stabbed her some thirty-one times."

Mandross then flicked a button on his hand remote, and a black-and-white photograph of the victim was instantly displayed on an electronic screen in front of the jury. The lead prosecutor then briefly summarized the sister's life, from her becoming a nun at 19 to her semi-retirement as sacristan at Mercy Hospital.

"Now the defendant, as he sits before you, is sixty-eight years old," Mandross told the jury, pointing at Father Robinson, a weary frown on an otherwise expressionless face. Later Mandross would speculate that the priest was medicated, as he appeared so far removed from what was going on.

Mandross hit his remote, replacing Sister Margaret Ann's picture with one of a handsome young priest.

"But this was the defendant back in 1980 at age forty-two," continued Mandross, pausing a short time to allow the jury to digest the picture of a youthful Father Robinson with a thick head of dark hair. A key part of the prosecution strategy throughout the trial would be to show old photographs of the defendant at every opportunity, installing that image into the jurors' minds, rather than one of the frail, harmless-looking white-haired priest sitting before them.

"Gerald Robinson will be described as a loner," continued Mandross. "Someone who avoided other people. No one really knew him."

Under Ohio law, he informed the jury, Mandross was under no obligation to provide a motive for Sister Margaret Ann's murder.

"But what the State is going to do," he said, "is tell you about the last hours of Sister's life. And you will learn how the defendant and the victim were together in the sacristy of that chapel. And how one of them died a horrible death."

He then dramatically outlined the events leading up to the murder. ·

"The chapel doors were locked," he told the jury, now listening intently. "The unspeakable was about to take place. There were two people inside this chapel. One was Sister Margaret Ann. She was working on the altar, preparing it for the evening service. And it was in the sacristy of that chapel that someone took her by the neck and choked her. Choked her so hard that two bones in the side of her neck broke. Choked her so hard that the blood vessels in her eyes burst. Choked to the very verge of death—but not quite.

"The killer laid her upon the floor, and after laying her on the floor, he covered her with a white altar cloth. And after doing that, he stabbed her over the heart nine times. Nine piercings of her flesh, in the shape of an upside-down cross.

"And after he does all that, he does still more. He takes off the altar cloth and stabs her twenty-two more times. This crime is still not over. Because after doing these things, he carefully rolls up her dress, her smock, up over her breasts. He pulls her girdle, her underpants, her hose down to her ankles and leaves her exposed, naked, stretched out as if in a coffin on the sacristy floor. Only then does he leave."

Mandross then outlined the 1980 police investigation, with Father Robinson becoming the prime suspect and being brought in for questioning.

"The defendant made statements that were just plainly not true," he declared, looking straight at the priest, whose eyes were closed as if asleep. "He denied ever having a key to the sacristy. He even claimed that someone else had confessed to doing the killing to him. And when pressed on the matter, he admitted, no, he'd made that up. That wasn't true at all."

The assistant prosecutor then explained how Kina and Marx had searched Father Robinson's rooms after the interview, finding a heavy metal letter opener shaped like a dagger. On its handle was an ornamental, nickel-sized medallion of the Capitol building, which had later tested positive for blood.

At the end of April 1980, said Mandross, the Lucas County District Attorney's Office had decided there was insufficient evidence to charge Father Robinson with murder.

"So the case lay dormant, and years passed," he said. "And Sister's killer went free and unprosecuted."

Then in 2003, the newly created Lucas County cold case task force had reopened the case. And with new technology, not available at the time of the murder, had discovered physical evidence proving Father Robinson's letter opener to have been the murder weapon.

"Next," continued Mandross, "they exhumed the body of Sister Margaret Ann Pahl. And they studied some depressions found in her skeletal remains, particularly one in her mandible—her jaw. A small hole. And you will learn that the tip of that letter opener fits exactly in that depression. Fits like a key in a lock."

Mandross told the jury how Father Robinson had lied, claiming to have been in his room when the murder took place. He promised to present witnesses who had seen the defendant at the doors of the chapel at the time of the murder.

"Now, ladies and gentlemen," he concluded, "in a perfect world, everyone would be held accountable for their criminal conduct. In a perfect world, this would happen sooner than later. But later is better than never.

"And it may have taken twenty-six years to get the evidence to solve this murder, but we have done so. And over the course of the next two weeks, you'll hear the evidence and you'll be convinced that this defendant, on April fifth, 1980, purposely caused the death of Sister Margaret Ann Pahl. Thank you."

Then, after twenty-five minutes on his feet, Dean Mandross returned to his seat at the prosecution table, and the balding, white-bearded lead defender Alan Konop rose to his feet.

"Ladies and gentlemen of the jury," he began in his folksy way, his glasses precariously perched on the end of his nose, "we will share a long journey together—and again, thank you very much for giving up your time to share this journey."

Comparing opening statements to coming attractions, Konop asked the jurors if they'd ever seen a movie after watching a preview, finding it a disappointment.

"We've all had the experience," he said. "Coming attractions aren't the same as the movie."

The prosecution, he told the jury, had nothing but circumstantial evidence, with important "inconsistencies and discrepancies" in key witnesses' statements between the time of the murder and Father Robinson's arrest.

"The circumstantial evidence are pieces of a puzzle," he said. "The puzzle will not fit. The pieces won't fit. As much as you want to jimmy them together."

The experienced defender then attacked the Toledo Police Department for arresting Father Robinson with insufficient evidence.

"He's arrested," he said. "He's condemned, humiliated, cuffed, booked—based upon evidence which doesn't fit the standard of proof beyond a reasonable doubt."

Konop told the jurors that prosecutors had only exhumed Sister Margaret Ann Pahl's body after his arrest. DNA discovered on the victim's underwear, he declared, did not match Father Robinson's. Foreign material found under the sister's fingernails contained an unknown male chromosome.

"Maybe it's time to get another puzzle," he declared, "because this puzzle's not working."

Concluding his opening statement, Konop told jurors that there was just not enough evidence to convict Father Robinson.

"There will be reasonable doubt," he stated. "Reasonable doubt, reasonable doubt—to the point where you will see that those puzzle pieces don't fit. You can jam them, shove them, carve them—whatever you want to do. You will not be able to say beyond a reasonable doubt that Father Robinson is responsible for this killing."

IMMEDIATELY AFTER OPENING STATEMENTS, THE JURY WAS bused to Mercy Hospital to view the murder scene. On the way, they were instructed not to talk to each other at the hospital or take notes.

At Mercy Hospital they were given a forty-minute tour by Lucas County Court Bailiff Tanya Butler. She read from a set of notes, previously agreed upon by both sides, instructing jurors on what to pay particular attention to.

Although parts of the hospital, now known as Mercy College, had changed since 1980, the 11' × 17' sacristy remained the same.

Beginning on the ground floor, jurors were asked to look around the lobby and elevator area. Then they were taken up to the second floor and the two-roomed apartment where Father Robinson had lived at the time of the murder, but were not told its significance.

Back on the ground floor, they viewed St. Joseph's Chapel and the adjoining sacristy. There was total silence as the jurors stood there solemnly, absorbing the atmosphere. Each and every one of them was aware of the terrible crime committed there, and how they would have to decide if Father Robinson was responsible.

THE NEXT DAY, THIRTY OF FATHER GERALD ROBINSON'S supporters gathered in the Resurrection Polish National Catholic Church in Sylvania for a special Mass in his honor. The church had only been founded a couple of months earlier by former members of St. Anthony's, where Father Robinson had once served.

Outside stood several local TV crews and reporters who had been barred from covering the event.

"It is not because of the trial," explained Resurrection Church pastor the Reverend Jaroslaw Nowak. "We don't judge. We just ask God for truth and justice and healing."

Mass organizer Jack Sparagowski said that everyone there supported Father Robinson.

"We wanted everyone to feel like they can [come] here and pray," he said, "even those not certain about Father Robinson's innocence."

CHAPTER THIRTY-SIX
Chilling Evidence

AT 9:00 A.M. ON MONDAY, APRIL 24, DEAN MANDROSS called his first witness, Sister Phyllis Ann Gerold. The 79-year-old former CEO of Mercy Hospital was now confined to a wheelchair, but her mind was razor sharp. Over the last few months, the lead prosecutor had visited St. Bernardine's retirement home several times, preparing her for this moment. On one occasion he had brought along the gray-haired mannequin representing Sister Margaret Ann Pahl, to get her used to it. He would use it several times to demonstrate to the jury how the victim had been found before the "Mr. Swift" team had moved it and the crime-scene photographs were taken.

"He practiced that with me," she would later explain, "so that I wouldn't pass out on him."

Mandross began by asking when she had first met Sister Margaret Ann Pahl.

"I first truly met her around 1954," said Sister Phyllis Ann, who was wearing her Sisters of Mercy blue habit, a gold cross pinned to her lapel. "I was assigned to Mercy Hospital, Tiffin, as a nursing supervisor, and she was getting ready to leave, and orientated me to my duties."

They had then gone separate ways, but in the early 1970s she had received a letter from Sister Margaret Ann, asking for a position at Mercy Hospital, Toledo, which Sister Phyllis Ann was then running.

"We were happy to have her," she said.

Mandross then asked if she had any specific recollections of the sister's 1980 murder.

"Yes, I do," she replied. "It was Holy Saturday, which is a special day. I got up early with the sun and showered, and then I prayed. Then I went down to breakfast with another sister at about 8:00 a.m. and I heard this terrible screaming."

She described running from the sisters' dining room to the chapel, where Sister Madelyn Marie was still screaming, then going into the sacristy, discovering Sister Margaret Ann Pahl dead on the floor.

"It was terribly strange and sad and horrifying," she remembered, her voice cracking with emotion. "She was laid out on the floor very neatly with her clothes pulled up . . . I don't remember how far up to above her breasts or below her breasts. And her other clothes pulled all the way down to her ankles."

Then Mandross asked for her first impressions on seeing Sister Margaret Ann's body on the sacristy floor.

"The horror," she replied. "I think it was the weirdness of it and that she needed to be saved. And then the afterthought was, 'Why the ritualistic kind of layout of a dead body?' "

The lead prosecutor then asked how the nun's body had been positioned.

"I remember that it was so neat and so different," said Sister Phyllis Ann softly, as if transporting herself back to the scene. "I told them it was ritualistic. She was lying in the center on the floor and I saw no blood. If I remember correctly, her arms were straight. Her legs were straight. And all her clothes from probably her brassiere all the way down [were] rolled down to her feet. People don't usually die very straight."

"You could see her nakedness?" asked Mandross.

"Yes, I saw her nakedness," she replied sadly.

Judge Osowik then called a ten-minute recess, so the mannequin, wearing a blue habit and underwear, could be brought into the courtroom and laid out in front of the jury box.

"Sister," began Mandross after the recess, "let's spend some time talking about how Sister Margaret Ann's body was presented . . . when you walked into the sacristy. I want to do a little demonstration for the jury, so they can better understand what you saw."

He then had Sister Phyllis Ann advise him on positioning the mannequin's clothes, in a dramatic re-creation of what she had seen. Under her instructions, he pulled down the mannequin's panties and girdle to its ankles, hoisting the habit up to its breasts.

"I'm sorry to ask this," probed Mandross, "but we need to be as specific as we can. Her genitals were exposed to you?"

"Yes," replied the nun.

"Were her breasts still covered by her jumper, or were uncovered?" asked Mandross.

"I don't remember that," said the elderly nun. "There may have been a white cloth over . . . I can't remember that."

He then showed her the crime-scene photographs, graphically depicting the victim's dead body. It was the first time she had ever seen them, and she was shocked by the extent of the stabbing injuries.

"It's Sister Margaret Ann," she said. "It's so strange. I do not remember seeing any blood."

Then Alan Konop stood up to cross-examine Sister Phyllis Ann, homing straight in on her use of the word "ritualistic." The sister admitted only using it as a general term.

"It was just such a strange scene," she explained. "Strange the way her body was laid out. The way her clothes were arranged."

AFTER LUNCH RECESS, SISTER MADELYN MARIE GORDON took the stand. The former Mercy Hospital chapel organist, celebrating her sixtieth year as a Sister of Mercy nun, described Sister Margaret Ann as a perfectionist.

When Mandross asked if she remembered Holy Saturday 1980, she said she did because it was "so traumatic."

She told the jury how she had gone into the chapel at about 7:15 a.m. to prepare music for Mass later that day. Then she had wandered into the sacristy, searching for a telephone to call Father Robinson about a particular piece of music.

Her first thought, she said, on seeing Sister Margaret

Ann's body on the floor, had been that it was a mannequin used in CPR training.

When she'd bent down to take a closer look, she realized it was Sister Margaret Ann's dead body, and ran out of the sacristy in shock, screaming.

Mandross then pointed to the mannequin, still lying in front of the jury, asking how the victim's body had been positioned.

"In a very straight position," the nun replied. "Her legs were together. Her arms were down by her side. Her head was in alignment. Her clothing was up around her waist and she was bare down to her ankles. It looked like someone had placed her in that position."

Beginning his cross-examination, Alan Konop asked if she needed a rest, but she said that, although it was "difficult," she could continue.

"I'll try and be as brief as I possibly can," said the lead defender. "Bear with me."

Then Konop asked what she'd done after she had discovered her friend's body.

"I went to the middle of the chapel and sat down," she replied.

"That was a very tough moment, too?" asked the defender.

"Yes," she agreed. "I was kind of restless."

Sister Madelyn Marie was then excused, and Judge Osowik called a short mid-afternoon recess.

THE NEXT STATE WITNESS WAS BILL KINA, WHO HAD SUPERvised the 1980 homicide investigation. Now in his early eighties with a full head of thick gray hair, the long-retired veteran investigator still retained the tough build of a boxer.

Under Mandross' questioning, Kina told how Deputy Chief Vetter had called him into his office two days after Sister Margaret Ann's murder, assigning him the investigation. Within a few days, he told the jury, he and his lead detective Art Marx had eliminated robbery and rape as possible motives, believing that the killer had known his victim.

"It would take somebody with a very strong vendetta," explained Kina, "to go in and kill a person in that ferocious manner. She had thirty-one stab wounds."

On April 9, he told Mandross, referring to notes, they had learned that Sister Margaret Ann had become "distraught" after the Good Friday service had been shortened. And three days later, two hospital employees had described hearing "frantic footsteps" running along the floor above, coming to a halt outside Father Robinson's quarters.

"Was there anything," asked Mandross, "about the time of when these footsteps were heard, that you thought was significant?"

"Yes," replied Kina. "They fell within the timeframe of the homicide itself."

Kina then described bringing Father Robinson to the detectives' bureau on April 18, and he and Marx's ensuing interrogation from 8:00 p.m. to midnight.

"Was there anything you found significant that the defendant said during that interview?" asked the assistant prosecutor.

"Yes," said Kina. "He said at one point that someone had come to him and confessed to killing the nun."

"Did you hear him say that yourself?" asked Mandross.

"Yes, I did," said Kina. "Marx continued to question him on it and he eventually relented and admitted it was a lie."

After the interrogation had finished around midnight, Kina said that he and Marx had gone to Father Robinson's quarters searching for relevant evidence.

"As you sit here twenty-six years later," asked Mandross, "do you have a specific, a real memory, of going into his apartment?"

"Yes," said Kina emphatically. "It stands out very vividly."

He described how Detective Marx had found "the blade" in Father Robinson's desk, resembling the type of weapon that Deputy Coroner Dr. Renate Fazekas had told them they should be looking for.

"Detective Marx opened the large center drawer of the

desk," explained Kina, "pulled it out and reached inside, and said, 'Oh, what have we got here?' " That's his exact statement. It was a dagger-shaped letter opener with probably a six-inch blade, center medallion and a handle grip with a knuckle guard."

The next day, they had summoned Father Robinson back to the Safety Building for a polygraph test. He and Marx had then resumed the interrogation, hopeful of getting a confession.

"It was a very short interrogation," Kina recalled. "Maybe an hour, an hour-and-a-half after we entered the room, there was a knock on the door. I was in the room alone with Father Robinson at the time. I got up, answered the door and it was Deputy Chief Vetter, my immediate superior, and behind him was Monsignor Schmit from the Catholic Diocese.

"The deputy asked me to step outside . . . and they went into the room with Father Robinson. They stayed in there five, ten minutes. Then the door opened and they walked out of the Safety Building."

Kina said that toward the end of April 1980, Deputy Chief Vetter had ordered him to scale down the investigation and reassign detectives back to their original jobs. Two weeks later, Vetter had him take the case file over to Lucas County Prosecutor Curt Posner, to decide if there was enough evidence to indict the priest.

"The prosecutor felt we did not have enough evidence at that time," said Kina.

Then Alan Konop stood up to cross-examine the veteran detective, immediately going on the attack.

"Would it be fair, Officer," he declared, "to say there's not a single report in this entire investigation that you have signed and prepared?"

"That's true," answered Kina nonchalantly.

"Not a single one?"

"Right."

"So everything you're testifying here today," said Konop, his voice rising with each word, "is either your recall from twenty-six years ago, or going over reports that have been supplied to you by the prosecutor's office. Correct?"

"That's true," Kina agreed.

Then Judge Osowik broke for the day, discharging the jury and recalling Kina to the stand the following morning.

CHAPTER THIRTY-SEVEN

"Memories Fade"

ON TUESDAY MORNING, THE FATHER ROBINSON TRIAL MADE headlines all over America. The tabloid *New York Post* ran a two-page spread with the headline " 'Satan Cult' Priest on Trial in '80 Nun Slay." It featured a quarter-page picture of clerical-collared Father Robinson in court the day before, staring blankly ahead, three fingers of his right hand supporting his forehead, and his little finger over his mouth.

Across the page was a dramatic photograph, showing prosecutor Dean Mandross bending over the realistic gray-haired mannequin, its clothing in disarray.

"Sister Margaret Ann Pahl may soon be able to rest in peace," began the story.

The Toledo *Blade* was more restrained, with a front-page story headlined "Witnesses recall scene in priest's murder trial—Testimony begins in nun's slaying."

On the third day of the trial, Lieutenant Bill Kina retook the stand, as lead defender Alan Konop resumed cross-examination, focusing on Father Robinson's two 1980 interrogations.

"You took no notes?" asked Konop incredulously.

"No, sir," replied Kina.

"Notes are important, are they not?"

"Yes, they are."

"Because notes memorialize what was said," said the defender, turning to the jury to emphasize his point.

"Correct," replied Kina.

"Memories fade," he continued. It was a mantra he would repeat continuously throughout the trial.

Konop then demanded to know why the only detail he remembered from the two long interrogations was Father Robinson's initial claim that someone had confessed the murder to him.

"That was the outstanding statement," said Kina.

"In four to six hours of testimony, that's what you remember?" the defender asked, raising his eyebrows incredulously.

"That's what I remember," stated Kina.

"So one thing stands out," continued Konop. "And that's it over all those hours?"

"Yes."

THE NEXT PROSECUTION WITNESS WAS JOSH FRANKS, WHO, in 1980, had been senior criminalist in the Toledo police crime lab. In direct examination, Assistant Prosecutor Christopher Anderson asked about the presumptive blood test Franks had performed on the letter opener, two-and-a-half weeks after the murder.

Then Anderson handed him an envelope, asking him to open it, telling the jury what it contained.

"This is the medallion," said Franks, who had only retired from the Toledo Police Department four years earlier. "The Capitol building in D.C. It was glued to the circular portion of the letter opener."

Franks explained that he had first placed it under a microscope, looking for traces of blood.

"It was sumptuously clean," he told the jury. "It didn't have any fingerprints, no stains, no smear marks. It appeared as if it had been polished, and that was interesting."

Further examination had revealed the nature of "the material" under one of the notches of the medallion, which was tested for blood with the chemical phenolphthalein.

"It had a positive reaction," said Franks. "It turned purple or blue. It indicated the possible presence of blood."

"And are you able to say," asked Anderson, "that it was

possible for the presumption of blood to a reasonable degree of scientific certainty?"

"Yes," he replied emphatically.

Then there was a rare light moment in the trial, when the assistant prosecutor asked if Franks had performed a DNA test in 1980.

"No DNA. No e-mails either," quipped Franks, raising a laugh from the jury.

In cross-examination, Alan Konop immediately started damage control, trying to lessen the impact of Father Robinson's letter opener testing positive for blood.

"You cannot say with certainty," he asked, "after doing a presumptive test for blood, that it is blood, can you?"

"No," agreed Franks.

"It could be blood, yes?" asked the defender.

"It gave an indication that would cause me to believe that it was blood," replied Franks.

THE NEXT PROSECUTION WITNESS WAS DETECTIVE TERRY Cousino, of the Toledo Police Department's Scientific Investigations Unit. Over the next two hours, he would recount the crucial role he'd played in the 2004 murder reinvestigation.

Under Christopher Anderson's direct examination, he told how on February 27, 2004, Sergeant Steve Forrester had first brought him the letter opener and altar cloth. After a cursory look at the cloth, he'd discovered distinctive bloodstains, closely resembling the highly unusual letter opener.

The ten-foot-long reddish-brown–stained altar cloth was then laid out on the floor in front of the jury box. With Judge Osowik's permission, the sixteen jurors were invited to come over and inspect it. For the next several minutes they slowly walked around the cloth, bending over for a closer look at the stains and the numerous stab holes.

As they studied the altar cloth, Father Robinson stared from the defense table, without a trace of emotion.

When the jury retook their seats, Detective Cousino projected various photographs of the altar cloth on a large screen, pointing out the long pointed stains, and explaining how they tracked the shape and curve of the defendant's letter opener.

The jury sat transfixed as Cousino moved to the various stab holes in the cloth, made by the diamond-shaped blade. And using the mannequin, which had been brought back into the courtroom, he described the pattern of stab wounds in detail.

"There are eighteen," he explained, "and they're pretty much centered in the altar cloth."

He said he'd immediately realized the cloth had been folded in half, and when he did so, nine holes—representing the first nine stab wounds into Sister Margaret Ann's body—lined up perfectly, forming an inverted cross.

"[It] jumps out at you," he told the jury, now hanging on his every word. "Not only did it fit the form of a cross, the symmetry and the precision of it would suggest to me that something was used as a template to put down on the cloth and stab around."

Detective Cousino said the weapon used to murder Sister Margaret Ann was highly unusual, with a diamond-shaped blade and a distinctive medallion depicting the U.S. Capitol building from the defunct National Historical Wax Museum. Cousino said he had spent hours searching eBay and other sites for a similar one, with no success.

He also pointed out that the stab holes in the altar cloth were highly unusual.

"I've seen many different stab defects in clothing," he testified, "but I have never seen ones like that. They're normally just a slit. Even if it's a wider blade, it usually looks like a fat slit. But this 'Y' shape was very unique."

From this, Cousino had deduced that the cutting edge became wider as it went up. He also noticed that not all the threads were cut, making him think it was not a very sharp instrument.

Then Chris Anderson handed him the letter opener, asking him to describe its blade to the jury.

"It's fairly unique," he said. "It's definitely got four

plains and four distinct corners to it. So it's a pretty unusual blade."

After lunch, John Thebes cross-examined Detective Cousino, asking if cold case detectives had been looking for crucifixes when they had searched Father Robinson's home after his arrest.

"Yes," said the detective.

"And you were looking for that," said the defender, "to see if you could match the holes and defects in the dress or the altar cloth with the crucifix?"

"Yes," replied the detective, "we were trying to find one that fit those dimensions."

"And to this date you have not found one?" said Thebes.

"That's correct," he confirmed.

The next witness was Dr. Diane Scala-Barnett, a founding member of the Lucas County cold case task force. A deputy coroner for twenty-one years, Dr. Scala-Barnett said she had performed almost 7,000 autopsies in her career.

Referring to the original autopsy report prepared by her predecessor, Dr. Renate Fazekas, Dr. Scala-Barnett told the jury that Sister Margaret Ann had probably been choked from the back with a soft ligature like a cloth, because her necklace and cross, inscribed "I AM A CATHOLIC. PLEASE CALL A PRIEST," had made an impression in her skin.

"That could be consistent with a soft ligature strangulation," she told the jury. "Because it's not leaving any other marks."

"Was that the cause of death?" asked Assistant Prosecutor Christopher Anderson.

"No," replied Dr. Scala-Barnett. "We need to move on to the stab wounds."

Using a medical model of a human neck, the deputy coroner showed the jury how Sister Margaret Ann had been choked with such force that the two hyoid bones in her neck had broken.

"That is commonly seen in strangulations from side-to-side pressure applied," she explained. "It's easier to break them in an older person, because they have more calcification."

Moving on to the numerous stab wounds on the victim's face, neck and chest, Dr. Scala-Barnett said her predecessor had noted that all the wound edges were sharp, meaning the murder weapon did not have a blunt edge.

"That can rule out some weapons," she explained. "For instance, a scissors has a cutting edge and a non-cutting, which is not sharp. It's flat."

"So based on her observation," asked Anderson, "scissors could not be the weapon?"

"Yes," replied Dr. Scala-Barnett.

The deputy coroner told the jury about the various clusters of stab wounds, counting six on the face, fifteen to the neck, and nine on the chest, including one straight through the heart. There had also been terrible internal injuries caused by the frenzied stabbing.

"How long could she survive after being stabbed like that?" asked Anderson.

"Probably no more than five to ten minutes," replied Dr. Scala-Barnett.

She then told the jury that Dr. Fazekas had found blood in the victim's left and right chest cavities, caused by internal bleeding.

"Now that tells you that Sister Pahl had a blood pressure when she received the stab wounds," explained the coroner, "or you wouldn't have the accumulation of blood."

"Are you able to determine whether she was strangled first or stabbed first?" asked Anderson.

"[Dr. Fazekas] doesn't actually address that," replied Dr. Scala-Barnett. "She says in her opinion, she died of stab wounds, and there was also evidence of strangulation."

"Are there any indications that she was alive and moving when she was being stabbed?" said Anderson.

"There was no indication of any movement," she replied. "If a person was alive and moving . . . you'd also expect defense wounds. If a person is conscious . . . fighting. Shielding themselves, or trying to grab the weapon."

"Were any defense wounds noted?" asked the assistant prosecutor.

"None," she replied.

Then Dr. Scala-Barnett read out Dr. Fazekas' reported cause of death in her April 1980 autopsy report.

" 'This seventy-one-year-old white female, Sister Margaret Ann Pahl, died of multiple—thirty-one—stab wounds to the left side of the face, neck and chest. There was also evidence of strangulation.' "

Then Dr. Scala-Barnett described her second autopsy on Sister Margaret Ann's remains in May 2004, after her body had been exhumed. A series of photographs of the body were then displayed on the electronic screen, causing some jurors to turn away.

"Believe it or not," Dr. Scala-Barnett told them, "twenty-four years later, you could still see many of the stab wounds in the actual skin and in the soft tissue."

The deputy coroner said she had gone through similar protocols to the first autopsy, starting with an external examination. Besides taking DNA samples, she had removed some small pieces of bone for later examination.

"We extracted teeth from the mandible," she explained, "because they are an excellent source of DNA. And we also took a scalp hair standard and a section of femur bone."

A few days later, Julie Saul examined the mandible and discovered a "small diamond-shaped defect." The prosecutor's office had then asked Dr. Scala-Barnett to conduct a test, determining if the letter opener could have caused it.

In the experiment, the tip of the letter opener blade was carefully placed in Sister Margaret Ann's mandible bone.

"It was a perfect fit," declared Dr. Scala-Barnett. "There was absolutely no damage to the bone. We did not alter the defect in any way."

"Based on your testing," asked Anderson, "did you draw a conclusion, based on a reasonable degree of scientific or medical certainty, as to what caused this injury to this mandible?"

"It was my conclusion," said the deputy coroner, "based on my experience, my knowledge, my training, that this weapon caused these injuries, or a weapon exactly like this."

After a ten-minute recess, defender John Thebes began his cross-examination, attempting to show that a larger man, like Father Swiatecki, had been the real killer.

He first projected a photograph of Sister Margaret Ann's body, taken in April 1980, on the screen.

"I believe it shows some bruising around her neck, does it not?" Thebes asked.

"It does," replied the deputy coroner.

"Would you agree with me, Doctor," continued the defender, "that those look like two very large hands around her neck?"

"Absolutely not," she declared.

THE NEXT WITNESS WAS FORENSIC ANTHROPOLOGIST JULIE Saul, of the Lucas County Coroner's office. The highly experienced expert underlined Dr. Scala-Barnett's opinion about the mandible fit test.

"The fit is very, very good," said Saul, who helped conduct the experiment. "The bone surrounds the blade very, very nicely. Very snugly."

Using slides to illustrate the experiment for the jury, Saul said that if the letter opener blade was tested in one direction, it fitted quite well.

"But then, when Dr. Barnett removed it and turned it one hundred and eighty degrees," she explained, "and then carefully put it within the defect, it just seemed to lock into place. And that's because it's not symmetrical. One side of the blade is a little longer because of [its] curve. And it just locked in when turned in that direction."

In his cross-examination, John Thebes asked if the letter opener was the only instrument tested in the mandible.

"Yes," said Saul.

"Not other objects?" continued the defender. "No other blades. No other items that had a blade. Correct?"

"That's true," said Saul. "That was the one that was brought to us as a possible weapon. We were not brought anything else."

CHAPTER THIRTY-EIGHT

Anointed in Blood

ON THE FOURTH DAY OF THE TRIAL, THE PROSECUTION
called Cassandra Agnosti to the stand. The forensic scientist
had examined all the DNA evidence relating to the cold case
when she was with the Ohio Bureau of Criminal Investigation and Identification, which she had recently left for personal reasons.

In an effort to disarm the defense's contention that foreign DNA found on Sister Margaret Ann's panties had come
from the real killer, Prosecutor Christopher Anderson seized
the initiative, immediately asking about it.

"I compared Gerald Robinson's DNA," Agnosti testified,
"and I excluded him as a contributor."

She said the trace amount of the foreign DNA was far too
small to develop a genetic profile, as one in eighty-three
Caucasians possessed this type.

Anderson then asked if the trace DNA on the victim's underwear could have come from any medical personnel or investigators coming into contact with the body.

"Four hundred thousand skin cells come off an average
person a day," he said. "Could the trace have been skin cells?"

"It could," agreed Agnosti.

"Could anyone [who] had been in the sacristy left that
DNA?" asked the prosecutor.

"Yes," said Agnosti. "Anybody [who] came into contact
with that particular item could have left the DNA."

"So people [who] transported the body out of the sacristy?"

"Yes. Anybody [who] could have been around the item."

Not surprisingly, in his cross-examination, John Thebes suggested that the unknown DNA belonged to Sister Margaret Ann's killer.

"There's other DNA on the underwear that is not consistent with him," declared the defender, pointing a finger at his client.

"That's correct," said Agnosti.

THE NEXT WITNESS WAS T. PAULETTE SUTTON, ONE OF JUST five people in the world certified in bloodstain-pattern transfer. The co-author of the definitive work on the subject, *Principles of Bloodstain Pattern Analysis: Theory and Practice*, would prove a powerful witness for the State.

Sutton told the jury she had first examined the bloody altar cloth and Father Robinson's letter opener on March 12, 2004, at her laboratory at the University of Tennessee in Memphis. After a cursory examination, she believed that some of the blood transfer stains matched Father Robinson's letter opener.

Then, using photographs, diagrams and charts, Sutton showed the jury blood transfer patterns on the altar cloth and Sister Margaret Ann Pahl's clothing. Over the next 100 minutes, Sutton held their rapt attention, demonstrating various transfer patterns and how they related to the letter opener.

The jurors paid special attention to a faint reddish-brown nickel-sized stain on the altar cloth that Sutton said mirrored the Capitol building outline on the letter opener's souvenir medallion.

"If another object made it," she testified, "it would have to basically be the same shape, same size and same configuration."

She then laid a transparency of the medallion over the stain on the altar cloth, pointing out several instances where the bloody lines actually defined the domed roof of the Capitol building, complete with columns.

"I believe the medallion is consistent with the object that created [this transfer pattern]," she declared.

Not only that, she said, but there was a semicircular bloodstain on Sister Margaret Ann's forehead, matching another part of the letter opener.

"[It] is certainly consistent," she told the jury, referring to a projected image of the stain on the screen in front of the jury box. "You can see the stars imprinted in."

Sutton said the killer had actually pressed the bloody handle of the letter opener into his victim's forehead.

In cross-examination, John Thebes suggested the circular blood transfer on the sister's forehead could have been caused by a doctor's stethoscope.

"Now when Sister was found in a hospital," he said, "doctors rushed to her aid. Certainly doctors have stethoscopes. Do you know what they are?"

"Yes, sir, I do," replied the doctor.

"And they're kind of circular at the end. So can you rule out a stethoscope as making that transfer pattern?"

"No, sir, I [can] not," replied Dr. Sutton.

THE PROSECUTION'S THIRD EXPERT WAS DR. STEVEN SYMES, a renowned anthropologist and a professor at Mercyhurst College in Pennsylvania. He had been called in by Julie Saul to recheck her findings that the tip of the letter opener "perfectly fitted" the tiny defect in the victim's mandible bone.

He admitted to being "somewhat skeptical" at the beginning, and even after testing, still had reservations.

"It is a nice fit," he told Christopher Anderson. "But this is anything but definitive evidence. We're just dealing in class characteristics."

In cross-examination, defender Thebes zeroed in on Dr. Symes' less-than-certain opinion.

"A single defect two millimeters in diameter in bone," he stated, "provides anything but definitive evidence?"

"Correct," said Dr. Symes.

" 'Definitive' means?" asked the defender.

"There's nothing there by class characteristics," replied the forensic anthropologist. "And it's very small."

"It's not conclusive, correct?" contended Thebes.

"That's correct," conceded Dr. Symes.

ON THURSDAY, APRIL 27 — DAY FIVE OF THE TRIAL — DR. Henry Lee took the stand. In just forty minutes, the world-famous Taiwanese-born forensic investigator would tell the jury his conclusions of how Sister Margaret Ann Pahl had been murdered.

Charming and charismatic, Dr. Lee began by telling Christopher Anderson he couldn't remember which Toledo detective had initially approached him, as "all Caucasians look alike."

When Prosecutor Anderson asked him to inspect some 1980 black-and-white crime-scene photographs, Dr. Lee opened his briefcase, bringing out an oversized magnifying glass.

"Doctor," asked Anderson, "do you always carry a magnifying glass, or are you just prepared for this court?"

"I always carry one," he replied. "They're my basic tool. You don't know when you're going to be called to a crime scene to examine evidence. [It's] impossible to carry a microscope around."

During often-riveting testimony, Dr. Lee displayed photographs of the altar cloth bloodstains on the large flat screen, pointing out similarities between transfer patterns and the letter opener. He told the jury that certain elements of an image in one of the bloodstains could have been made by the Capitol building medallion on the letter opener.

"I cannot exclude it," he said. "It is consistent. I cannot come here to tell you this pattern is produced exactly by this. I can only say similar to."

He believed Sister Margaret Ann had been murdered in a "quick attack," and probably strangled before being stabbed.

"She was not standing up," he declared. "If she was standing, we should see vertical blood drops and see blood running down. . . . Some of the blood patterns were running against gravity. In one direction and then in the other direction, which is consistent with the body, the face especially."

John Thebes' cross-examination was extremely brief.

"Just so we are clear," said Thebes, "your opinions today in court are ones of similarity and consistency, correct?"

"Correct," agreed Dr. Lee.

Then after asking if his report was "accurate and thorough in all respects," the defense had no further questions.

ON FRIDAY MORNING, THE PROSECUTION CALLED WITNESSES to show Sister Margaret Ann's state of mind at the time of her murder. Her former cleaning woman, Shirley Lucas, testified that just hours before her murder, the sister had been distraught after the Good Friday Mass had been shortened.

Lucas said that Sister Margaret Ann had burst into tears outside the chapel, asking, "Why do they cheat God out of what belongs to him?"

"She squeezed my hand," testified Lucas, "and turned around and walked away."

Another housekeeper named Valerie Berning testified how she had been ordered to clean up the chapel and sacristy several hours after the murder.

"There was a lot of blood on the floor," she told the jury.

She had also cleaned Father Robinson's two rooms several times before the murder, observing the dagger-shaped letter opener on his desk.

"It was long and had a large handle," she told the jury.

Then Assistant Prosecutor Larry Kiroff showed her the letter opener, asking if it was in the same condition as she had last seen it.

"As I can remember it," she said, suddenly becoming emotional. "When I see the letter opener, I just had a bad feeling and I walked out of the room."

Former janitor Wardell Langston then testified how he and receptionist Margaret Warren had both heard "running feet" at about 7:30 a.m. Holy Saturday morning. The "frantic" footsteps had been along an overhead pathway, leading from the main part of the hospital, housing the chapel, to the professional building where Father Robinson lived.

"It was kind of odd," he testified, "because most of the building was empty."

In cross-examination, Alan Konop pressed him as to exactly where the footsteps stopped, with Langston admitting he was uncertain if they had gone to Father Robinson's quarters or stopped earlier. This was a blow to the prosecution, as he had never expressed any previous reservations about them finishing up at the defendant's door.

CHAPTER THIRTY-NINE
"Violated in the Most Violent Kind of Way"

AS THE TRIAL FINISHED ITS FIRST WEEK, PRESS COVERAGE reached saturation point, threatening to turn it into a three-ring circus. Dozens of reporters from all over the world had descended on Toledo, working the story from every conceivable angle.

Court TV was broadcasting the complete trial to thousands of viewers coast to coast, with legal experts dissecting the action like a sporting event. All four local network affiliates devoted hours of daily coverage to the case. The major players became instant celebrities in Toledo.

"We didn't like the publicity," explained Lucas County Prosecutor Julia Bates. "We would have preferred no cameras, no reporters, no Court TV. None of that. Just let us do our job. [We didn't need that] constant barrage of Monday morning quarterbacking that went on."

From the outset of the trial, Bates told her team to avoid seeing any television coverage.

"I told the team, 'Don't watch that stuff,'" explained Bates. "'Don't second-guess yourself.' There's been a lot of commentary over the years about what happened in the O. J. Simpson [trial]. That the prosecutors lost their way and the message got lost because they spent too much time trying to prove that Detective Fuhrman was or was not a racist, instead of trying to prove that O. J. Simpson was or was not a murderer.

"My guys are good," she said. "I said, 'Stay on message. It doesn't matter what the media says. Stay on message.'"

Lead prosecutor Dean Mandross had already worked one homicide case broadcast by Court TV, but even he was not prepared for such intense interest.

"It was worldwide," he said. "It was reported literally around the world. And the power of television . . . But it didn't get to me, because my family wouldn't let it."

Mandross avoided all local news programs, saying he saw "maybe three minutes of Court TV" throughout the entire trial.

But the prosecution's biggest concern was the unsequestered jury being exposed to any television and Internet coverage.

"That was our fear," explained Prosecutor Bates. "That they were going to get stuff."

None of the defense or the prosecution attorneys were talking to the media because of the gag order. But others were.

"There were fringe people," explained Bates, "and some of the stuff they were talking about was pretty far-out. So that stuff gets in the paper. Gets on TV. It somehow filters its way back to the jury. That was the fear for us. We wanted to keep them pristine, so they only heard the evidence from the trial. Not the nonsense that was going on outside."

THERE WAS AN AIR OF ANTICIPATION ON MONDAY MORNING, May 1, when lead prosecutor Dean Mandross called Father Jeffrey Grob to the stand. The Chicago archdiocesan priest had written a doctoral dissertation on the history of modern exorcisms, and is nationally recognized as an expert in unorthodox religious practices.

And while his colleague Christopher Anderson questioned Father Grob about the Satanic significance of the murder, Dean Mandross scrutinized the defendant for any hint of emotion.

As usual, Father Robinson seemed totally unfazed, chatting with his supporters by the defense bench and sharing the occasional joke. But as soon as the jury entered, he would become his usual dispassionate self.

"There was much discussion about his demeanor," Mandross later said. "He was so unemotional."

After a couple of days, the lead prosecutor observed how Father Robinson would talk to his supporters, often becoming "animated" during jury breaks.

"They must have been trying to keep his spirits up," he said, "because he was laughing at certain times."

But Mandross saw the dramatic change that came over the defendant when the jury entered the courtroom.

"My personal opinion," he said, "is that he was able to almost remove himself from the room. Almost like he was meditating and could take himself away. He was just able to disembody."

ANDERSON FIRST ASKED GROB IF THE SISTER'S KILLER would possess specialized knowledge of "ritual practices."

"Certainly," replied Father Grob, "a priest would have had that kind of knowledge, possibly a seminarian. All these things have deep symbolic meanings."

The soft-spoken bespectacled exorcist told the jury it was highly significant that the murder had taken place on Holy Saturday in the sacristy, where the Eucharist had been temporarily moved, making it *the* holiest place.

Asked by Anderson to detail ritual aspects of the murder, Father Grob sighed and threw up his hands, declaring, "Where does one begin?"

Explaining the significance of the inverted cross to the murder, Father Grob told the parable of St. Peter, who felt unworthy to die like Jesus, asking for the crucifix to be inverted.

"It's an effrontery to God," explained Father Grob, holding his crucifix upside down for the jury. "And if you want further proof, for those who are computer literate, go do a Google."

Father Grob told the jury that Sister Margaret Ann Pahl had been murdered on a deeply significant Catholic holy day, the middle of three days of services, culminating with Easter.

The prosecutor then displayed a photograph of the sister's

body, clearly showing a small semicircle of blood on her forehead, asking what it meant.

Father Grob theorized that the killer had performed a "perverse" version of last rites, using the sister's own blood to anoint her, instead of oil, as in the Catholic sacrament.

"It's a reversal," he explained to the jury, four of whom were Catholics. "Normally, what should be a good Catholic person going to meet God, getting anointed, is now all of a sudden a mocking. [She is] anointed with blood, her own blood."

Attempting to mitigate damage caused by Father Grob's testimony, John Thebes had the priest admit he had never seen a crime scene before. He also acknowledged that doctors and nurses from the "Mr. Swift" team may have moved the victim's body before it was photographed, and that blood on the sister's forehead did not prove someone had made the sign of the cross.

AFTER A SHORT RECESS, JURORS WERE SHOWN DETECTIVE Tom Ross's eighty-minute interview with Father Robinson on the night of his arrest. It would be the only time the jury would hear Father Robinson speak during the entire trial.

In the interrogation, Father Robinson claimed to have woken up and was drying off after a shower, when he received a phone call informing him of Sister Margaret Ann's death. He also maintained he had not been anywhere near the chapel at the time of the murder.

"I was not there," he told Detective Ross.

The jury heard Father Robinson acknowledge being accused of the murder by Father Swiatecki, telling the detective he had been stunned by the accusation. The priest said he had no idea what Swiatecki was talking about.

Then, pressing him further, Detective Ross asked how he could have just stood there and done nothing.

"But I'm not one to answer," replied Father Robinson. "I'm a calm and not a forceful person. That's my choice."

"What?" said Ross incredulously, "Are you going to stand there and take it?"

"Well, I took a lot," replied the priest cryptically.

Toward the end of the videotaped interview, the detective left the room with the recorder still on. The jury watched the screen, as the anguished priest lowered his head into his hands and bent over the table.

"Oh, my Jesus," he began mumbling, apparently in prayer, almost inaudibly. "Sister, won't you come through for me? Please. Won't you?"

As the videotape played, jurors listened intently, some staring over at Father Robinson to see his reaction. But he just stared blankly into midair, as if on another planet.

AFTER A SHORT RECESS, SERGEANT STEVE FORRESTER TOOK the stand. The youthful-looking boss of the Lucas County Cold Case Task Force told of his first interview with Sister Annie Louise, soon after the case was resurrected.

"One of the things that [she] told me," Sergeant Forrester told the jury, "was that we should be looking for an upside-down cross on the victim's chest."

Lead prosecutor Dean Mandross then methodically led Forrester through the complex chain of investigation, leading to Father Robinson's arrest. Forrester said the turning point had been Detective Terry Cousino's fresh look at the bloodstained altar cloth.

"He recognized the transfer patterns," said Forrester, "and he demonstrated those to us in a way that we had never guessed."

Other compelling evidence against the priest included two witnesses hearing "frantic footsteps" leading to his room, and that he knew the victim.

"This is overkill," said Forrester, referring to the huge number of stab wounds, "which is typical of someone who knows the victim."

In cross-examination, Alan Konop tried to trip up the detective about precise timing and places of several interviews.

Konop demanded to know why Forrester had not written reports about his interviews with T. Paulette Sutton and Dr. Scala-Barnett.

"Are we on the same wavelength?" a visibly frustrated Konop asked at one point after a heated altercation. "Sometimes we're not on the same wavelength."

"Sometimes we're not, Mr. Konop," agreed the detective calmly.

Then Konop turned to Father Grob's analysis of the inverted cross.

"As to that interview," began Konop, "I take it there was nothing with that person that indicated to you that Father Robinson was involved with inverted crosses?"

"I'm sorry, you've lost me," replied the detective.

"Sometimes I get a little ahead of myself," admitted Konop. "So his name didn't come up as to that issue?"

"Not directly," said Sergeant Forrester. "No."

AFTER A TWO-DAY DELAY TO ACCOMMODATE OUT-OF-STATE witnesses, the trial resumed on Thursday, May 4. The State, now nearing the end of its case, called three powerful witnesses to testify to having seen Father Gerald Robinson near the chapel around the time of the murder.

Leslie Kerner, a former EKG technician, told the jury that she'd seen Robinson by the chapel doors about 6:50 a.m., one hour before Sister Margaret Ann Pahl's body was discovered.

"He had dark clothing on," she testified.

Under Konop's cross-examination, Kerner admitted she was unsure whether the priest had been entering or leaving the chapel. Then the defender read out a 1980 police report, asking why Kerner had told investigators that she had not seen anyone in the hallway. She replied that she had not mentioned Father Robinson at the time, as she'd merely been asked if she had seen anything unusual.

When questioned on how she could be certain she hadn't seen the other hospital chaplain coming out of the chapel, Kerner replied, "Because Father Robinson was shorter and had more hair, and Father Swiatecki was larger and didn't have much hair."

A particularly strong witness for the prosecution was

Grace Jones, a wheelchair-bound African-American woman. The former Mercy Hospital laboratory worker testified that she had been waiting for an elevator when Father Robinson came out of the chapel and walked straight past her. Although she could not remember the exact time, she was certain it was before Sister Margaret Ann's body had been found.

"He had a duffle bag in his hand," she told the jury. "I nodded, and then he nodded, and then went on."

Then Dr. Jack Baron, chief resident at Mercy Hospital at the time of the murder, testified of responding to the 8:15 a.m. "Mr. Swift" call. He said he had taken a wrong turn and gone past the chapel, when he'd seen a man with a priest's collar and black clerical clothes walking toward it.

"He was within ten feet of me," testified Dr. Baron, "looking over his shoulder and going in the opposite direction. I'll never forget the stare that just kind of went right through me. He didn't say a word, and continued in the opposite direction."

Dr. Baron, who now runs a family practice in Florida, said he had told investigators at the time about seeing a priest near the chapel, but they had appeared uninterested and had never followed up.

The State's final witness was investigator Tom Ross. The heavily-built white-haired veteran detective, who had worked on almost 350 homicides during his nearly forty-year career in law enforcement, told the jury about the Lucas County cold case task force.

"Most of us have seen it on television," he explained. "We try to apply new technology to old cases."

He then described the historic cold case meeting in early December 2003, when Sister Annie Louise's letter naming Father Robinson was first mentioned.

"It was a name well known," Detective Ross told the jury. "We decided to review the case notes and case reports from 1980 . . . and then physically look at the evidence."

Guided by Dean Mandross, Detective Ross led the jury through the course of the investigation, culminating in Father

Robinson's arrest and subsequent interrogation on April 23, 2004.

Mandross then asked if there were any inconsistencies between what the defendant had previously told police and his videotaped statement. Ross said there were many inconsistencies, and Mandross started playing selections of the tape so Ross could illustrate.

Initially, Father Robinson had claimed that, after he'd received Sister Phyllis Ann Gerold's phone call, he "just quickly dressed up. Didn't finish anything else and ran. I put the cassock on and ran." But after Ross informed him that several witnesses had heard running footsteps near his quarters, he changed his story, saying he had been walking.

"I had a cassock on," he had told Ross. "I couldn't be running in that."

Then Mandross asked the detective about these inconsistencies.

"When we began talking about the running footsteps that the janitor and the receptionist heard," said Detective Ross, "he changes to 'walking' because of the long cassock. It's no longer 'running.'"

Another important discrepancy involved the keys to his quarters. During his first interview at his residence, he had told Ross and Forrester that he kept his residence locked.

"And did that position appear to change during the second interview?" asked Mandross.

"It did," replied Ross.

The pertinent extract of the tape was then played for the jury, where Ross asked if he kept his residence locked, and the priest seemed unsure how to answer, finally saying he did not.

"Do you have an estimate of how many seconds passed," asked Mandross, "before he can formulate a response to that?"

"I'd say at least five seconds," replied the detective.

In his cross-examination, Alan Konop zeroed in on the highly damaging videotaped interview.

"When Father went into the interrogation room," asked the defender, "he's not told it's being taped?"

"He's not," replied Ross.

Telling the jury he was "bringing in low-tech," Konop then played an enhanced version of when the priest was left alone in the interrogation room at the end of the interview.

After playing the extract to the jury, Konop asked Ross what he had heard and Ross admitted not being able to make out what Father Robinson had been mumbling.

Konop then showed the detective a Toledo *Blade* article from April 9, 1980, quoting from Father Swiatecki's homily at Sister Margaret Ann's funeral where the late priest apparently admitted being the celebrant of the Good Friday service, so upsetting Sister Margaret Ann.

Konop asked if it would be fair to say that Father Swiatecki had delivered the Good Friday service.

"Yes," admitted the detective.

Then Judge Osowik excused Detective Ross from the stand and Dean Mandross officially rested the State's case against Father Gerald Robinson. Over seven days of testimony, the prosecution had called a total of thirty-one witnesses, the exact same number of stab wounds inflicted on Sister Margaret Ann Pahl.

CHAPTER FORTY

The Defense

AT 8:45 A.M. FRIDAY MORNING, ALAN KONOP LAUNCHED HIS
defense by recalling Sergeant Steve Forrester to the stand.
For most of the first day, the lead defender would attempt
damage control for the three ex–Mercy Hospital employees'
damning testimony about seeing Father Robinson near the
chapel at the time of the murder.

He immediately attacked Sergeant Forrester for blatant
omissions and discrepancies between court testimony by
Leslie Kerner, Grace Jones and Dr. Jack Baron, and police
reports from both the 1980 and 2004/2005 investigations.

Under Konop's relentless questioning, Forrester agreed
that the 1980 police reports made no mention of Dr. Baron
making a wrong turn on the way to the chapel, or receiving a
cold stare from Father Robinson.

The defender also highlighted discrepancies in former
laboratory worker Grace Jones' timing of events, varying by
more than an hour in her several police interviews.

Konop also focused on Jones' uncertainty of whether Father Robinson was disappearing down a hallway, or walking
out through exit doors.

"Initially, she said she'd gone out the Madison Street [sic]
door!" snapped Konop. "Initially, that's what she said! Father Robinson is charged with murder, is that correct? Isn't it
vitally important to be as accurate as possible?"

"You've asked me that question a lot," replied Sergeant
Forrester, losing patience. "And I've answered it a lot. I try
to be as accurate as I can."

Then Konop asked about Leslie Kerner first contacting investigators in spring 2004.

"Any problems with that?" he demanded to know.

"I don't think you'd lie to me," answered Sergeant Forrester, sending a ripple of laughter through the courtroom."

Most of the remaining defense witnesses would be former police officers, a ploy playing right into the hands of the prosecution. Dean Mandross, who teaches trial practice, would later maintain he felt so confident about the State's case that he took a strategic decision not to call many of the original 1980 detectives.

"We felt that if we didn't call them, the defense would," he explained. "And that would give us an advantage. For when I call a witness, I can only use direct questioning and not any leading questions. But if they call a witness, when I cross-examine them, I can use leading questions. So I can control the testimony a thousand times more. The cross-examination is, in effect, the lawyer's opportunity to testify."

And Mandross' strategy began to pay off with the next defense witness, retired Detective Dave Weinbrecht, who had conducted the second search of the defendant's quarters. Alan Konop aggressively questioned Weinbrecht about a pair of scissors that had gone missing from the chapel after the murder.

"Sister Kathleen Mary did approach me back in 1980," agreed the ex-detective. "She reported to me that a pair of scissors was missing from the chapel."

The nun had then given him a similar pair of scissors, used for trimming candle wicks, which he'd brought to Deputy Coroner Renate Fazekas for testing.

"She had sample pieces of flesh preserved from the victim," asked Konop, "as well as photographs and slides? Is that correct?"

When Weinbrecht agreed it was, Konop noted that Dr. Fazekas had stabbed the sample flesh with the scissors, comparing the results to crime-scene photographs.

"You were there when the doctor rendered her opinion?" asked Konop.

"Yes, I was," replied Weinbrecht. "She stated that wounds on the victim's face appeared to have been made with a weapon sharper than the scissors."

In cross-examination, Mandross asked if Dr. Fazekas had ever seen the letter opener, rendering an opinion as to it being the murder weapon, after conducting test cuts.

"Yes, she did," replied Weinbrecht. "And her conclusion was that the [letter opener] was compatible with each of the wounds found in the body, and could have been the weapon used."

The defense next called Detective Art Marx to testify. The now balding lead detective in the 1980 investigation had prepared most of the police reports, and twice interrogated Father Robinson.

Konop immediately went on the attack, demanding to know why certain reports, including notes from Fathers Robinson's and Swiatecki's interviews, were missing.

"*Unavailable*," corrected Marx.

Konop then asked what had happened to them.

"I have no idea," shrugged Marx. "I can't tell you. It's been twenty-six years."

"And you said you wrote a report?" asked Konop, dismissively.

"I know I did," said the former detective.

Then Konop accused Marx of sloppy police work. He criticized the 1980 investigation for not looking for blood or fingerprint trace evidence in Father Robinson's room, on the doors of the sacristy and in other obvious places. In a heated exchange, he demanded to know why Marx had not had police crime lab technicians use chemicals to search the sacristy for clues.

"I don't even know if we had chemicals in 1980," Marx deadpanned.

"This is an important case, call someone up!" shouted the defender, asking sarcastically if he'd had a telephone in 1980.

In his cross-examination, Dean Mandross deftly steered his questions to any possible collusion between the Toledo

Police Department and the Catholic Diocese in protecting Father Robinson for so many years.

He asked if the last person with access to all the missing reports was Deputy Chief Ray Vetter.

"To my knowledge, yes," replied Marx.

"And this is the individual," continued Mandross, attempting to send a message to the jury, "who brought Monsignor Schmit and interrupted your interview with the defendant?"

"Same person, yes," confirmed Marx.

"Deputy Chief Vetter. Do you know if he's Catholic or not?" asked Mandross.

"Yes," said the former lead detective. "A very strict Catholic."

Then Mandross asked Marx his reaction to Father Robinson's recanted 1980 claim that he had taken the murderer's confession.

"I said, 'Someone confessed to you?'" Marx told the jury. "'Was it a male? Was it a female?' I kind of pressured him to give me some answers about who did this. And that's when he told me it wasn't the truth. He'd made this up to protect himself."

THROUGHOUT THE TRIAL THERE HAD BEEN MUCH DISCUS-sion amongst Court TV pundits about Alan Konop's effectiveness at trial. One of the cable TV channel's anchors had labeled his opening statements "namby-pamby." Another court-watcher questioned why the well-regarded Toledo defense attorney had never once told the jury that Father Robinson was innocent, calling the case a question of reasonable doubt.

Alan Konop did often seem ill-prepared during crucial questioning of witnesses. And on several occasions he brought the trial to a halt, fumbling through notes and files in order to make a relevant point.

On Friday afternoon, Court TV anchor Ashleigh Banfield cynically remarked that the "vibrancy" usually associated with Cinco de Mayo was missing from the courtroom that day.

Later, when contacted by the Toledo *Blade* to elaborate, Banfield backpedaled.

"Overall, the defense has done an admirable job in a very difficult case," she explained diplomatically.

ON MONDAY, MAY 8, THE DEFENSE CALLED DEPUTY CHIEF Ray Vetter to the stand. The 82-year-old devout Catholic had been criticized for years over his handling of Sister Margaret Ann Pahl's homicide investigation.

Under Konop's direct examination, Vetter vehemently denied ever allowing his faith to interfere with his police work.

"My job came first," he told the jury.

But he did admit asking his "close personal friend," Monsignor Schmit, to talk to Father Robinson, see what he could discover and then report back.

When questioned about halting Father Robinson's second 1980 police interrogation, Vetter could not recall anything about it.

But he did admit collecting Monsignor Schmit that day, and bringing him to the Safety Building, so he could speak to Father Robinson.

"It was twenty-six years ago," he explained.

"You did the very best job you could in this case, is that correct?" asked Konop.

"Tried to," said the former deputy chief.

"It wasn't a Catholic investigation?"

"It was a police investigation of murder," said Vetter.

During cross-examination, Dean Mandross suddenly produced a letter that Father Ray Fisher had written to the late Bishop John Donovan, then in charge of the Catholic Diocese of Toledo. The letter had been seized from the Catholic Diocese several years earlier under a search warrant.

Mandross then read out several portions of Father Fisher's letter, claiming Deputy Chief Vetter had given a personal assurance that the Toledo Police Department "has remained silent about their suspicions" of Father Robinson. It also mentioned that Father Swiatecki had told people at Mercy Hospital that Father Robinson was a suspect in the murder.

Father Fisher's letter to Bishop Donovan also claimed that Monsignor Schmit had been warned that Vetter said he would have to take information to the prosecutor, who would ultimately decide if Father Robinson should be charged. Father Robinson's lie about Sister Margaret Ann's real killer confessing to him was also mentioned.

Vetter told Mandross that he would only state facts about a case and never suspicions.

On re-direct, Alan Konop asked about the letter and whether he had protected Father Robinson.

"Absolutely not," Vetter replied resolutely.

AFTER MORNING RECESS, THE DEFENSE CALLED ITS STAR witness, Kathleen Reichs, the nationally recognized forensic anthropologist, best-selling crime author and inspiration for the Fox-TV prime-time hit show *Bones*.

"I'm fairly distinguished," the blonde scientist with laboratories in Charlotte, North Carolina, and Montreal, Quebec, told the jury.

First she explained that she wrote fiction under the name "Kathy Reichs," but used her full name, "Kathleen J. Reichs, Ph.D.," for her forensic work.

Dr. Reichs said she had studied the late Dr. Renate Fazeka's autopsy report, the 1980 police reports, Dr. Diana Scala-Barnett's exhumation report, and the skeletal analyses by Julie and Frank Saul. She'd also received Dr. Steven Symes' report, along with his photographs of the mandible and other bones.

Then John Thebes asked her professional opinion on the experiment of placing the tip of the letter opener into Sister Margaret Ann's mandible bone.

"In my opinion," said Dr. Reichs, "you would never do that, because of the potential for damage or modification of the defect."

"You did not look at that mandible itself?" asked Thebes. "Why?"

"Given that something was inserted into it at least once," she replied, "any analysis subsequent to that becomes compromised. You don't know if damage was done at the time that the object was stuck in there. So for me to look at it would be irrelevant."

In cross-examination, Assistant Prosecutor Christopher Anderson asked Dr. Reichs if she had actually examined any of the evidence firsthand. She admitted she had not.

"Is it normally a protocol for anthropology," asked Anderson, "if you're given a problem, you define it, and then take steps towards analyzing it or coming up with a solution?"

"Yes," she replied.

"And normally that involves viewing or handling the actual material?"

"Most cases," said the forensic anthropologist. "Not all cases. Sometimes you might work from images."

"How many times have you testified in court strictly from images?" asked the prosecutor.

"I've never testified strictly from images," she admitted.

"This is the first one?" asked Anderson, turning toward the jury.

"I'm testifying here on protocol and methodology," she stated.

"You're not testifying as to the results?"

"No."

The defense then rested its case after less than two days of testimony and just eleven witnesses, one third as many as the prosecution's.

Immediately the state recalled Lieutenant Bill Kina to the stand as a rebuttal witness.

Kina testified that he had been "livid" when Deputy Chief Vetter had walked into his interrogation with Monsignor Schmit and stopped it.

He also testified that Vetter had ordered all three copies of the police reports to be given to him, many of which have since disappeared. Kina testified that his boss kept a locked file cabinet in his office, containing all sensitive police reports. The question of how those files were lost has never been answered.

ON TUESDAY MORNING, ATTORNEYS FROM BOTH SIDES WERE back in the courtroom, finalizing Judge Osowik's jury instructions. As the State's case relied heavily on circumstantial evidence, the defense urged the judge to adopt a law in effect in 1980, where a jury would be told not to convict on circumstantial evidence alone, if there was a reasonable theory of innocence. That was changed in the 1990s, and now juries are instructed that circumstantial evidence carries as much weight as direct evidence.

"Certainly," defender John Thebes told the judge, "part of the defense is going to be that the circumstances presented in court are wholly inconsistent with the State's theory in this case. You have, as the judge, discretion in order to give this instruction. The crime occurred in 1980. This was the instruction given in 1980."

But Assistant Prosecutor Christopher Anderson said the court must use the revised instruction.

"He's asking you to give an instruction on the law that has been overruled," said Anderson. "It was found to be improper."

Judge Osowik sided with the prosecution, saying he would apply the current law regarding jury instructions.

"If it was declared invalid," he said, "how do we keep it in?"

CHAPTER FORTY-ONE

"He Wasn't Going to Take Any More"

ON WEDNESDAY, MAY 10, JUDGE THOMAS OSOWIK'S COURT-room was "standing room only" for closing arguments. All forty-five seats in the public gallery were packed by re-porters, representatives of the Sisters of Mercy order and cu-rious members of the public. Also present were Thomas and Barbara Robinson and Father Robinson's supporters, sitting across the courtroom from Lee Pahl and Claudia Vercellotti and other members of SNAP.

Court TV and all four local television stations would broadcast it live, and there was much activity as cameras were set up and audio equipment checked.

But before the closing arguments could begin, the prose-cution called two more rebuttal witnesses, challenging Dr. Kathleen Reichs' assertion that Sister Margaret Ann Pahl's mandible bone had been damaged by inserting the letter opener in the fit test.

First, Lucas County Deputy Coroner Dr. Diane Scala-Barnett returned to the stand, telling jurors that the mandible bone was so hard, she had needed a power saw to remove it. She testified that she had performed the test between fifty and sixty times in her career, and was confident the bone had not been contaminated in any way.

"Dr. Reichs presumed that I may have altered the defect," she told Prosecutor Christopher Anderson. "Scientists don't presume. They test."

The next rebuttal witness was forensic anthropologist Julie Saul, who stated that the fit test conducted on the mandible was carefully conducted and had not damaged it in any way.

Then, taking a swipe at the defense's expert, Anderson asked if it was possible to reach a scientific conclusion by just examining photographs and reports. "How important is it for a forensic anthropologist to review the bone?"

"It's very, very important to do this in person," replied Saul.

Shortly before 10:00 a.m., Judge Osowik dismissed the jury for a brief recess before the start of closing arguments.

A FEW MINUTES LATER—AFTER THE SIXTEEN JURORS HAD reentered the jury box—Dean Mandross strode out to the front of the courtroom to deliver his closing argument. Dressed in a somber black suit and plain striped tie, it would be the lead prosecutor's final address to the jury, and he'd prepared it well.

Once again he would take every opportunity to project an old photograph of the young and powerful Father Gerald Robinson, hoping the jury would relate to that image, rather than the feeble-looking figure now cradling his head at the defense table.

"This is not a case that can be tried without talking about God and religion," he began, clasping his hands behind his back. "And after all, we have a Roman Catholic priest as a defendant, a Roman Catholic nun as a victim. So whether you believe in God or providence or destiny or fate, it may be that this was a case that had to wait twenty-six years before it could be fairly tried."

In 1980, he told the jury, it was "doubtful" that twelve people could have been found who could accept that a priest was capable of murder.

"It just may be that we had to wait until 2006," he told them, "for you folks to decide this case."

The prosecutor then told the jurors that although twenty-six years was a long time, witnesses did remember significant details of major events in their lives, such as a nun being killed at their workplace.

"Some things don't really change with the passage of time," he said. "And the heart of the State's case is just the same now as it was on April fifth, 1980. The letter opener is just the same now as it was back in April of 1980, when it was put in that police property room, where it stayed for some twenty-four years. This altar cloth, these stains are just the same."

Mandross then reviewed the physical evidence proving that the defendant had murdered Sister Margaret Ann Pahl. He told the jury that Father Robinson's letter opener, found at his apartment, had been used to stab Sister Margaret Ann repeatedly. The proof, he said, was the "diamond-shaped hole" in her mandible, which three experts had testified was a perfect fit with the blade tip of the letter opener.

Moving to the blood transfer evidence, Mandross said that the State had sought the help of Paulette Sutton and Dr. Henry Lee, two of the world's top five experts.

"And they both testified about something exceptionally unique," said Mandross, projecting an enlarged photograph of the letter opener medallion onto the large digital screen in front of the jury box.

"The U.S. Capitol building," declared Mandross. "You can see the dome. You can see the rectangle."

He asked the jury to pay particular attention in deliberations to the two exhibit photographs, showing the semicircular smear of blood on Sister Margaret Ann's forehead.

"You look," he told them. "Because you can clearly see the top of the dome that matches the emblem. You can see the rectangle of that building. Study these, because these two photographs, perhaps more than any other item of evidence, prove that that was the murder weapon."

Mandross told the jury that in 1980, the Toledo Police Department had accounted for everyone at Mercy Hospital at the time of the murder, with the sole exception of Father Robinson.

"Now if you don't think he's the murderer," Mandross said, looking straight at the defendant, who displayed absolutely no emotion, "then you believe in an amazing series of coincidences that have to be called mind-boggling. First you have to believe it's just a coincidence that he's the only one with religious training [who] can't be accounted for. You recall the testimony of Father Jeffrey Grob, who took the stand and told you about the significance of what he felt took place in the sacristy, that only someone, maybe a nun or maybe a priest, would understand."

Mandross then asked if it was coincidence that Sister Margaret Ann was upset eighteen hours before her murder, after Good Friday Mass had been shortened. And was it a coincidence that a bloodstain on the altar cloth matched his letter opener?

"Is he just the victim of more bad luck?" asked Mandross.

Then the deputy prosecutor called the jury's attention to Father Robinson's initial claim to Detective Art Marx that someone had confessed committing the murder to him.

"That false confession," declared Mandross, pointing at the defendant, "that story, he made up. 'Well, I know who the killer was. He just confessed to me.' And then when Detective Marx called him on it, he said, 'Well, all right. No, that really didn't happen.'

"Now we don't expect priests to kill, do we? But do we expect them to lie to the police during a murder investigation? Who lies to the police during a murder investigation? Maybe the one [who] did the crime."

Then Mandross said that although the State did not have to provide a motive, he was going to suggest a possible one.

"Is this some sort of Satanic cult killing? No. Was this part of some ritualistic black Mass? No. Sorry to disappoint. This case is about perhaps the most common scenario there is for a homicide. A man got very angry at a woman and the woman died. The only difference is, the man wore a white collar and the woman wore a habit."

Mandross told the jurors that in April 1980, Father Robinson had been at Mercy Hospital about six years, giving last rites almost daily.

"His world was about darkness and death," he said. "So who could blame him if he didn't want to be there?"

And Mandross urged the jury to listen again to his video-taped interview with Detective Ross to gain real understanding into Father Robinson's mindset at the time of the murder.

"He said, 'It's their hospital. I just worked there.' Listen to that statement. Find it. Play it over and over."

Turning to Father Robinson's relationship with Sister Margaret Ann, Mandross noted that during the 1980 investigation, he had told a detective she had a "dominating personality."

"Now does that give you some insight in terms of their relationship?" he asked the jury.

Another clue to Father Robinson's state of mind during this period, said Mandross, was the reason he had given Detective Ross for his lack of assertiveness, when Father Swiatecki publicly accused him of the killing.

"The defendant's response is, 'I took a lot,'" said Mandross, his voice rising with every word. "That's what he says, 'Well, I took a lot.'

"In less than eighteen hours after Sister's interaction with Shirley Lucas, she's found butchered on the sacristy floor. He had had enough. The man had decided he had had enough. He had taken a lot and he wasn't going to take any more and he knew where Sister Margaret Ann Pahl would be that morning. The others may sleep in, but not Sister Margaret Ann Pahl. She would be up and she would be out early."

Then the lead prosecutor gave the jury the State's version of what had happened that 1980 Holy Saturday morning.

Father Robinson had slipped into the chapel and locked the door behind him, just before 7:00 a.m., before entering the sacristy, where Sister Margaret Ann was preparing the altar.

"He came up to her," he told the jury. "He wouldn't even have had to sneak up on her. They knew each other. And he got behind her and he choked her down, either with his arm or a ligature—that altar cloth [later found] in the hallway. It would have taken a minute or two to get her to the point where she's very, very near death.

"Then what does he do? What does he always do? What did he do over the dead or dying? He performed last rites. And that's what he did. Oh, a bastardized version of last rites, to be sure, but that is what happens. He covers her with that blessed altar cloth and he marks her with the sign of the cross. But an upside-down cross.

"Why? Father Grob told us why. To degrade her. To mock her. To humiliate her. To bring her down to the lowest point he possibly could. He marks her with an upside-down cross in front of the Eucharist, the very person of Jesus Christ, to whom she is wed. He carves that in her. Does that make him a Satanist? No. If she had been Jewish, he would have carved a swastika in her chest. It was about how he could humiliate her the most.

"And then is he done after that? No. No. There's more to do. What can we do? Well, you'd have to anoint her. What would be the worst possible way? What would be the most offensive way to do that? Well, with blood. Her own blood.

"So he pulls off that altar cloth and he stabs her to get her blood. But the dead don't bleed. So he has to stab her again, and again, and twenty-two more times he stabs her. To do what? To what end? You see that bloodstain? That's this one here. And what we know from that bloodstain is that the entire length of this blade at one point was covered with blood.

"Now does that make sense? No matter how bloody a scene this was—and we know that it wasn't, but—you're not going to get the handle all covered with blood. How did that happen? Because after those twenty-two stab wounds, after he finally got blood out of that dead body it seeps out. He depresses it all in the blood. Covers it all with blood. To what end? To anoint her. He presses it across her face like that. He anointed her with her own blood as one more means of humiliation.

"Well, that should be enough, shouldn't it? Enough humiliation for one murder? No. It's not enough. We have to do more. What else can we do? We'll strip her. We'll strip her naked. That's what we'll do. We'll roll up that smock. We'll take that girdle down. We'll leave her naked in front of that

Blessed Sacrament. Is that enough? No. Even that is not enough.

"And we know that he does more. Imagine what it took to pull that girdle down off a dead body. Why is he doing all that? Notice this picture. Notice that the girdle is actually off her left foot. Her shoe is still on, but for some reason he struggles to get it off and free up that leg so it wouldn't be bound together to the other one.

"Why would he do that? Well, for the final act of degradation. The final act of humiliation. He needs to free that leg. He needs access because he wants to penetrate her. With the blade? With the crucifix? With his finger? We don't know. It doesn't matter. But he does it, and we know, because in the autopsy report you will find that this virginal nun had a red scratch inside her.

"And so he finishes. And he straightens up her body. Just like Phyllis Ann said, it looked posed to her. People don't die straight like that. And he stands up and he looks at his work. And what is it that he has left there on the floor? He's left a message. A message to Sister Margaret Ann Pahl? To be sure. Maybe to the Church. Maybe to God himself: 'See how angry I am? See what you have made me do? This is how angry I am.' He's left a message for everyone to see."

Then, said the deputy prosecutor, Father Robinson attempted to return to his quarters, but was seen leaving the chapel by laboratory worker Grace Jones. So he had to decide whether to run back to his room, or just walk casually past her.

"They didn't teach you what to do in seminary school after you kill a nun," said Mandross. "So he had to make a decision."

Ultimately, he told the jury, Father Robinson had decided to walk past her, making it irrelevant whether he actually went out the Madison Avenue exit or doubled back after she'd left.

But then, at 7:35 a.m., maintenance worker Wardell Langston heard footsteps running from an overhead bridge down the hallway, where only Father Robinson lived

Then, fifteen minutes later, at 7:50 a.m., receptionist Margaret Warren heard a second set of "frantic footsteps" that scared her.

"What happened during that fifteen minutes?" Mandross asked the jury. "Is that enough time to go back to your room, clean off that murder weapon, change your cassock, clean yourself and wipe off anything that may be on a shoe?

"But there is a problem," observed the prosecutor. "He dropped that cloth that also has blood on it."

Mandross now speculated that Father Robinson had gone out again to try to retrieve it.

"Is that what the second set of footsteps is about?" he asked. "That he comes back down and he sees that the nuns are going in and out of the chapel? Or maybe it's gone by then . . . Sister Madelyn Marie said she picked it up on her way to the chapel and left it on the back pew."

Or perhaps, suggested Mandross, Father Robinson had become "confused," unable to decide whether to remain in his room, or if being so late would look "suspicious," even on a slow Holy Saturday.

"So he comes back out," said Mandross, "and is out in that hallway when the 'Mr. Swift' call sounds."

Suddenly the emergency medical crews came running toward the chapel, and he encounters Dr. Jack Baron, who had taken a wrong turn.

"He doesn't know what to do," Mandross told the jury. "So he decides again to go back to his two small rooms he called home. And he waits to be called."

Finally, the phone rang and Sister Phyllis Ann Gerold informed him that Sister Margaret Ann was dead, telling him to come to the sacristy. But when he arrived, Father Swiatecki, having just completed last rites, demanded to know why he had done this.

"Ten, fifteen minutes after the body has been discovered," Mandross told the jury, "he's being accused by Father Swiatecki of her murder. What does Father Swiatecki know? No wonder [the defendant] started taking Valium."

When detectives contacted him two weeks later, he'd had

plenty of time to clean the letter opener blade and wash his clothes, making sure there was nothing incriminating in his quarters.

But when the police brought him in to the Safety Building on April 18, 1980, they asked "tough" and "difficult" questions.

"And what do you do when you're asked these tough questions?" asked Mandross. "You lie. You make up a story. You want to divert attention from yourself, so you say, 'Well, someone else did it. They just told me.' And when the police don't buy it, you have to admit that 'You know, I just made that up.'"

Then the next day Father Robinson was brought back for "another marathon session," with more and more questions.

"Suddenly, there's a knock at the door," said Mandross. "It's Monsignor Schmit. And they walk out together. He's out of that room. He's out of the police station. He's back out in the air of that April night. Maybe he can breathe again for the first time in two days.

"But it's back. Back to those two small pitiful rooms. And he sits and he waits. He waits for the police to come back and knock again. He knows they will. But the days pass. He waits. And no one comes. And the days turn into weeks. And he waits, and no one comes. And the weeks turn into months. And the months turn into years. And he's still been waiting all this time."

Then, slowly turning to Father Gerald Robinson, sitting impassively at the defense table, Dean Mandross told the jury: "And if that white collar means anything to him, he has always known that one day he is going to have to be held accountable for what he has done. So for all these years, he's been waiting. And now he's waiting for you."

Finally, after more than two hours on his feet, Dean Mandross slowly walked back to the prosecution bench, staring straight at Father Robinson.

Later, in his office, Mandross explained how he had carefully studied the priest, looking for the slightest reaction.

"I was suggesting that he was being called to account

either here on Earth or when he meets his Maker. And I purposely turned and made eye contact with him during that portion. And I was looking to see if there would be any kind of reaction from him. But he was impassive."

THEN ALAN KONOP WALKED OUT TO THE FRONT OF THE court, announcing that John Thebes would deliver the first of two closing arguments.

"You've given up a lot of time, a lot of energy," said the white-bearded defense attorney, who had been fighting off the flu for several days. "You've been a very attentive jury, and for that, I thank you. All of the counsel on our table thank you, and Father Robinson especially. So John will at this point discuss the forensics." Konop would return later to address the jury.

"Ladies and gentlemen of this jury," began Thebes, pacing up and down the jury box, as he would do throughout his speech. "Father Robinson is not guilty. He's not guilty. And that's solely and simply because the State of Ohio has not proven to you beyond a reasonable doubt that this letter opener is the murder weapon. Their whole prosecution is premised on that fact.

"They need to show to you beyond a reasonable doubt that that's the murder weapon. And if they cannot do it, ladies and gentlemen, the ballgame's over."

For the next forty-five minutes, Thebes dismissed all the prosecution's expert witnesses one by one, characterizing their findings as not objective.

"This forensic evidence takes many forms," said Thebes. "I think you could group it into four basic areas. We had blood transfer. We had forensic pathology. We had forensic anthropology—the bones—and we had DNA."

The defense attorney then invited the jury to consider if each particular prosecution expert and their discipline was a subjective or an objective field.

"Every [State] expert called," he told them, "was an expert in a subjective field. They rely on experts in those fields of subjectivity."

Thebes then picked up the letter opener, telling the jury that the real murder weapon was the missing pair of scissors, matching the holes in the altar cloth and victim's clothing far better than a curved letter opener. He told the jury that the late Lucas County Deputy Coroner, Dr. Renate Fazekas, had found the stab wounds consistent with being caused by scissors.

"But Dr. Scala-Barnett," said Thebes, "who is part of the cold case team, contradicts her mentor and said it had to be the dagger. This letter opener is not that sharp and can't cut flesh."

He maintained that the semicircular bloodstain on Sister Margaret Ann's forehead, which T. Paulette Sutton and Dr. Henry Lee had testified was an imprint of the U.S. Capitol building, could just as easily have been made by a nickel. (Later, Prosecutor Christopher Anderson would note that Thomas Jefferson's house in Monticello was on the back of a nickel coin.)

The defender claimed the prosecution had first arrested Father Robinson, before trying to fit a case around him and ignoring any evidence supporting his innocence.

"Do we really want a prosecution," he asked the jury, "that arrests us first and then does an investigation? Your common sense says, 'That's not how we do things in this country.' We expect more."

Thebes said when evidence was lacking, the State turned to other means.

"And they turned their head west and their eyes west to Chicago, Illinois, and Father Grob," he declared. "They can't win on the facts. Make Father Robinson look bad."

Thebes told the jury that DNA evidence was objective, but after the results had shown none of Father Robinson's on the victim's underclothing, the State had "turned a blind eye."

If Father Robinson was guilty, said the defender, his DNA would have been found on the evidence taken from the murder scene.

"So when you go into that jury room, have your common sense." said Thebes. "Your eyes and your ears will take dif-

ferent routes, but will all come to the same conclusion . . .
not guilty.

"They say a picture is worth a thousand words. I would
tell you it's only worth two words. And I'll settle for two at
this point. Those words are 'Not guilty.' Thank you and may
God bless you."

By the time Alan Konop began his closing argument, the
jurors were noticeably restless.

"I'll try and be as brief as possible," he told them. "Fa-
mous last words of a lawyer."

And for the next eighty minutes the lead defender delivered an impassioned, but often rambling, soliloquy, pleading
his client's case.

"They've got a circumstantial evidence case," he declared
at the beginning. "And they've got to put those circumstantial pieces together for a true picture beyond a reasonable
doubt, before you can do anything other than find him not
guilty. So let me begin."

The veteran defense attorney then methodically tore apart
the 1980 investigation, claiming it was "poor" and inept.

"Was a proper job done?" he asked. "I submit: In no way."

The murder scene, he told the jury, was never processed
properly, with no fingerprints taken and few trace evidence
samples. He accused the State of being so short of evidence
they had played the Catholic card.

"They must be pretty darn desperate to have to blame it
on the Church," he told the jury. "Maybe they should blame
it on their own investigation."

Then Konop tried to neutralize the damaging testimony
that his client had lied about taking the killer's confession.

"Think about Father's personality," said Konop. "After all
that grilling—and you can imagine how that was."

He asked the jury to imagine being interrogated for four
to eight hours by police in a small room. And, Konop said,
the only thing Bill Kina and Art Marx could "salvage" from
the hours of questioning was one statement from Father
Robinson that a parishioner had confessed to the murder,
which he then withdrew.

"Father Robinson's explanation was, 'Look, he was pressuring me. I just wanted to get him off.' OK. It's a human quality. Priest or no priest. It's a human quality. He was pressured."

Then Konop turned to the reopening of the case, calling Father Robinson's arrest a rush to judgment.

"They have committed themselves to arresting a priest for the murder of a nun," said Konop. "There's national publicity. They can't turn back."

Finally, Konop delivered one last emotional appeal to the increasingly restless jury, asking them to acquit.

"I've been so proud to have been able to be involved in this case, as have all my colleagues," he said, brushing a tear from his eyes. "So proud. So proud to stand up for Father Robinson. Now it's your turn to stand up for Father Robinson. It's your turn to render a verdict based upon the evidence as it comes from the witness stand, from the law as it comes from the court, with reason, with common sense. To stand up for Father Robinson.

"To render a verdict so that when you see Father Robinson with his friends and family, you can go up to him and say, 'Father Robinson, I was on the jury that did the right thing. And the right thing was this—the State didn't have a case beyond a reasonable doubt, and we stood up for the law. We enforced the law to find you not guilty by law.'"

Then, just before 2:00 p.m., Judge Osowik called a thirty-minute lunch break, before Christopher Anderson delivered the prosecution's rebuttal.

"THERE ARE STATEMENTS MADE BY BOTH THE DEFENSE counsels that I vehemently disagree with," began Christopher Anderson, when court resumed that afternoon. "It's the evidence that I heard during the course of the trial. It's going to be up to you to determine what those are."

Anderson told the jury that he would not waste time listing each of the defense's claims individually, as they would have the opportunity to "sift through" the evidence later in the jury room, and make their own decisions.

"I do want to counsel, though," said Anderson with a twinkle in his eye, "that if you see John Thebes on the street, do not take a nickel from him, because the Capitol building is not on the back of the nickel."

It was a rare light moment in an otherwise solemn day.

Anderson then took the jurors once again through the scientific evidence, before turning his attention to the defendant's personality and behavior in April 1980, after he became the prime suspect.

"This is a case, I submit to you, that the evidence supports the conviction of Gerald Robinson. [The] murder weapon was in his exclusive control. It was taken from his room. Nobody else went in there and took it. When questioned about it, he lied, and he continued to lie all the time. . . .

"You have a Catholic priest lying to police about a murder investigation. But there was humiliation in this, but this humiliation occurred back in 1980. And it was Sister Margaret Ann Pahl [who] was humiliated. [Who] was stabbed through an altar cloth, [who] had her clothes pulled up and her undergarments pulled down in front of the Holy Eucharist in the sacristy of the church. That was the humiliation, and in this particular case, Father Gerald Robinson did not suffer humiliation—he caused it. And he caused it in 1980."

Then, as a twenty-six-year-old photograph appeared on the screen in front of the jury box, Anderson continued: "The State of Ohio is not asking you to convict a sixty-eight-year-old man, as they keep referring to him in court here today. We're asking you to convict a forty-two-year-old man, twenty-six years late. And that's why I have this photograph up on a lot of the board, because you've got to remember that's what he looked like back when this murder occurred.

"Mr. Mandross talked about—back in opening statements— you can't not talk about God and religion in this particular case, because you have a Catholic priest and a nun involved in this. But this is a court of law. And the laws that apply here are the laws of man. Gerald Robinson may be judged by some other authority at a later date, but this is his focus of judgment of man's law. And he's up for judgment today with you.

"Based upon man's law, the State of Ohio has proven its case beyond any reasonable doubt. I submit to you that your verdict will finally bring justice to the Bride of Christ—Sister Margaret Ann Pahl."

JUDGE THOMAS OSOWIK THEN ISSUED HIS INSTRUCTIONS TO the jury, saying it was time for them to decide the "disputed facts." He reminded them that as the defendant had pleaded not guilty, he was legally presumed innocent until his guilt was established beyond a reasonable doubt.

"Proof beyond a reasonable doubt," he told the jury, "is proof of such character that an ordinary person would be willing to rely and act upon it, in the most important of his or her own affairs."

He also instructed them on the differences between direct and circumstantial evidence. Direct evidence is testimony from a witness who has personally seen or heard the facts, and includes exhibits admitted into evidence. Circumstantial evidence is the proof of unrelated facts or circumstances by direct evidence, that, when considered together, can be used to infer a conclusion, according to common sense.

"Direct evidence and circumstantial evidence are of equal weight," he told the jury.

Judge Osowik also told them not to take into account the fact that Father Robinson had not taken the stand to testify on his own behalf, as there is no legal requirement for a defendant to do so.

Then, shortly before 4:00 p.m., Judge Osowik excused the four alternates, sending the seven men and five women of the panel off to the jury room, to sift through the 200 pieces of evidence and decide Father Gerald Robinson's fate.

JUST A FEW MINUTES AFTER THE JURY BEGAN DELIBERA-tions, it asked for a list of all forty-two witnesses who had testified over the course of the trial. Then, a few hours later, it sent a note to the judge requesting a DVD player for another look at the video of Father Robinson's interrogation by Detective Tom Ross.

Just before 8:00 p.m., Judge Osowik dismissed the jury for the day, warning them not to speak about the case to anyone, or watch TV, read a newspaper or check the Internet.

THAT NIGHT, AS THE JURY DELIBERATED ON WHETHER HE should spend the rest of his life in jail, an unusually upbeat Father Gerald Robinson gathered with his family, friends and supporters at his Nebraska Avenue home. The atmosphere was positive as everyone agreed that the jury would soon bring his nightmare to an end.

By Sunday, they assured him, he'd be back in church saying Mass like in the old days.

CHAPTER FORTY-TWO

Day of Judgment

AT PRECISELY 11:00 A.M. THE NEXT MORNING, THE JURY SENT word that it had reached a verdict, after just six-and-a-half hours of deliberation. No one had expected such a rapid decision, least of all Dean Mandross.

That morning the deputy prosecutor had been at his desk on the second floor of the courthouse. "When we're waiting for a jury, I can't do any real work," he explained. "What I do historically is take that opportunity to start cleaning my office, which always looks like a tornado by the end of the trial."

Minutes after news of the verdict came through, Lucas County Prosecutor Julia Bates led her team upstairs to the fourth-floor courtroom. But before leaving his office, Mandross tore off a piece of yellow legal paper, writing down his prediction of "GUILTY." Then he folded it up, and put it in his pocket.

"I was confident at that point," he later explained, "just because I didn't think the twelve could go not guilty in that short a time. If it had been twenty hours later, I may well not have been so confident."

A few minutes later, Father Robinson walked up the court steps in his clerical collar and cassock, flanked by his defense attorneys Alan Konop and John Thebes. He was immediately assailed by half a dozen television crews and news reporters, but walked stoically by without a word.

Then, as he entered court, he took off his rosary beads and kissed them, placing them in a small plastic tray with his wallet, as he went through the metal detector.

Father Robinson and his attorneys then took an elevator up to the fourth floor, entering Courtroom 5 at 11:37 a.m. and taking their place at the defense table.

The atmosphere inside was electric, as everyone felt the awful anticipation that something historic was about to happen.

As usual, Thomas and Barbara Robinson and several friends sat behind Father Robinson, who occasionally turned around to acknowledge them. But there were no representatives from the victim's family, as Lee Pahl had returned to Edgerton the previous day, not expecting such a swift verdict. But SNAP coordinator Claudia Vercellotti was sitting in the public gallery with several other supporters, as they had done every day of the trial.

The much-anticipated verdict was being carried live on Court TV, and on all local television and radio stations, which had broken into regular programming.

Just before Judge Osowik entered, Dean Mandross discreetly handed his prosecution colleague Larry Kiroff the folded paper with his prediction.

When the twelve members of the jury solemnly filed into the jury box, not one looked at the defendant. They all seemed conscious of the huge responsibility that was resting on their shoulders.

At 11:40 a.m., court bailiff Tanya Butler handed Judge Osowik the jury's verdict form. The judge looked at it and then told Father Robinson to rise.

"We, the Jury," read the judge, "find the defendant guilty of murder."

At the word "guilty," there was a gasp from the gallery, as Barbara Robinson broke down in tears. All four defense attorneys looked shaken, but Father Gerald Robinson's craggy face registered no discernible reaction whatsoever, as he just stared blankly ahead.

Then Judge Osowik polled each of the twelve jurors by name.

"Is this your signature," he asked each one, "and does this reflect your verdict?"

One by one, each confirmed that it did.

Then the judge asked if the defendant had anything to say, and Alan Konop replied that he had not.

Judge Osowik then turned toward Father Gerald Robinson, to pronounce sentence.

"The statute in effect in 1980 is the same as it is today," he told the priest, now a convicted murderer. "And that is that whoever is convicted or pleads guilty to murder in violation of section 290302 of the Ohio Revised Code, shall be imprisoned to an indefinite term of fifteen years to life.

"The court imposes the life imprisonment pursuant to that code section. Mr. Robinson, you have thirty days from today's date to appeal my decision."

Then a Lucas County Court Deputy walked up behind the priest, slipping a pair of handcuffs over his wrists.

"All right," said the judge, "anything further from the defense?"

"No, Your Honor," replied Konop wearily.

"Anything from the State?"

"No, Judge," replied Dean Mandross.

The convicted murderer was then led out of the court by armed bailiffs as his supporters applauded him. He was then placed into a waiting elevator, to be taken to the basement for the walk through a connecting tunnel to Lucas County jail.

As reporters dashed out of the courtroom to file stories and get reaction interviews, Father Robinson's relatives and supporters were in a state of despair and disbelief. On her way out of court, Barbara Robinson briefly stopped in front of Claudia Vercellotti to vent her venom on the woman she blamed for the trial ever taking place.

"I hope you rot in hell!" she hissed at the SNAP leader, before exiting the court with her husband Thomas.

A FEW MINUTES LATER, THE COLD CASE DETECTIVES AND attorneys from both sides held a press conference in the jury assembly room. The conference was being broadcast live, and it would be the first time these key players could discuss the case under the strict gag order in force up to the verdict.

First to speak was Lucas County Prosecutor Julia Bates, who had taken the controversial decision to indict a Roman Catholic priest for murder.

"This was an extremely long and involved investigation," she declared. "I'm extremely proud of the very professional and very tactful performance displayed by the members of [my] office."

Fielding reporters' questions, Bates said the earliest Father Robinson could be released on parole was in 2021.

She was asked how much the trial had cost the taxpayers of Lucas County.

"Approximately $38,000," she said. "I guess I'd put it to you this way: 'What is the cost of a life?' [It] really is a small price to pay for justice in a twenty-six-year-old case."

Then Lead Prosecutor Dean Mandross took the microphone, saying that Father Robinson's murder conviction was no cause for celebration.

"It isn't something to applaud," he said. "It's a homicide case. We were trying to hold the person accountable. We didn't go back to the office high-fiving."

And Mandross also applauded Julia Bates' bravery for taking on the Catholic Church.

"Mrs. Bates had a lot of courage," he said. "The Catholic Church is an institution, it's something that you're not anxious to necessarily be on the other side of."

Then visibly shocked defense attorneys Alan Konop and John Thebes came over to the microphone, vowing to appeal the verdict.

"Obviously," said Thebes, on the verge of tears, "we are extremely disappointed with the outcome. Today is difficult, but the jury has spoken and, unfortunately, that's the way it is."

Last to speak was Alan Konop, who was asked what, in hindsight, he might have done differently.

"I'm not going to talk about second-guessing," he said dismissively, with a wave of his hand. "What was done was done. The verdict was rendered. We respect the verdict."

He was then asked how he thought his client would fare in prison.

"He's not well," said Konop. "He's not very well. That's a real, real serious concern. That's a pretty rough environment."

Later that day, Father Leonard Blair issued an Internet press statement on behalf of the Catholic Diocese of Toledo, calling for healing in the wake of the verdict:

> This is a sad day for the Diocese of Toledo. In the matter of the State of Ohio versus Gerald Robinson, a jury of his peers has convicted him of the 1980 murder of Sister Margaret Ann Pahl.
>
> I ask for prayers for all those involved—Sister Margaret Ann, her family and the Sisters of Mercy, as well as those witnesses who testified at the trial, the jury, the judge and the attorneys who participated, and for Father Robinson. . . .
>
> Father Robinson's present status is that of a retired priest of the Diocese of Toledo. He continues to be barred from any public ministry.

Sister Marjorie Rudemiller, President of the Sisters of Mercy of the Americas, who had been in court for the verdict, also issued a statement, calling for forgiveness for Sister Margaret Ann Pahl's killer:

> We have prayed for truth to prevail and for a fair and just trial. The jury has spoken and we respect their decision. We will never forget Sr. Margaret Ann Pahl. As a Sister of Mercy for 53 years, she lived her life dedicated to the healing ministry of Jesus through her service in many healthcare institutions until her untimely death.
>
> God's grace enables us to forgive the person who caused her death. God's love and the love of others will heal our aching hearts and bring peace to us. We trust that God's mercy is extended to all of us, as we move forward with our lives.

LATER THAT DAY, LEE PAHL GAVE A TELEVISION INTERVIEW on behalf of his family.

"I really truly believe justice has been served," he said,

welling up with emotion. "And I think my aunt's probably looking down and smiling today."

AFTER HE WAS BOOKED IN THE LUCAS COUNTY JAIL, THE convicted murderer exchanged his black clerical suit and white collar for a regulation brown jail jumpsuit. His rosary was taken away, in case he used it to harm himself, and he was held overnight in the jail's medical area under suicide watch.

Reportedly, as he was being processed, several inmates recognized him and asked, "Did you do it?"

A few days later, Robinson was transported by bus to the Correctional Reception Center outside Columbus, Ohio, for psychiatric evaluation and assessment.

And on May 18, Inmate #519811 was moved to the close-security Warren Correctional Institution in Lebanon, Ohio, to serve out his sentence, with some of the most violent criminals in the state.

His earliest possible parole board hearing will be March 2021, when he will be 83 years old.

IN THE WAKE OF FATHER GERALD ROBINSON'S CONVICTION, he still enjoyed much support from the Polish Catholic community of Toledo. Many now believed him to be a martyr.

CHAPTER FORTY-THREE

"As I Shall Answer to God"

ON JUNE 6, 2006, JOHN THEBES FILED A TWO-PAGE NOTICE OF appeal against Father Robinson's guilty verdict, without outlining the grounds. Within two weeks, the incarcerated priest had fired his old legal team, hiring a new attorney named John Donahue to represent him in his appeal.

A chain-smoking 59-year-old criminal lawyer, Donahue had watched Court TV coverage of the trial from his office in Perrysburg, Ohio, and was so "shocked" by the conviction, he agreed to handle the appeal pro bono.

He had first contacted Thomas Robinson, outlining his proposal for an appeal, before writing to Father Robinson at the Warren Correctional Institution. A few days later he had received a collect call from the priest, asking him to represent him.

"An innocent man is in prison," declared Donahue. "I would not be representing this man if I thought he did this. I believe he's innocent."

The former Wood County prosecutor also criticized Father Robinson's defense.

"The lawyers [who] represented him," said Donahue, "I wouldn't have representing me in a traffic case, let alone for murder. It's the most unbelievable performance I've ever seen."

And he told reporters he was starting the appeal process by donating $15,000 of his own money to pay for a complete transcription of the trial.

IN MID-SEPTEMBER, ST. HEDWIG CATHOLIC CHURCH—WITH long ties to Father Robinson—held a chicken dinner fundraiser, to generate cash for his appeal. In its church bulletin, the organizers were listed as the "Friends/Supporters of Fr. Robinson." A flier advertising the event was also posted in the back of the church.

After several complaints to the diocese, the Reverend Michael Billian, Episcopal vicar for the Toledo diocese issued a statement, reading:

> The bishop's office and the Diocese of Toledo did not grant permission for this advertisement to be placed in parish bulletins. In fact, the contrary is true. We have told parishes NOT to advertise this event.

But a reported 300 supporters did attend the dinner at the Scott Park Banquet Room, where they were met by a small band of protesters led by SNAP's Claudia Vercellotti, holding up a picture of Sister Margaret Ann Pahl.

"I want my Church not to be a conduit to raise money for a convicted murderer, who murdered a Roman Catholic nun," she told the Associated Press.

In mid-October, John Donahue filed papers requesting Father Robinson's release from prison on a $250,000 property bond. In an affidavit with the motion, Father Robinson spoke out about his conviction for the first time.

"I do solemnly swear," wrote Robinson, "as I shall answer to God, that I did not kill Sister Margaret Ann Pahl."

Lucas County Prosecutor Julie Bates called Robinson's statement "highly inappropriate," saying she would be filing a motion to oppose his release.

A week later, a twelve-page motion prepared by Dean Mandross was filed in Lucas County Common Pleas Court:

> A cynic might think that this claim would have carried more weight had it been made before the jury. But then, a cynic might think that Robinson wanted to avoid being cross-examined by the state. A cynic might believe that Robinson didn't want to be forced to explain his many lies.

On October 30, 2006, Judge Thomas Osowik refused to release Robinson from state prison, pending his appeal. In his six-page decision, the judge wrote: "The defendant has not presented any argument that would warrant any suspension of the sentence imposed."

A week later, John Donahue unsuccessfully appealed to an Ohio appellate court, in a further bid to free Robinson.

"I will have to think about what the next step will be," Donahue told a reporter. "Obviously, the Court of Appeals has spoken."

On December 7, Gerald Robinson was rushed from Hocking Correctional Facility to the Ohio State University Medical Center, suffering from an unspecified kidney complaint. Two weeks later, he was returned to Hocking to continue his life sentence.

In January 2007, Jean Marlow's civil action against Robinson and Jerry Mazuchowski was dismissed by Lucas County Court Judge Ruth Ann Franks, finding that the allegations of their involvement in ritual abuse ceremonies forty years earlier were past the statute of limitations.

"This is a huge victory for Father Robinson," declared John Donahue. "It was this type of allegation that started the ball rolling on the murder investigation. The fact that it was dismissed is good news."

EPILOGUE

On Saturday evening, September 23, 2006, Catherine Flegal, a sister of Sister Margaret Ann Pahl, Martha-Jane Dietsch, Catherine Flegal's daughter, myself, Sister Margaret Ann's nephew and Karen Pahl, wife of Lee Pahl, gathered at my home to view the A&E "Cold Case Files" show, about Father Robinson and the murder of Sister Margaret Ann Pahl.

We all sat in the great room and began to watch the show. The dining area in our home is adjacent and fully open to the great room. There is a chandelier over the dining table with nine bulbs on it. We had the chandelier on but it was dimmed down.

We were in the midst of watching the show about the murder of Sister Margaret Ann Pahl, when we heard loud snapping and cracking. And all of a sudden all the bulbs in the chandelier went full bright and illuminated the entire room. (The dimmer wall switch burnt out.)

I remember looking out to the dining room and saying, "What's that?" Aunt Catherine, Martha-Jane and Karen all did a slow look, as if in disbelief that this had just happened. But said nothing and went back to watching the show.

Strange! Why did the dimmer burn out at this precise moment? It made me think back to the violent storm at my aunt's funeral. I feel certain Sister Margaret Ann was acknowledging for us that justice had finally been done and was having the last word.

Lee Pahl
May 2007

In the American legal system, a criminal defendant is presumed innocent until proven guilty beyond a reasonable doubt by a jury of his peers. In this case, a jury rendered its verdict of guilt, ultimately accepting the prosecution's theory that Father Gerald Robinson killed Sister Margaret Ann Pahl.

A convicted defendant is entitled under American law to appeal his conviction in an effort to overturn the jury's finding of guilt. As of press time, Father Robinson's appeal has not yet been resolved.